Evaluating
Democracy
Assistance

Evaluating Democracy Assistance

Krishna Kumar

LYNNE
RIENNER
PUBLISHERS

BOULDER
LONDON

The views expressed in this book are the author's and should not be attributed to either the Department of State or the US Agency for International Development.

Published in the United States of America in 2013 by
Lynne Rienner Publishers, Inc.
1800 30th Street, Boulder, Colorado 80301
www.rienner.com

and in the United Kingdom by
Lynne Rienner Publishers, Inc.
3 Henrietta Street, Covent Garden, London WC2E 8LU

Library of Congress Cataloging-in-Publication Data
Kumar, Krishna, 1940–
    Evaluating democracy assistance/Krishna Kumar.
        p. cm.
    Includes bibliographical references and index.
    ISBN 978-1-58826-858-7 (alk. paper)
    ISBN 978-1-58826-883-9 (pbk. : alk. paper)
    1. Democratization—International cooperation. 2. Technical assistance. I. Title.
JC423.K85 2012
327.1—dc23

                                                                2012028227

British Cataloguing in Publication Data
A Cataloguing in Publication record for this book
is available from the British Library.

Printed and bound in the United States of America

The paper used in this publication meets the requirements
of the American National Standard for Permanence of
Paper for Printed Library Materials Z39.48-1992.

5 4 3 2 1

*To the memory of my late father, Mohan Murari,
who, through his lifelong struggle for freedom
and democracy, taught me to cherish them,*

*And to my late friend Ram C. Malhotra,
who sparked my interest in evaluation.*

Contents

Acknowledgments   ix

1 Why This Book?   1

2 The Why and What of Evaluating Democracy Assistance   7

Why Democracy Evaluations? *8*
The Meaning of Evaluation *10*
Types of Democracy Evaluations *13*
Evaluation Modalities *22*
Obstacles to Evaluating Democracy Interventions *28*

3 Democracy Indicators: Their Use and Misuse in Evaluations   31

Micro-Level Indicators *32*
Macro-Level Indices and Evaluations *38*
Meso-Level Indices *43*
Use of Meso-Level Indices in Albania *48*
Disaggregating Macro-Level Indices *51*
Conclusion *54*

4 Designing Realistic Monitoring Systems   57

The Meaning of Monitoring *58*
Guiding Principles *60*
Designing a Monitoring System *62*
Operating a Monitoring System *67*
Collaborative Critical Reflections *68*

5 Planning and Managing Evaluations   71

The Manager's Role During the Planning Phase *72*
The Manager's Role During Implementation *79*
The Manager's Role During Review and Follow-Up *84*

6 Experimental and Quasi-Experimental Designs   87

The Logic Behind Experimental and
   Quasi-Experimental Designs *89*
Different Designs *91*
Methodological and Practical Obstacles *96*
The International Republican Institute's Experience *102*
The National Democratic Institute's Experience *108*
Conclusion *113*

7 Nonexperimental Designs   117

Pre- and Postdesigns *118*
Cross-Sectional Design *120*
Case Study Evaluation Designs *121*
Steps to Improve Methodological Rigor *130*

8 Methods for Data Collection   137

Quantitative and Qualitative Methods *138*
Sample Surveys and Censuses *140*
Structured Direct Observation *148*
Secondary Analysis of Data *151*
Document Reviews *153*
Key Informant Interviews *155*
Focus Group Discussions *159*
Group Interviews *162*
Multimethod Approach *165*

9 Communicating Findings and Recommendations   167

Guiding Principles for Effective Communication *168*
Critical Elements of Evaluation Reports *173*
Written Products *184*
Verbal Communication *187*

10 Concluding Observations   191

Appendix 1: Acronyms   199
Appendix 2: Glossary of Evaluation Terms   201
Appendix 3: A Note on Democracy Assistance Programs   209
References   219
Index   231
About the Book   241

Acknowledgments

Although I cannot individually acknowledge all the friends, colleagues, and democracy experts who have helped me in this endeavor, I will always remain indebted to them. A few deserve special mention, however.

Before deciding to write this book, I discussed my proposal with many leaders of democracy nongovernmental organizations and democracy experts, including Kenneth Wollack, president of the National Democratic Institute (NDI); Tom Carothers, vice president of the Carnegie Endowment for International Peace; Richard Blue, vice president of Social Impacts; and Gerry Hyman, senior adviser, Center for Strategic and International Studies. Kenneth Wollack invited me to present the proposal at an NDI directors' meeting, and I also discussed ideas for the book with Rebekah Usatin, program officer for monitoring and evaluation at the National Endowment for Democracy. David Black from the Democracy/ Governance Office at the US Agency for International Development (USAID) organized a small meeting to discuss the proposal. They all encouraged me to write this book and promised their full support. I am grateful for their encouragement and trust.

Many staff members at NDI, particularly Linda Stern, Peter Manikas, and Sef Ashiagbor, shared their experiences and thoughts and provided valuable evaluation reports. Linda also contributed two sections to the book—one on NDI's experience with experimental designs and a note on case study design. My friends at the International Republican Institute (IRI)—Jeffrey Lilley, Liz Ruedy, and

Jonathan Jones—were also very generous with their time. Jonathan contributed to Chapter 6 with a note on IRI's experience with experimental designs.

I am grateful to Lorne Craner, president of IRI, and Larry Garber, deputy assistant administrator at USAID, for reading the entire manuscript. Tom Carothers, Peter Manikas, Linda Stern, Jonathan Jones, Liz Ruedy, Sef Ashiagbor, Michael Patton, and Harry Blair read earlier drafts of the manuscript and gave valuable suggestions about its contents and organization. There are not sufficient words to thank them.

I wish to acknowledge the continual support of Melissa Schild and Peter Davis in the Office of the Director of Foreign Assistance Resources at the State Department. I am also thankful to the staff of the department's library, particularly Linda Schweizer, for their timely assistance in getting me needed books and articles for writing the book.

I would be remiss if I did not thank my wife, Parizad, for allowing me to work on the book most weekends and holidays during 2011, and also my daughters, Sonia and Sanaz, for their support.

Finally, I would also like to acknowledge Lynne Rienner, who has published my previous five books and has taken yet another gamble on this one. Senior project editor Lesli Brooks Athanasoulis and copyeditor Diane Foose did a superb job in editing the manuscript.

—*Krishna Kumar*

Evaluating
Democracy
Assistance

1

Why This Book?

Unlike development assistance, results chain of democracy assistance is non-linear and can be obscured by multiple factors and actors at play in the dynamic contexts where our programs take place.

—Kenneth D. Wollack, president of the NDI

I am not convinced if you can evaluate democracy programs. The types of evaluations you do are of little help to us. You should trust the judgment of those who are struggling to promote democracy at great personal risk.

—A Russian democracy activist

During the past two decades, international aid to promote democracy in developing and transition countries has significantly increased.[1] While precise figures are not available, it is estimated to be more than $3 billion.[2] The international community increasingly treats democracy assistance on a par with assistance to improve health, education, or economic growth. It now provides assistance to promote human rights, the rule of law, and gender equality. It also assists in developing electoral institutions for competitive elections and gives support for holding free and fair elections. In addition, it gives technical and financial assistance to strengthen civil society, political parties, and independent media, which are essential for the functioning of a democratic society. Finally, the international community assists in improving governance, as it is now recognized that the institutionalization of democracy also depends on the functioning of efficient and accountable public sector institutions. This book focuses on the monitoring and evaluation of democracy assistance programs.

The underlying premise of the book is that caution is necessary in applying to the democracy domain the evaluation concepts, models, and approaches that have paid rich dividends in the evaluation of development programs. There are significant differences between development and democracy programming. While these differences are of degrees—it is a matter of lighter versus darker gray—they are nonetheless significant and should not be ignored. I will briefly mention them here.

First, most democracy assistance goes to countries that are in a period of political transition or recovering from civil wars and strife. In such countries, the established political order has collapsed, but a new political system is yet to emerge. The political landscape is constantly changing, and there is a great deal of uncertainty about the future with different political forces pulling in different directions. For example, during the Arab Spring, many established authoritarian regimes collapsed, but their future remains uncertain; we do not know what types of political institutions and regimes will evolve in these countries. And yet the international community has to develop democracy interventions to take advantage of political openings. As a result, many democracy programs[3] have to be rapidly designed without conducting a thorough assessment of the local conditions and circumstances. Moreover, they are implemented in an era of rapid change and uncertainty. In such conditions, a high probability exists that many targets, indicators, and activities, which were formulated at the launch of an intervention, may not remain relevant.

Second, democracy interventions can affect and unsettle existing power relations and therefore they often are viewed with suspicion, if not hostility, by some governments and entrenched political interests. For example, some ruling parties that want to keep their hold on power at all costs tend to regard free and fair elections as threats to their interests. Although they hold elections and even accept electoral assistance, they do not desist from undermining the integrity of elections by manipulating electoral commissions, denying opposition parties access to government-controlled media, or limiting the access of election monitors to geographical areas that are the stronghold of opposition parties. Similarly, police, entrenched security forces, and other vested interests are typically suspicious of human rights interventions and reluctant to support them. It also is not uncommon that, at the same time as they publicly praise anticorruption programs, corrupt political leaders, government officials, and their cronies take every opportunity to undermine them. The situation is even worse in semiauthoritarian states that are positively hostile to even modest international programs for training journalists, supporting prosecuted human rights organizations and activists, or helping nascent civil society organizations. In such countries, the organizations or activists receiving small grants from foreign donors are under constant surveillance of the intelligence agencies.

International development assistance, on the other hand, has limited impact on existing political structures at least in the short term. Successful implementation of these programs can enhance rather than undermine the legitimacy and authority of the ruling elites. For example, increased agricultural production and productivity generated by foreign assistance avert the threat of famine and starvation, and assistance to fight HIV/AIDS takes the pressure off government to spend money on that battle. Therefore, programs in agriculture, health, microfinance, or basic education are generally welcomed by the ruling regimes. This is a major difference in the political environment of development and democracy assistance that is often overlooked by policymakers.

Third, as compared to development interventions, the conceptual models that underlie democracy interventions have weaker empirical and theoretical foundations. The international community often finances awareness programs to mobilize public opinion against corruption. Yet there is no solid empirical evidence that such efforts have any lasting influence on public policies, much less on the prevalence of corruption. It also invests heavily in nongovernmental organizations (NGOs) that support democracy, but there is little hard evidence on the sustainability of the assisted NGOs or their impacts on strengthening democracy. One obvious explanation is that, as compared to development assistance, the field of democracy assistance is relatively new. The development community has more than a half-century of experience in designing, implementing, monitoring, and evaluating development programs and policies while democracy assistance is barely thirty years old and has not accumulated the rich programming experience. The situation is improving, however. To cite an example, the knowledge of electoral assistance has vastly improved as a result of past experience so that the international community now has quite sophisticated models, intervention strategies, and analytical tools to design and implement electoral assistance projects and programs.

Fourth, it is more difficult to establish a causal relationship between an intervention and the observed changes in democracy interventions than in most development programs. One can be certain that immunization will prevent the occurrence of a particular disease and, therefore, if a major immunization initiative is launched in a country, it will reduce the incidence of the disease. Agricultural experts know that the introduction of a high-yielding variety of seeds with assured supply of agricultural inputs in a stable economic environment will increase agricultural production and productivity. But no such relationship can be established in most democracy promotion programs. We cannot be certain if assistance to civil society in a transition country will contribute to its enhanced role in promoting democracy or if human rights training of security officials will result in fewer human rights violations. Many long-term outcomes of democracy interventions tend to remain what Jonathan Morell (2005) calls "unforeseen" and "unforeseeable." Unforeseen consequences arise because of the paucity of knowledge and/or the failure to take advantage of the existing knowledge while unforeseeable consequences can be attributed to the uncertainties of the changing, dynamic environment, which cannot be predicted by the social science community in advance. Many democracy interventions have ripple effects that were not anticipated by their designers. For example, media interventions undertaken in the Balkans to promote social reconciliation among conflicting parties helped to institutionalize independent media outlets. And anecdotal experience indicates that some alumni of democracy projects funded by the United States have participated in the recent uprisings in the Middle East. As a result of ongoing empirically grounded evaluations and academic research, designers of democracy programs in the future will be in a better position to anticipate what are at present unforeseen consequences.

The case of unforeseeable consequences is undoubtedly different. These arise because the long-term outcomes of democracy interventions cannot always be predicted. A wide variety of factors, forces, and unpredictable events as well as their constant interactions in a changing environment affect the outcomes of democracy interventions. For example, the international community has been providing significant assistance to build and strengthen democratic institutions in Afghanistan, but the future of democracy in that troubled country remains in question. We do not know what kinds of political compromises will take place, how the Islamist ideology will affect its emerging political culture, and what will be the shape of its political institutions. If the past is a guide, social scientists are not very good at predicting long-term political changes or events. Despite the huge investments in sophisticated models based on empirical data, the US intelligence services and the academic community conspicuously failed to predict the fall of the Soviet Union, the disintegration in the Balkans, or the uprisings in the Middle East in 2011 and 2012. The situation, on the other hand, is much better in many fields of development assistance. Demographers can estimate the likely impact of family planning interventions on birth rates and economists can approximate the effects of agricultural interventions on agricultural production and productivity.

Finally, the primary focus of democracy assistance tends to be on institution building rather than service delivery. Programs are designed to strengthen civil society organizations, electoral commissions, election monitoring organizations, and independent media outlets. Institution building is a complex process and it is difficult to develop reliable and valid measures for evaluating the effects of assistance. The impacts of assistance are not always visible and can be captured only in the long term, if at all.

The above-mentioned differences between development and democracy programming have implications for the planning, conducting, monitoring, and evaluation of democracy programs. They indicate the need for a nuanced approach in applying evaluation concepts, approaches, and tools to the domain of democracy assistance. And this book attempts to articulate a nuanced approach.

The book presents a comprehensive discussion of the issues surrounding the planning, conducting, and managing of evaluations of interventions. It is designed to provide conceptual clarity about key evaluation constructs; outline steps that are essential for establishing sound and flexible evaluation and monitoring systems; explore the use and misuse of indicators in the monitoring and evaluation of democracy interventions; explain the various designs that can be used for evaluating democracy initiatives, programs, and policies, including their relative strengths and limitations and the type of the data collection methods that they require; suggest ways for formulating evaluation recommendations and communicating them to policymakers and decisionmakers; promote accountability and learning; and encourage critical reflection about the effectiveness and impacts of democracy interventions.

Chapter 2 explains the meaning of evaluations, their different dimensions, and the rationale for conducting democracy evaluations. Chapter 3 focuses on democracy indicators and examines their nature, strengths, limitations, and use. It looks at three categories of indicators: micro (performance and outcome), meso (sector specific), and macro levels. Chapter 4 discusses the meaning of monitoring, identifies the requirements for effective monitoring systems, and explains the steps in developing realistic monitoring for democracy interventions. Chapter 5 presents an overview of the evaluation process and suggests appropriate roles for evaluation managers. Chapter 6 focuses on experimental and quasi-experimental evaluation designs and explains the reasons why these designs cannot be widely used in multifaceted, long-term democracy evaluations. Chapter 7 discusses three other designs (pre- and posttest, cross-sectional, and case study designs) and mentions their relative strengths and limitations. Chapter 8 explains the distinction between qualitative and quantitative methods and then discusses seven specific methods: surveys, structured direct observation, secondary data analysis, document reviews, focus group discussions, key informant interviews, and group interviews. Chapter 9 focuses on communicating the findings and recommendations of democracy evaluations to stakeholders and the public. The final chapter makes a set of recommendations for the future.

Notes

1. There is often confusion between democracy promotion and democracy assistance. *Democracy assistance* is a subset of democracy promotion that, in addition to aid, includes a wide range of policy instruments such as diplomatic pressure, economic and political sanctions, incentives to join a wider union (e.g., the European Union), and even use of force under certain circumstances to foster and strengthen democratic institutions, procedures, and culture. A distinct advantage of democracy assistance is that it is relatively less threatening than, say, economic sanctions or intense diplomatic pressure to introduce political reforms. Its purpose is not to impose democracy, but to give a helping hand to those who are struggling to establish a more open, pluralistic political order. It is targeted to governmental organizations, civil society institutions, private sector firms, and even selected leaders and activists.

2. The United States budgeted more than $3.6 billion for FY 2010/11.

3. Although the meanings of the terms *project* and *programs* are different (please see the glossary in Appendix 2), in this book I often use the terms interchangeably.

2

The Why and What of Evaluating Democracy Assistance

Our understanding of the actual impacts of USAID DG [democracy and governance] assistance on progress towards democracy remains limited—and is the subject of much current debate in the policy and scholarly communities. Admittedly, the realities of democracy programming are complicated, given the emphasis on timely responses to fluid political circumstances. These realities pose particular challenges for the evaluation of democracy assistance programs.

—Report of the National Research Council

You (donor agencies) should encourage managers of democracy programs to do their own evaluation. That is the only way to institutionalize evaluations. They (managers) are threatened when evaluations are commissioned by funding agencies.

—An official of an international NGO

In this chapter, I focus on the evaluations of democracy programs and answer a broad range of essential questions: Why should democracy programs be evaluated? What is the meaning of evaluation? What types of evaluation are usually conducted or should be conducted by bilateral and multilateral agencies, their implementation partners, NGO communities, and private foundations engaged in democracy promotion? What are the major modalities for democracy evaluations? What are the elements of a sound evaluation system? And finally, what obstacles do evaluators face in evaluating democracy programs?

Why Democracy Evaluations?

Usually, the first question asked is why do we need evaluations of democracy assistance? It is not uncommon to hear responses that evaluations impose unnecessary burdens on management and that the time and resources devoted to evaluations can be better spent on developing new interventions. Such remarks are based on misconceptions about the very purposes of evaluations. Unlike audits or inspections, evaluations should be viewed as problem-solving and learning exercises, not fault-finding missions. In fact, evaluations of democracy assistance can improve its effectiveness, impacts, and legitimacy in various ways.

Evaluations can and do improve the performance of democracy interventions by solving implementation problems. Like other internationally supported interventions, democracy programs routinely encounter implementation problems caused by various factors. For example, they were not properly designed and the underlying conceptual models were flawed, the political context has changed so that programs are not getting the expected cooperation from host-country institutions, or managerial and technical staff proved to be incompetent. Whatever the reason, evaluations can identify the problems and their causes as well as make concrete recommendations for addressing them. For example, a midterm evaluation of a civil society program in an African country could inform managers about why it is not reaching the targeted organizations, what concerns and reservations these organizations have about the program, and what can be done to solve the problem. Such information will help managers and stakeholders to make midcourse corrections if necessary.

Evaluations also help international agencies make informed decisions about the future of a program or its follow-up. For example, a multilateral donor agency might have to decide about the future funding for its project on community radio stations or a private foundation might need to decide whether to continue its democracy fellowship program that provides in-house training for promising journalists. In both cases, performance and/or impact evaluations can aid in decisionmaking. By commissioning evaluations to find out about the effectiveness and outcomes of these interventions, concerned officials will be able to decide future courses of action on the basis of solid data and independent analysis rather than hunches or hearsay.

Moreover, evaluations of democracy assistance are needed to codify organizational and programming experience, thereby facilitating learning. Democracy assistance is relatively recent in origin, and there is a dearth of codified knowledge that can be fed into developing new interventions, strategies, and policies. Evaluations can fill this information gap. For example, during the 1990s, the international community was successful in brokering peace accords in several countries (e.g., Angola, Cambodia, El Salvador, Ethiopia, Guatemala, Mozambique, and Nicaragua), which called for electing new governments. The international community provided assistance to hold these elections, which, albeit not totally free and fair, contributed to their democratic transitions. The US Agency for International Development (USAID) conducted a program evaluation of international assistance for these elections. Its evaluation report and the individual case studies, which were also published in the form of a book, generated a set of findings and lessons that were used in subsequent electoral assistance (Kumar 1998). More importantly, they stimulated new evaluations and academic research and, as a result, there is now a corpus of data, information, and empirically grounded theoretical insights, which are routinely used for designing elections not only in war-torn societies but also in other countries that have embarked on a transition to democracy.

Finally, democracy evaluations are essential for accountability purposes. Accountability is needed at two levels—the intervention and the agency or organization level. At the intervention level, evaluations promote a culture of accountability among managers by examining whether the concerned intervention achieved what it was expected to achieve and, if not, why it did not and what should be done to solve the problem. At the agency or organization level, evaluations put pressure on senior policymakers and managers to determine whether the assistance is making a difference, or whether the investments justified the results. Generally, agencies and organizations are unable to answer these questions on the basis of credible evidence if they do not conduct evaluations. International agencies can use evaluation findings to document the successes and failures of their programs and their possible contribution to strengthening and consolidating democracies.

In the United States, there is a growing demand from the White House, Office of Management and Budget (OMB), and US Congress for rigorous evaluations of foreign assistance programs, including those for promoting democracy. OMB recently issued a directive to all federal agencies requiring them to institute effective mechanisms that can generate empirical data to evaluate the effectiveness of existing programs and explore alternate approaches that may better achieve their objectives. There are also legal and regulatory mandates for performance management and evaluation under the US Code and Government Performance and Results Act (GPRA) of 1993, which was changed to the GPRA Modernization ACT in 2010. The act articulates a comprehensive approach to planning and performance in which agencies collaborate on achieving federal goals as well as their individual agency goals.

Thus, evaluations of democracy assistance are not an intellectual luxury, but a necessity for democracy promotion. Sound evaluations not only improve the effectiveness and impacts of democracy assistance, but also promote its legitimacy. Above all, they save taxpayers money by eliminating programs that do not accomplish what they were intended to achieve.

The Meaning of Evaluation

The *Encyclopedia of Evaluation* defines evaluation as

> an applied inquiry process for conducting and synthesizing evidence that culminates in conclusions about the state of affairs, value, merit, worth, significance, or a quality of a program, product, person, policy, proposal or plan. Conclusions made in evaluation encompass both an empirical aspect (that something is the case) and a normative aspect (judgment about the value of something). It is the value feature that distinguishes evaluations from other types of inquiry, such as basic science research, clinical epidemiology, investigative journalism or public polling. (Fournier 2005, p. 140)

Thus, evaluations involve both investigating programs as well as determining their worth. Both of these dimensions are recognized by the Development Assistance Committee of the Organisation for Economic Co-operation and Development (OECD), which defines evaluation as

> the systematic and objective assessment of an on-going or completed project, program or policy, its design, implementation and results. The aim is to determine the relevance and fulfillment of objectives, development efficiency, effectiveness, impact and sustainability. An evaluation should provide information that is credible

and useful, enabling the incorporation of lessons learned into the decision-making process of both recipients and donors. (OECD 2002, pp. 21–22)

Three general observations can be made on the basis of the above definitions. First, evaluations involve systematic and credible collection and analysis of data, which can be gathered from a wide range of sources such as surveys, direct observation methods, key informant interviews, or focus group discussions. Most evaluations also draw heavily from planning documents, progress reports, and monitoring information if and when available. Finally, they can use secondary data available from governments, private sector firms, universities, and research organizations. The data can be quantitative, qualitative, or both.

Second, evaluation involves making judgments. Evaluation is the process of "determining the worth or significance of an activity, policy or program" (OECD 2002, p. 21). Such judgments may pertain to the program's design, components and activities, implementation, outcomes, or cost-effectiveness. For example, examining the performance of a media project or its training component also involves determining its worth. Such assessments about the worth of a project can be made on the basis of criteria that are implicit or explicit in the intervention's design documents or criteria that are established by evaluators.

Third, the value of an evaluation lies in generating information, findings, and recommendations that can be used by a project's stakeholders. During the early phase of the evaluation discipline, most evaluators viewed evaluations simply as social research endeavors that should be judged solely by their methodological rigor. While many still adhere to this view, a majority of evaluators now believe that the real test of evaluations is that their findings and recommendations are relevant and usable. A methodologically sound evaluation that does not produce usable information for managers, policymakers, and/or stakeholders is of little value. What distinguishes evaluations from academic research is their practical utility; therefore, considerations such as relevance, timeliness of the findings, and practicability of the recommendations are critical.

Democracy evaluations can focus on one or more of the following five sets of issues (also called "criteria" or "dimensions" in evaluation literature):

1. *Effectiveness.* Effectiveness refers to the extent to which an intervention's objectives are likely to be achieved. Evaluations seek to determine whether an intervention's services and products are reaching the targeted populations, whether the intended beneficiaries are using them, whether the coverage of the target population is as planned, and whether the intervention is likely to achieve its targets. Most midterm evaluations focus on effectiveness.

2. *Efficiency.* Efficiency measures the output of an intervention in relation to its costs. The most widely used method in development programs is cost-benefit analysis, which determines the net benefits of an intervention. Such analyses are most appropriate when (1) economic values can be assigned to outputs and outcomes; (2) reliable data are available or gathered; and (3) causation can be established between inputs and outputs and outcomes. Cost-benefit analysis of democracy programs is not feasible simply because it is unrealistic and unwise to assign economic values to constructs such as human rights, liberty, or freedom. Instead of utilizing a cost-benefit analysis, evaluators can measure the cost-effectiveness, which involves comparing the costs of different approaches for achieving a given objective. For example, for a voter education project, evaluators can measure the costs of different methods of reaching voters. They can compare the per unit cost of reaching voters through radio, newspapers, or public meetings. By comparing the per unit costs of different methods, evaluators can identify the most cost-effective method for undertaking voter education programs.

3. *Impact.* In evaluation parlance, impacts refer to results or effects that are caused by, or are attributable to, a program or policy. Impact evaluations often focus on higher-level effects of a project, program, or policy that occur in the medium or long term. The essential questions are, Did the intervention make a difference? How did it make a difference? Did it have unintended consequences? In the case of democracy interventions, while the outputs can usually be documented, it is not always easy to establish medium- and long-term results. For example, while evaluators can often establish that the assistance has strengthened human rights NGOs, which have begun to undertake many educational and lobby activities, they cannot establish, much less measure, the impact of NGOs' activities on the state of human rights in the country.

4. *Sustainability.* Sustainability refers to the continuation of an intervention's services and benefits after assistance ends. Three dimensions of sustainability—financial, institutional, and environmental—

can be examined in evaluations. *Financial sustainability* indicates the capacity of the assisted organization to be financially self-sufficient, either through revenue-generating activities or substitution of other funding sources. *Institutional sustainability* refers to the assisted organization's capacity to manage its operations independently. Finally, *environmental sustainability* refers to the capacity of an intervention's services and benefits to survive in the changed or changing environment.

5. *Relevance*. Evaluations also examine the continued relevance of an intervention's objectives and approach in light of changing political problems, policies, or priorities. The political, economic, and institutional environments in which programs are designed and implemented can change over time. Some of the changes can have major consequences for a program. For example, the decision of a host government to impose restrictions on the existing human rights organizations could undoubtedly affect human rights programs funded by the international donor agencies. As a result, new strategies would have to be developed to help them. On the other hand, the fall of a semiauthoritarian regime would open new opportunities for existing democracy interventions. In such circumstances, an evaluation can be undertaken to find out if ongoing interventions remain relevant and, if not, what changes can be made so that they can be appropriate and useful.

Types of Democracy Evaluations

Performance or Process Evaluations

Performance or process evaluations focus on the performance of a program and examine its implementation, inputs, outputs, and likely outcomes. They are undertaken to answer a wide range of important questions: Did the program take off as planned? What problems and challenges, if any, did it face? Was it or is it being effectively managed? Did it provide planned goods and services in a timely fashion? If not, why? Were the original cost estimates about the program realistic? Did a change in the host country's political circumstances affect the performance and outcomes? Did the program meet its targets or is it likely to meet them? What are its expected effects and impacts? Is the program sustainable?

Performance evaluations can be conducted during the midcycle of an intervention or near its end. When conducted during the midcycle of an intervention, they can provide recommendations to improve its implementation and solve the challenges and problems it faces. When conducted at the end of an intervention, they can aid in developing follow-up programs. There is no hard or fast rule about when a performance evaluation should be conducted. However, for a democracy intervention with a life cycle of five years, it should be undertaken during the midcycle of the program so that managers and stakeholders can have an objective assessment of the progress, problems, and challenges of implementation, which would enable them to make midcourse corrections if necessary. On the other hand, for a two- or three-year intervention, it is preferable to conduct a performance evaluation at its end because it usually takes eight to twelve months before a project becomes fully operational and its outputs are visible. Moreover, many short-term democracy interventions tend to have follow-up activities and performance evaluations that can help identify them.

The resources and efforts required for performance evaluations differ depending on variables such as the size, component activities, sites, and duration of projects. For example, USAID generally sends two- or three-person teams to the field to evaluate its multiyear and multicomponent democracy programs. However, for smaller interventions, even a one-person team assisted by a junior researcher would serve the purpose. When evaluations are done by expatriates, as often is the case, they require a local partner who is fluent in the country's language and understands its social and political landscape. Most performance evaluations of democracy interventions can be completed within three to four weeks. Box 2.1 shows an example of a performance evaluation of a National Democratic Institute for International Affairs (NDI) project by the Swedish International Development Cooperation Agency (Sida).

Impact/Summative or Expost Evaluations

These evaluations differ from performance evaluations in that their focus is on the outcomes and impacts. The Development Assistance Committee of the OECD defines *impacts* as "the positive or negative, primary and secondary long-term effects produced by a development intervention, directly or indirectly, intended or unintended" (OECD 2002, pp. 21–22). While this definition emphasizes long-term impacts, impact evaluations include short- or medium-term impacts as

Box 2.1 Performance Evaluation of the NDI Program to Strengthen Women's Political Participation

During 2005–2008, the Swedish International Development Agency supported the NDI program "Strengthening Women's Political Participation in Political and Decentralization Processes" in Burkina Faso. Sida commissioned an evaluation of the program in 2008. In addition to the review of program documents, the evaluation team conducted an e-mail survey, key informant interviews, and focus group discussions. Here are some key findings.

Relevance. The program used participatory approaches that were relevant and strategies that were pertinent given the country's complex and sensitive elections context. Further, the relevance of the program in relation to Burkina Faso's political vision is evidenced by the fact that it promotes the country's international commitments such as the Convention on the Elimination of Discrimination Against Women (CEDAW), the Millennium Development Goals (MDGs), and the strategic objectives of the national Poverty Reduction Strategy Plan (PRSP).

Effectiveness. The program achieved its objectives as measured by the indicators specified in the original project document. However, objectives and indicators as currently elaborated tend to capture mainly quantitative results and activities undertaken. Although the program set realistic targets in order to ensure their effective fulfillment, it is regrettable that important lessons learned and qualitative effects are neither captured nor analyzed in reports.

Results and possible impact. The substantive difference that the program made at the political and legislative level can be identified in a unanimously recognized improvement of intraparty political dialogue; a clear understanding that the political participation of women could be a precious election asset; advances made in relation to the 30 percent quota legislation; and, consequently, advances toward equality (at least in numbers) in political participation at national and local levels between women and men. With regard to having a substantive contribution to poverty alleviation, women's rights, and inequalities in the poorest strata of the population, the program made a difference by creating discussion forums where citizens (or their representatives) could voice their concerns. However, given the limited time frame of the program and the early stages of election processes as well as the fact that poverty reduction was neither part of the objectives of the program nor part of its indicators, the impact on the poorest citizens cannot be measured at this stage.

(continues)

Box 2.1 continued

Efficiency. NDI is in a unique position in terms of combining the use of local NGO expertise and remaining external and neutral to internal political parties' interests. By choosing to collaborate and support local expertise, NDI has succeeded in anchoring its action within Burkinae's civil society while ensuring a cost-efficient strategy compared with the use of internationally based expertise. In terms of weaknesses, NDI's human and financial resources are limited.

Sustainability. Although the main challenge to the sustainability of the training is the considerable turnover of elected representatives, NDI succeeded in maintaining a core participant group to regularly attend the training sessions. Whereas the sustainability of the program activities cannot be fully ensured given the nature of the training activities, NDI could nevertheless improve it by providing trainings of trainers and reusable pedagogical material and by ensuring sustainability is captured in the monitoring systems with relevant indicators.

Source: Consulting firm COWI A/S, Parallelvejz, Denmark (2008).

---

it may take years before the long-term impacts of democracy interventions are visible.

These evaluations are designed to answer questions such as, What changes were observed in targeted populations, organizations, or policies during and at the end of the program? To what extent can the observed changes be attributed to the program? How did the intervention affect the recipient country organizations that participated in it? Were there unintended effects that were not anticipated at the planning stage? Were they positive or negative? What factors explain the intended and unintended impacts? The essence of impact evaluation lies in establishing that the changes have occurred as a result of the intervention or, at least, that it has substantially contributed to the changes. This is the greatest conceptual and methodological challenge that all impact evaluations face.

USAID defines *impact evaluations* narrowly and uses the term to refer to those summative/expost evaluations that use control groups to measure the precise impacts of an intervention. In such evaluations, two groups—treatment and control/comparison—are established at the launch of an intervention. One group receives the services and goods from the intervention (e.g., technical assistance, training, advice, and financial support) while the other does not. The overall impacts of the intervention are measured by comparing the performance, conditions, or status of the two groups.

As much as possible, summative evaluations should be carefully planned at the design stage so that necessary baseline data can be collected.

Global Evaluations

Global program evaluations, which are designed to examine the performance and outcomes of a major subsector of democracy assistance, are indeed complex intellectual endeavors. They seek to draw general findings, conclusions, and lessons about a subsector, drawing from the experience of a large number of interventions implemented in different countries. The purpose of a global evaluation of electoral assistance, for example, is not to evaluate the success or failure of individual projects but to determine the efficacy and outcomes of electoral assistance programs per se. The methodology for such evaluations was developed by the now defunct Center for Development Information and Evaluation (CDIE) of USAID, which conducted numerous global program evaluations of USAID assistance. These evaluations generated a wealth of empirically grounded knowledge that affected subsequent USAID policies and programs. Since global program evaluations are not common, I will briefly mention a few steps that CDIE followed in conducting them.

The first step was to identify a critical program area that needed global evaluation. CDIE identified each topic after intensive consultations with senior USAID officials and a thorough review of policy and program documents, budgetary allocations, and legislative interests. Once it was satisfied that a global evaluation would be useful, CDIE prepared a brief evaluation proposal, which was submitted for approval to the senior officials. If a proposal was approved, CDIE undertook an intensive review of literature to develop a conceptual framework, refine evaluation questions, and explore data collection approaches for the proposed evaluation. The principal investigator then prepared a comprehensive evaluation proposal, which included the rationale for evaluation, evaluation questions and hypotheses, the primary stakeholders, data collection approaches, the countries in which fieldwork would be undertaken, a time frame, and an estimated budget. The proposal was presented at planning workshops attended by senior managers, technical experts, members of the evaluation team, and outside experts. Such workshops proved to be extremely helpful in revising the proposal. An unintended consequence of the workshops was that many participants developed an interest in the evaluation and continued to provide intellectual and political support to the evaluation team.

CDIE evaluations treated a country as a unit of analysis, which meant that all interventions in the concerned sector or subsector in a country were covered by the evaluation. A major challenge was the selection of the countries to be covered in evaluation. Usually, the countries were selected by taking into consideration factors such as the volume of assistance, coverage of different regions, the willingness of the country to host evaluation teams, and the feasibility of data collection. The global evaluations generally—though not always—followed a multiple case study approach. Six or seven country case studies were prepared by evaluation teams; each team usually consisted of two or three expatriates and one or two local researchers. In addition to review of documents, each team conducted key informant interviews, focus group discussions, and direct observations. In many cases, they also conducted minisurveys. Each country case study was reviewed both at USAID headquarters and in the field. Once all case studies were completed, the principal evaluator wrote a synthesis report. Writing the synthesis report was an iterative process. Often, the principal investigator found that there were information gaps and additional data were necessary. Whenever possible, the needed data and information were solicited from overseas missions or other sources. A workshop was usually organized at this stage to solicit the comments and suggestions on the synthesis report from the authors of different case studies, USAID managers, and outside experts. The principal evaluator took all the comments and suggestions into account when producing the final report.

There is a need for undertaking global program evaluations for the core areas of democracy assistance (see Appendix 3). They would provide insights, understanding, and lessons that cannot be obtained by evaluations of a single program. A finding that rings true across multiple countries is more robust than a finding coming from an individual case study. Global evaluations enable senior policymakers and decisionmakers to observe trends that occur across multiple countries, which adds weight to key findings. Two examples of global program evaluations are shown in Boxes 2.2 and 2.3.

Box 2.2 Global Program Evaluation of USAID's Media Assistance

During July 2002–June 2003, the Center for Development Information and Evaluation conducted a global program evaluation of USAID's international media assistance programs. CDIE brought together managers and former managers of media programs, media experts, senior policymakers, senior staff of congressional committees, and outside experts to share their experiences, insights, recommendations, and expectations on the subject during a two-day workshop in July 2002. The workshop examined different dimensions of media assistance and assisted in developing a coherent evaluation proposal. The proceedings of the workshop were published as a separate document. CDIE also undertook an intensive review of more than 300 documents, reports, and papers that it had collected on international media assistance.

CDIE prepared detailed background papers on media assistance programs to Afghanistan, Bosnia and Herzegovina, Indonesia, Russia, Serbia, and Central America. These papers gave a brief background of the country and its media sector, the nature and progress of USAID media interventions, the challenges that these programs faced, and other relevant material. CDIE then sent evaluation teams to these countries to conduct in-depth interviews with project managers, staff of the media organizations that had received or were receiving assistance, civil society organizations, and democracy experts. Teams also organized focus group discussions and, in a few cases, commissioned surveys. Teams spent two to four weeks in a country depending on the nature of projects and volume of USAID investments. The teams wrote detailed case studies based on their fieldwork, which were reviewed both at USAID headquarters and in the country.

Because there was a dearth of information on several aspects of the media assistance program, CDIE commissioned a few additional studies. One such study focused on the international media assistance provided to Sierra Leone, which was designed to promote social and political reconciliation in the aftermath of prolonged civil war and bloodshed. The second study focused on the workings of community radio stations in Africa.

The major findings of the global evaluation were as follows: media assistance was effective in promoting and strengthening independent media; while training programs had multiplier effects on upgrading the professional skills of journalists and instilling the norms of free press, they suffered from poor implementation; progress in promoting legal and regulatory reforms was slow and halting; economic viability of independent media outlets in war-torn societies remained a major problem;

(continues)

Box 2.2 continued

built-in safeguards to ensure the independence and integrity of media programs from political manipulations worked well; and independent media building has served US national interests. The evaluation made specific policy and programmatic recommendations for USAID.

In addition to the main report, six country case studies were published by USAID. In addition, several other reports including the findings of the workshop were also published. Finally, I directed this evaluation and wrote a book titled *Promoting Independent Media: Strategies for Democracy Assistance*. It was the first book published on the subject that articulated a coherent framework for media assistance and presented eight case studies of media assistance programs.

Sources: Kumar (2004, 2006b).

Experience Reviews

As the name suggests, experience reviews involve systematic analysis of the past experience. They focus on a limited range of questions that are of paramount interest to policymakers and decisionmakers. Experience reviews do not involve fieldwork; the needed information is gathered from sources such as literature reviews supplemented whenever possible by key informant interviews or expert workshops. Framing of the right questions is critical to the success of experience reviews. As far as possible, questions should be such that they can be answered on the basis of available data and information. For example, if there is no information about the cost-effectiveness of different methods of voter education, there is no sense in conducting an experience review on this topic.

When resources are limited and there is an urgent need for information for policy formulation or designing new policies and programs, experience reviews can be worthwhile. The ideal course is to combine a literature review with key informant interviews or an expert workshop. An example might be that an agency wants to know about donors' experiences in establishing journalism training institutes. The evaluator would begin by framing a set of researchable questions and conduct a review of documents including evaluations on the subject. Since these documents are not likely to be available to the public, the evaluator may have to contact the organizations and

Box 2.3 IRI Evaluation of Political Party Assistance Programs

The International Republican Institute (IRI) has supported political party building programs for the past twenty-five years. To identify results, lessons learned, and best practices from this experience, IRI conducted an eight-country case study initiative of its political party building programs.

To frame the research, IRI first identified six principles for political party development derived from a literature review on the topic of political parties and an extensive period of internal discussion and reflection among its staff. The principles encompass the key aspects of a fully functioning political party and its activities, including party organization, party identity, message development and delivery, party competition, governance, and strengthening of the legal system. The case study effort then sought to determine the types of programs that IRI conducted to promote progress toward these principles, the extent to which IRI programs influenced that progress, and what the parties' progress looked like over the course of a country's democratic development.

The institute used various criteria in the selection of the countries researched, including length of time of IRI's party program in the country, democratic progress, and location to ensure balance and breadth of scope. For each country in the case study, IRI researchers spent several weeks conducting a desktop review of program documentation and then undertook two to three weeks of field research. On average, the team conducted thirty in-depth interviews in each country. Using the collected data, the team then assessed the extent to which targeted parties developed both according to and outside of the principles as well as the contributions that the institute made in that development process.

The team then analyzed findings for each country that focused on results of the party development programs in the country as well as programmatic lessons learned based on IRI's experiences and changing country contexts. This analysis informed the development of a final synthesis report that covered program strategy, general results, and lessons learned with respect to party development that resonated across multiple countries. The synthesis report explores not only how IRI's activities and results contributed to party development across varying political contexts, but also why some strategies may have been more effective than others. The synthesis report presents seventeen overarching program recommendations to help inform the Institute's party building programs going forward.

(continues)

Box 2.3 continued

For example, the study found that IRI's public opinion polling played an important role in several country programs in encouraging parties to develop issue-based messages and platforms. The case studies also revealed, however, that public opinion research work was often a long-term undertaking. In many cases, IRI faced challenges in terms of getting parties to understand the value of polling since there was sometimes a level of misinformation and distrust about polling methodology. This distrust does make sense: polling is a sophisticated tool and various attributes of polling (including the use of small samples to predict public sentiment overall) must be understood before stakeholders (including political parties) can be expected to accept and use results. The research revealed that a long-term approach to polling programs, where the introduction of polling was phased in slowly and initially involved basic instruction on what polls are and how to use them, had payoffs down the road in terms of changing the perceptions of parties that did not initially appreciate the importance of polling in the democratic process. Based on this finding, the report recommends that IRI consider polling efforts to be a long-term endeavor since it can take several years for parties to understand and use polling in sophisticated and effective ways.

Source: Personal communication from Jonathan Jones of the International Republican Institute.

agencies involved in producing them. The Center for International Media Assistance (CIMA) has fashioned an interesting approach to experience reviews. It commissions a few papers on a specific topic and then organizes an expert workshop to draw conclusions and lessons about the media assistance. Such workshops have generated interesting ideas and lessons on different dimensions of media assistance. The findings of a workshop on community radio stations are shown in Box 2.4.

Evaluation Modalities

Using the criterion of who conducts them, evaluations can also be classified in the following four categories.

Box 2.4 Findings of a Meeting on Community Radio Stations

On October 9, 2007, National Endowment for Democracy's CIMA convened a working group of twenty-seven experts to examine the role and challenges of community radio development. The working group included community radio developers and activists, representatives from donor and implementing organizations, scholars, and policymakers. The goal of the one-day meeting was to draw a few lessons and make recommendations for policymakers on whether and how to address community radio development within larger media assistance initiatives. The group's major findings can be summarized as follows:

1. The impact of independent media on society is cross-cutting and encompassing and, thus, should be regarded as a unique development sector. Within media development, it is essential to focus on community radio as a powerful source for empowerment, especially for disenfranchised and marginalized groups in society. Research efforts to quantify, analyze, and draw conclusions regarding the impact of community radio are essential and can serve as a sound basis for assistance advocacy.
2. The most important aspects of community radio, which serves a geographic group or a community of interest, include the broad participation by community members—often on a volunteer basis—and the ownership and control of the station by the community through a board of governors that is representative of the community and responsive to the diversity of its needs.
3. Where local need and potential are present, but the legal and political environment conducive to community radio development is absent, the international development community should find ways to encourage governments to adopt and enforce legislation and regulations necessary for community radio to operate.
4. Financial sustainability is a major challenge for community radio stations. Possible solutions to boost struggling community radio efforts include a well-coordinated pooled funding source, or a microcredit loan system for community radio development that is not subject to donor priorities.
5. Although sustainability of funding recipients should not be the primary objective of donors, funding strategies and development models should encourage sustainability in the long run. Donors should provide equipment and technological support adequate for the local setting and comprehensive training to prepare funding recipients for sustainability even in changing environments.

(continues)

Box 2.4 continued

6. Networks of community radio stations can serve as effective and efficient instruments for exchanges of programming and creation of national news and information programs. Professional associations can play a vital role in establishing professional codes of ethics, identifying training needs, and establishing training programs. They can also serve as advocates for the community radio sector, soliciting more funds for development. Associations and networks can thus become focal points for donor assistance.
7. The media assistance community should be alert to new prospects for community radio development through digitization and the Internet.

Source: CIMA (2007).

Internal Evaluations

Internal evaluations are conducted or commissioned by program managers to assess the progress of their interventions, identify problems and bottlenecks, and find ways to improve performance and possible outcomes. Their defining feature is that the evaluation findings and recommendations are meant <u>for internal</u> use only. Internal evaluations can be conducted by internal and outside specialists. Since most staff members of a democracy intervention do not have expertise in evaluations and are too close to its implementations, it is <u>advisable to hire outside</u> experts.

There are many advantages that make internal evaluations suitable for democracy evaluations. They can be undertaken quickly. Evaluators receive full cooperation of the management in obtaining necessary data and information. Moreover, since these evaluations are commissioned by managers, their findings and recommendations tend to be readily utilized by management. Moreover, their recommendations tend to be actionable since managers are often involved in framing them. In fact, some recommendations may even be implemented before formal reports are submitted. Internal evaluations also facilitate organizational learning. Managers and concerned staff learn how to evaluate their own efforts. This is particularly important for the nascent NGO community in developing and transition countries where the management of NGOs often rests with charismatic leaders with limited experience in managing formal organizations.

In addition, managers do not feel threatened as they often do
when evaluations are conducted by their headquarters or by donor
agencies. They are not worried that the shortcomings of the program
would become widely known to sully their image. Many democracy
interventions operate in highly sensitive political environments; consequently, there remains the possibility that adverse information
about their implementation can undermine their legitimacy. For
example, an evaluation finding that a few NGOs, which received
human rights assistance from the international community, failed to
keep financial records may provide ammunition to opponents of
democracy assistance to question the very rationale for human rights
assistance.

While internal evaluations are both necessary and desirable, they
should not be treated as substitutes for rigorous external evaluations.
Their obvious limitation is that, because evaluators are responsible to *downside*
managers of the programs, they may be reluctant to criticize management's performance. As a result, questions can be raised about their
objectivity and credibility.

External Evaluations

External evaluations are administered by a management unit that is
separate from or higher in rank than the unit managing the program
and are carried out by an independent outside evaluator. For example, the evaluation of a USAID program to provide technical assistance and support to a national election commission would be managed by the office of the mission director or program officer or by a
bureau at USAID headquarters, not by the democracy officer who is
in charge of such assistance.

External evaluations tend to be more objective and credible than
internal evaluations since evaluators are not responsible to managers
of the interventions being evaluated. These evaluators enjoy greater
freedom than they do in internal evaluations and are able to express
their criticisms more freely and candidly. They can call attention to
managerial problems without the fear that they will be criticized for
it. Often, such evaluations are more formal than internal evaluations.
Since the findings and recommendations can be shared widely, they
are relatively better documented than internal evaluations.

The strengths of internal evaluations are the weaknesses of external evaluations. Their principal weakness is that many program
managers are apprehensive about them and feel that evaluators do not

appreciate the constraints under which they operate. As a result, they may withhold their full cooperation and may be guarded in sharing inside information. Moreover, unlike in internal evaluations, they do not feel a sense of ownership of recommendations.

Participatory Evaluations

Participatory evaluations involve the active participation of multiple stakeholders. Michael Quinn Patton identifies several features of participatory evaluations, which include (1) evaluation involves "participants in learning evaluation logic and skills, for example, setting evaluation objectives, defining priorities, selecting questions, interpreting data and connecting activities to outcomes"; (2) ownership of the evaluation is vested in the participants, who determine its focus and priorities of evaluations; and (3) the role of the evaluator is to help "the group in making the collective inquiry" (2008, p. 175). Participants are accountable primarily to themselves and only secondarily to external actors, if at all.

A common modality involves the program managers or the funding agency's appointing an evaluator who, after extensive discussions with the stakeholders, prepares a draft proposal reflecting their views, suggestions, and expectations. Participants in a stakeholder workshop discuss the draft proposal and make decisions about evaluation questions, scope, design, data collection requirements, modes of data collection, and utilization of findings and recommendations. If necessary, specific responsibilities are also assigned to different stakeholders. Once data and information are gathered, stakeholders analyze the material and explore its implications in a subsequent workshop or series of workshops. Findings and recommendations are formulated by a panel of the participants.

Participatory evaluations have obvious advantages. They enable managers to listen and respond to stakeholders. Face-to-face interactions facilitate better understanding of the workings of an intervention and its achievements and problems. Participants often come up with fresh ideas for solving problems or improving performance. Since the managers themselves participate in the evaluation process, they are inclined to use the resultant information and recommendations. Participatory evaluations also have limitations. They tend to be less objective because participants have vested interests that they articulate and defend. In many cases, developing consensus among stakeholders can be difficult. Also, such evaluations are not suitable for addressing complex technical issues that may require specialized expertise. Because they are less formal, their credibility is often low.

Collaborative (Joint) Evaluations

Collaborative evaluations are conducted jointly by more than one office, agency, or partner of a program. For example, all major agencies and organizations that provided electoral assistance to a post-conflict society can work together in conducting a joint evaluation of their individual electoral assistance programs. While collaborative evaluations have been used in evaluating international assistance programs, there are only a few examples of their use in evaluating democracy assistance.

The modus operandi for such evaluations tends to vary. In a major evaluation, collaborative organizations form an implementing committee responsible for designing and managing it. The committee develops the statement of work/terms of reference (SOW/TOR), selects an evaluation team, and provides necessary support and advice to it. The committee holds meetings to review the progress and solve bottlenecks and other problems that may arise. Once the report is ready, the committee is responsible for its review, necessary revisions, and follow-up actions. For small projects, the process can be simpler. One of the participating organizations can take the lead and work closely with sponsoring organizations and agencies in the planning and conducting of evaluations.

Collaborative evaluations have many advantages. They can facilitate mutual learning among partnering organizations. The burden for conducting evaluations is shared among collaborating entities, as a single evaluation is undertaken instead of multiple evaluations by collaborating organizations. Since more than one organization is involved, evaluators usually enjoy greater flexibility and independence than in evaluations commissioned by a single organization. Finally, as a result of the pooling of resources, more intensive and systematic data collection and analysis can be undertaken, which enhance both the quality and credibility of the evaluation.

On the negative side, collaborative evaluations can be time consuming. Collaborating organizations may find it difficult to agree on a common SOW/TOR for the proposed evaluation. They may differ about appropriate evaluation designs and data collection strategies, the qualifications of evaluators, and the composition of the evaluation team, and it may require time to evolve a consensus around these issues. Collaborative evaluations also require a strong management team that can keep in touch with different partners and reconcile their concerns and expectations. Unless carefully planned, the findings of collaborative evaluations may not meet the needs and requirements of all partners.

The choice of modality for an evaluation depends on perceived information needs, resources, and circumstances. If objectivity and credibility are key requirements, an external evaluation may be the appropriate choice. If stakeholder ownership and acting on findings are priorities, participatory approaches are usually better. When there is a need to draw common lessons from programs supported by different agencies and organizations, collaborative evaluations may be advisable.

Obstacles to Evaluating Democracy Interventions

As any evaluator will probably testify, conducting an evaluation is not an easy enterprise. Every step toward designing and implementing an evaluation is fraught with numerous obstacles that range from a lack of credible data and limited time and resources to bureaucratic apathy, if not hostility. The situation for democracy evaluations is even worse for the three reasons that follow.

First, the underlying intervention models for many democracy programs remain questionable. They are grounded neither in sound theory nor in hard empirical evidence. Although during the past two decades, knowledge about and understanding of the workings and outcomes of democracy interventions have improved, the situation remains far from satisfactory. For example, we still do not know if assistance to political parties in drafting their election manifestos makes much of a difference in elections and yet most political party training focuses on it. Most anticorruption programs support public education programs and yet there is no hard evidence that such programs have any long-term effects on the prevalence of corruption. As Michael McFaul notes, there is no consensus among political scientists about suitable designs for democratic systems:

> Big debates also continue over institutional design. Are parliamentary systems more stable and more democratic than presidential systems or is semi-presidentialism best design? Is proportional representation a better electoral system than first-past-the-post electoral laws? When are unitary states preferable to federal systems?

> There is also disagreement on the best sequence for democratic re-
> forms. Which should come first: elections or a constitution? Should
> regional elections be held before national elections? Is the rule of
> law a necessary precondition for effective elections? . . . Among
> democratic theorists, no consensus exists on the relative impor-
> tance of political parties, civil society, and courts. (2010, p. 15)

It may be argued that democracy is not alone in this respect.
Many other areas of international assistance ranging from economic
growth to humanitarian support also are not immune from controversy. While this is true, democracy promotion has more than its le-
gitimate share, partly because democratization is a complex process
and its various facets and elements have not yet been fully explored.

Such a state of affairs often creates problems for evaluations of
democracy interventions. One precondition for evaluations is that the
underlying intervention model on which the intervention is based is
sound and verifiable. If there are serious reservations about the underlying rationale for a program, then the evaluations not only have to examine the outputs and outcomes of democracy interventions in relation
to the implicit or explicit evaluation model, but also must reexamine
the model itself. This can become a challenging task that evaluators
often are not able to accomplish given time and resource constraints.

Second, as alluded to earlier and explained in detail later, while
we can examine the issues pertaining to the implementation and outputs of democracy programs, it is extremely difficult to assess, much
less measure, their outcomes and long-term effects. For example, an
international donor has provided assistance to a transition country for
training election monitors. Whereas evaluators can examine the effects of assistance on the quality of election monitoring training and
the knowledge and skills the trainees acquired, and in some cases
their placement during national elections, they cannot attribute the
freeness and fairness of elections to the assistance itself. Nor can they
examine the long-term effects of the training on the institutionalization of democratic competition in a country. The obvious reason is
that a large number of factors and forces (e.g., the commitment of political elites, the strength of independent media, the vibrancy and independence of the judiciary, the strengths and weaknesses of political
parties, and public awareness) also affect the freeness and fairness of
elections. The problem is that evaluators are frequently expected to
answer critical questions about the outcomes and impacts, which can
be answered only by long-term research by the academic community.

Third, in many cases, the political environment is not conducive to the collection of necessary information and data. In many semiauthoritarian states, there are established boundaries that evaluators cannot cross without jeopardizing the welfare of organizations and individuals receiving democracy assistance. Several evaluators, who evaluated democracy interventions in Middle Eastern countries before the Arab Spring, told me that they felt both dismayed and frustrated by their inability to freely interview key informants.[1] Many felt that that they were being watched. In war-torn societies such as Afghanistan and Iraq, where the international community launched well-funded programs to pave the way for democratic transition, many evaluators could not even venture into the field to gather needed data. Evaluators of media interventions during civil war in the former Yugoslavia encountered a hostile environment, which undermined the rigor and relevance of their reports. These examples can be multiplied, but the essential point is that evaluations of democracy programs require a political landscape in which evaluators can freely seek information and ideas. This can be a question mark in many cases.

Note

　　1. This interview and all others in this book were conducted confidentially by the author.

3

Democracy Indicators: Their Use and Misuse in Evaluations

A problem that confronts the managers of all production agencies is that by plan or inadvertence they may give most of their attention to more easily measured outcomes at the expense of those less easily observed or counted.

—*James Q. Wilson*

Development officers focus on what they can measure because the counter-bureaucracy demands it. In practice it means more funding for those development sectors in the hard sciences, such as public health and medicine, and less to the soft sciences such as democracy and governance programs, the foundation of which is political science, the "softest" of the social sciences. The soft sciences are less visible, harder to measure, and much slower to demonstrate success than the hard sciences.

—*Andrew Natsios*

During the past three decades, the word *indicator* has entered the vocabulary of the international development community and has been accepted with enthusiasm that is unprecedented for evaluators and monitoring experts. An indicator is a measure used to determine change over time or in space. Indicators have been successfully used in a wide variety of sectors (e.g., health, education, family planning, and economic growth) and have enabled policymakers and evaluators to monitor progress, measure results, and make comparative analyses.

Social scientists also have been developing and refining democracy indicators with varying degrees of success. Such indicators can be classified in three categories. The first category consists of micro-level indicators that measure the performance and outcomes of democracy programs. Such indicators are increasingly being used by international agencies and their implementing partners. Second, a few efforts have been made to develop indices for specific sectors of democracy (e.g., the media or elections), which, for a lack of better expression, can be labeled as meso-level indicators. Finally, political scientists have constructed indices to measure the state of democracy in a country. Such macro-level indices are used to examine the progress toward democracy over time and to make cross-country comparisons. In this chapter, I explore the use of the above three categories of indicators in evaluating democracy assistance.

This chapter is organized as follows. First, I discuss micro-level indicators, provide examples of such indicators, and explain their use and limitations. Next, I discuss macro-level indicators, which are relatively more developed and have been tested in different political environments over time. Finally, I focus on meso-level indicators. After explaining their nature, I present a case study in which meso-level indicators were used to evaluate a democracy intervention.

Micro-Level Indicators

The purpose of the micro-level indicators is to measure the activities, outputs, and outcomes of democracy interventions. For the purposes of analysis, they can be divided into two subcategories: performance and outcomes. As discussed in the next chapter, performance indicators are essential for monitoring purposes. The data generated by these indicators can inform managers and other stakeholders about whether inputs are being delivered on time, whether the program is producing outputs as expected, and whether the program is likely to produce the intended results. For example, if a program was designed to provide technical assistance to ten new civil society organizations each year for five consecutive years to improve their internal organizational capacity, the indicator of "number of civil society organizations assisted" will inform the manager if the program is achieving its intended target. If it assisted only seven organizations, it is obvious that it did not achieve its target. On the other hand, if it assisted twelve organizations, it overachieved. Usually, it is the cumulative evidence of several indicators that enables us to learn whether programs are making progress. Good performance indicators also aid efficiency and effectiveness by specifying targets that sharpen the focus of management staff. A few examples of these indicators are shown in Box 3.1.

Most performance indicators used in democracy interventions are relatively simple and can generally pass the tests of validity and reliability. However, their general limitations should not be overlooked. By their nature, they provide minimal information and do not give details about the quality of the goods and services provided. For example, the number of election monitors trained does not inform the manager and other stakeholders about the quality of the training or its use.

More importantly, performance indicators often oversimplify reality as they cannot capture the intricate and complex interactions that take place among different actors in program settings. An example is a technical assistance program that provides assistance to develop a legal and regulatory architecture for independent media in a postconflict society. As those who have participated in such efforts

---

Box 3.1 Performance Indicators

1. Number of domestic election observers trained with project assistance:
   - Number of men.
   - Number of women.
2. Number of judicial officers trained with project assistance:
   - Number of men.
   - Number of women.
3. Number of domestic human rights NGOs receiving project assistance.
4. Number of public advocacy campaigns on human rights launched with project assistance.
5. Number of organizations receiving project support to promote development of and compliance with political finance regulations and legislation.
6. Number of civil society organizations using project assistance to promote political participation.
7. Number of independent and democratic trade or labor unions supported by the project.
8. Number of media civil society organizations and/or support institutions assisted by the project.
9. Number of media outlets that received project-supported training to promote financial sustainability.

know, it involves much more than helping to write the necessary legislation or regulations. It involves working with executive and legislative branches of the government, building political constituencies that favor independent media, and engaging foreign governments that have political leverage on the interim government. All of this has to be done in a subtle manner so that the government officials and political parties do not feel that they are being coerced into drafting media regulations. In fact, every effort has to be made to ensure that the government and legislative bodies have a sense of ownership of the changes. Indicators such as the number of technical experts provided, the number of consultations the technical experts had with legislative bodies, or the number of statutes they assisted in drafting cannot provide a realistic picture of the progress or failure of the program. The truth is that what can be quantified is not necessarily the most important in the political arena. Although in some cases qualitative indicators can be developed that can later be quantified, most indicators tend to focus only on those dimensions of performance that can be initially quantified.

The usual assumption behind the use of indicators is that the higher the scores of values of an indicator, the better the performance. This assumption is not justified in many cases. If a program assisted twenty community radio stations with an expenditure of $2 million and the other thirty with the same amount of the money, the performance of the second project is not necessarily better. It could well be that the first project had to deal with the radio stations that needed more intensive assistance or that they were located in remote areas that required additional expenditure on travel.

Performance indicators also are not good at tracking whether the situation would have gotten worse if it had not been for intervention. For example, if a program measures the success of electoral monitoring by the number of irregular practices observed, one cannot estimate how many irregular incidents have been prevented as a result of international monitoring. Other sources of data would be needed to make the estimation.

Outcome indicators go beyond measuring performance and are designed to measure the immediate results of interventions. For example, if a program provides training to the managerial staff of NGOs to improve their organizational effectiveness, outcome indicators would measure the trained managers' effectiveness in performing their functions, not the training per se. As compared to performance indicators, outcome indicators are more difficult to identify. Examples

Box 3.2 Voter Turnout as a Measure of Success

Voter turnout is usually used as an indicator for measuring the success of voter education programs funded by the international community. However, as Catherine Barnes, an election expert, has pointed out, voter turnout is influenced by many factors, such as "local actors independent of foreign funding, the dynamism and popularity of candidates, the importance of the election, the competitiveness of the election, the weather on election day, or the ability of workers to leave their jobs in order to vote" that cannot be related to international assistance. She mentions other factors that can affect the reliability and usefulness of voter turnout data. For example, in former communist countries in Europe, voter turnout was very high because of forced participation and intimidation. Once these countries became free, a decrease in voter turnout was indeed a better sign of "free and fair elections" than higher turnout.

Source: Personal communication with the author.

of a few outcome indicators that have been suggested or used are shown in Box 3.3.

A major problem with many outcome indicators is that they do not pass the test of reliability and validity. (Box 3.4 explains the meaning of the constructs of reliability and validity.) For example, the indicator "number of positive modifications to enabling legislation or regulations for civil society accomplished" can be interpreted differently by different observers. Observers may differ about their understanding of the meanings of "enabling" "legislation," or "regulations," or even the expression "accomplished." Similarly the "degree to which electoral laws or rules conform with international standards" is likely to be interpreted differently by observers doing the ratings in different countries. In addition, since ratings are subjective, they tend to be affected by current events. Their external validity is also questionable.

Another problem with many outcome indicators is that they cannot measure limited incremental change. The changes in the values of the type of indicators mentioned above happen slowly and, thus, cannot be captured in a year or two. While there are no empirical studies on the experience of using outcome indicators for measuring incremental outcomes of democracy programs, a majority of experts that I interviewed were skeptical.

Box 3.3 Outcome Indicators

1. Number of merit-based criteria or procedures for justice sector personnel selection adopted with project assistance.
2. Number of laws, regulations, and procedures designed to enhance or improve judicial transparency adopted with project assistance.
3. Number of program-supported consensus-building processes resulting in an agreement.
4. Percentage of project-assisted election polling places without major logistical problems during an election.
5. Number of program-assisted courts with improved case management systems.
6. Number of project-assisted political parties that are implementing programs to increase the number of candidates from women's, youth, and marginalized groups.
7. Number of positive modifications to enabling legislation or regulations for civil society accomplished.
8. Degree to which electoral laws or rules conform with international standards.
9. Number of donor-supported anticorruption measures implemented.

As compared to those of development assistance, evaluators of democracy interventions face a major handicap in using outcome indicators. In many sectors of development assistance, outcome indications can reasonably provide details about the impact of interventions. We can be sure that, if a program vaccinates 500,000 children against smallpox, practically all of them will be protected from the disease or, if farmers use a high-yielding variety of seeds, agricultural production will increase except in the case of physical disasters. This is not necessarily the case in democracy interventions. For example, even when a program successfully trains and deploys election monitors, it cannot ensure the freeness and fairness of elections. The problem is that many requirements need to be met between the training and the resultant free and fair elections: (1) an adequate number of monitors; (2) the resources to travel and observe elections; (3) the ability to monitor an entire election process, starting with the selection of candidates and continuing to the counting of ballots and declaration of results; (4) the ability to ensure that political parties or the government and other vested interests do not prevent the monitoring; and (5) the capacity to ensure that trained monitors are able to publicize their

Box 3.4 The Meaning of Reliability and Validity in Social Research

Reliability is the extent to which any measuring procedure yields the same result in repeated trials. It means that independent observers would achieve the same result by using the same procedure. Without establishing reliability, we cannot be sure about the generalizability of their findings.

Researchers usually mention the following four categories of reliability. (1) *Equivalency reliability* indicates that two procedures measure identical concepts with the same results. (2) *Re-test reliability* indicates the consistency of measuring instruments over time. (3) *Internal consistency* implies that research procedures assess the same characteristic, skill, or quality. For example, an evaluation team conducts a survey of journalism trainees to find out their satisfaction with the course. The analysis of the internal consistency of the survey items dealing with satisfaction will reveal the extent to which items in the survey focus on satisfaction. (4) *Interrater reliability* is the extent to which two or more individuals (coders or raters) agree. It addresses the consistency of the implementation of a rating system.

Validity refers to the degree to which an indicator accurately reflects or assesses the specific concept that the indicator is supposed to measure. While reliability is concerned with the accuracy of the actual measuring instrument or procedure, validity is concerned with with measuring the construct itself. Validity can be both internal and external.

Internal validity refers to the extent to which we have taken into account alternative explanations for a causal relationship. Scholars have identified several types of internal validity. (1) *Face validity* is concerned with how a measure or procedure appears. Does it seem like a reasonable way to gain the information the researchers are attempting to obtain? Does it seem well designed? Does it seem as though it will work reliably? (2) *Instrumental validity* demonstrates the accuracy of a measure or procedure by comparing it with another measure or procedure that has been demonstrated to be valid. (3) *Construct validity* seeks agreement between a theoretical concept and a specific measuring device or procedure. (4) *Content validity* reflects the specific intended domain of content. For example, if researchers measuring the attitude toward elections ask questions pertaining to only national elections, it can be argued that the survey lacked content validity because it asked questions about national elections but generalized for all elections.

External validity refers to the extent to which the results of a study are generalizable.

findings without fear and intimidation. Only when such conditions are met, can one realistically use training indicators to measure the conduct of free and fair elections.

Moreover, even when outcome indicators indicate that changes are taking place, it cannot be assumed that the observed changes are the result of a specific project. The State Department, UN, UNDP, USAID, European Union, and a host of European countries provide electoral assistance to African countries. The cumulative activities of these agencies, the diplomatic pressure exerted by the international community, the level of economic and social development of the concerned countries, and the valiant efforts of democracy NGOs and activists, affect the degree to which a country takes steps to ensure that its electoral laws and regulations conform to international standards. Therefore, any improvements in *the degree to which electoral laws/rules conform to international standards* cannot be attributed a single project or program funded by a bilateral or multilateral donor agency. At best, one can assume that the project or program has contributed to it.

It is also worth noting that data collection for outcome indicators can involve an extensive research effort. Often the local partners of donor agencies are spread around the country and data collection can be logistically difficult as well as time consuming. Sometimes the targeted organizations are not willing to release the necessary information for an indicator. For example, if the indicator measures improved organizational structure of a political party, it might be difficult for a party to release the necessary information (e.g., an organizational chart).

Despite their limitations, when carefully selected, micro-level indicators can serve two important functions. First, they can help to identify implementation problems that call for an evaluation. For example, if the data show that despite increased assistance, the number of NGOs engaged in democracy promotion is declining, the program authorities can commission a midterm evaluation. Such an evaluation can identify the reasons why the program is failing and suggest possible solutions. Second, micro-level indicators can provide useful data for midterm and final impact evaluations.

Macro-Level Indices and Evaluations

Macro-level democracy indices measure the state of democracy in a country. Political scientists have been developing and refining measures of democracy for nearly a half-century and have even constructed several large datasets that are widely used in scholarly research as well as in public discourse. These indices differ in their conceptualization of democracy, measurement strategies, and aggregation, and it is not possible to discuss them in detail. Therefore, I will briefly mention here only a few indices of democracy that are more policy oriented.

The Freedom in the World Index. The Freedom in the World Index developed by Freedom House is undoubtedly the most widely used among policymakers, the media, democracy activists, and academic scholars. It focuses on political rights and civil liberties that people enjoy in different countries, and it has been published annually since 1972. It presents global and regional breakdowns for freedom status, political rights, and civil liberties ratings for each country and territory; the number and percentage of electoral democracies over the past two decades; and the total number of free, partly free, and not free countries. It covers 193 countries and 15 related and disputed territories and provides empirically grounded narratives for each of them. Its data and reports are available at the Freedom House website. The procedures for assigning ratings are not fully transparent, however. Country experts assign ratings for each research question, using checklists of subquestions as guides. Academics and staff review ratings in regional team meetings. Each country and territory is assigned a numerical rating on a scale of 1 to 7 for political rights and an analogous rating for civil liberties; a rating of 1 indicates the highest degree of freedom and 7 the lowest.

The Economist Intelligence Unit's Democracy Index. This index is based on the premise that measures of democracy that focus simply on political freedoms and civil liberties are not robust enough and do not encompass sufficiently or at all some features that determine how substantive democracy is or its quality. Freedom is an essential component of democracy, but not sufficient. Therefore, the index focuses on multiple components of democracy: electoral processes and pluralism, civil liberties, the functioning of government, political participation, and political culture. It provides a snapshot of the current state of democracy worldwide for 165 independent states and 2 territories and, thus, covers the vast majority of the world's 192 independent states (27 microstates are excluded). The index has sixty indicators, and country experts use public opinion survey data, legislative data, and other statistical data to assign mostly dichotomous scores for each indicator, which are then aggregated to determine the score for each of the five categories. These scores and overall scores for a country are reported.

The World Bank's Worldwide Governance Indicators. The Worldwide Governance Indicators capture six key dimensions of governance: voice and accountability, political stability and lack of violence, government's effectiveness, regulatory quality, rule of law, and control of corruption. Its authors use both commercial and noncommercial sources of data and derive aggregated scores for each of the governance indicators through component modeling. The contribution of each of the forty datasets is weighted to reflect the precision of each dataset. Democracy researchers have used particularly the indices on voice and accountability, rule of law, and control of corruption. Virtually all of the individual data sources underlying the aggregate indicators are, along with the aggregate indicators themselves, publicly available.

Polity IV. The Polity IV focuses on governing authority that spans from fully institutionalized autocracies through mixed, or incoherent, authority regimes to fully institutionalized democracies. The Polity score captures this regime authority spectrum on a 21-point scale ranging from -10 (hereditary monarchy) to $+10$ (consolidated democracy). The Polity scheme consists of six component measures that record key qualities of executive recruitment, constraints on executive authority, and political competition. It also records changes in the institutionalized qualities of governing authority.

Global Barometer Surveys. The Global Barometer Surveys represent "an indigenous initiative to develop a global intellectual community of democracy studies surveying ordinary citizens." The underlying premise behind these surveys is that "public attitudes and orientations toward democracy are crucial to the process of political legitimacy and that political culture operates autonomously as a key factor mediating the impact of socio-economic modernization on the evolution of the political regime, particularly in democracies." Following the example of the Eurobarometer, which was funded in the 1970s to track mass attitudes in what was then the European Community, new regional barometers have further developed innovative approaches for regions undergoing rapid political and economic change. As more regions join the Global Barometer network, "a standard approach is being established to ensure that the data is comparable and reliable." The Global Barometer Surveys now cover three continents,

---

Box 3.5 Findings of *The Economist*'s Democracy Index

In *The Economist*'s index, the countries are categorized under four categories: full democracies, flawed democracies, hybrid regimes (all considered democracies), and authoritarian regimes. The following table lists the number of countries in each category according to 2008 survey.

Type of Regime	Countries	% of Countries	% of World Population
Full democracies	30	18.0	14.4
Flawed democracies	50	29.9	35.5
Hybrid regimes	36	21.6	15.2
Authoritarian regimes	51	30.5	34.9

World population refers to the total population of the 167 countries that are covered. Sweden had the highest score and North Korea the lowest. The United States ranked eighteen, which was below countries such as Australia, Denmark, Malta, Ireland, Spain, and Germany.

Source: Economist Intelligence Unit (2008).

---

more than 48 percent of the world's population, and are still expanding. Besides Africa, East and South Asia, Central and South America, and the Middle East, the Caribbean region is possibly the next region that will join the network once the surveys begin in the area.

Practically all major indices, including those mentioned above, have been criticized by scholars and experts on several grounds. A report by the National Research Council has summarized these criticisms under five categories: definitional, sensitivity issues, measurement errors and data coverage, aggregation, and lack of convergent validity (2008, pp. 73–81). Definitional issues arise from the fact that the different indices do not necessarily focus on the same elements of a democratic regime. For example, some emphasize electoral democracy while others focus mainly on civil and political rights. Still others include aspects of governance as a component of democracy. Such differences are not unexpected, as scholars and policymakers do not share a common definition of democracy.

Issues with indicators

A more serious criticism of democracy indicators is that the leading indicators are not sensitive to important gradations in the quality of democracy across countries or over time. As the National Research Council notes, "All extant indicators are bounded to some degree and therefore constrained. This means that there is no way to distinguish the quality of democracy among countries that have perfect negative or positive scores" (2008, p. 76). This is fine as long as there is no real difference in the quality of democracy among these countries. Yet the latter assumption is highly questionable. The report cites the example of the Freedom in the World Index, which assigned the highest score of 1 for political rights to fifty-eight countries in 2004. These countries included ones as diverse as the Bahamas, Barbados, Estonia, Malta, Mauritius, Suriname, Sweden, the United Kingdom, the United States, and Uruguay. The problem is that the substantive differences in the quality of democracy among these diverse polities are overlooked. In defense of Freedom House, it should be mentioned that this limitation is not unique to democracy indicators and indicators in many other areas of development are not immune from it.

There are also methodological limitations that should not be overlooked. A majority of indicators largely depend on opinion surveys or expert judgments. As we know, opinion polls reflect people's perceptions and not empirical reality. A small incident prior to polling may cause significant variations. Moreover, often people's expectations from democracy rise as a society marches toward democracy, with the result that the progress is not always reflected in opinion surveys. Moreover, expert judgments are always selective and their limitations have been widely accepted by researchers and political scientists.

Still another limitation of democracy indicators concerns the issue of aggregation, that is, how to weigh the components of an index. For example, the World Bank assigns weight to household surveys relative to the weights of expert assessments and firm surveys. For example, the Gallup world poll that asks citizens about their exposure to crime gets zero weight, while Global Insight Business Risk and Conditions, a US commercial business information provider that measures the crime risk to businesses, gets the third highest weight for "rule of law." The problem is that the rules for assigning weights are not clear and are ambiguous. But even when they are clear and unambiguous, because "they bundle a host of diverse dimensions into a single score, it is often unclear, which of the dimensions is driving a country's score in a particular year. It is often difficult to articulate what an index value of '4' means within the context of any single indicator" (National Research Council 2008, p. 79).

In a recent research article, Michael Coppedge and John Gerring (2011) raise questions about the validity and reliability of macro-level indicators. Some excerpts from their article are given in Box 3.6.

Despite the above-mentioned limitations, democracy indices provide useful information about the overall context in which programs are designed and implemented. They also provide an understanding of the changes in public attitudes and perceptions about democracy and the political system during the life of an intervention. The rich narratives, which often accompany statistical data, can be illuminating. For example, an evaluation team examining effects of an electoral assistance program in a country can learn from the Freedom House index about the country's political landscape when programs were designed, the political developments since their launching, and the current state of democracy in the country. Democracy evaluators have always found macro-level data generated by different indices highly useful, but not sufficient.

There is a broad consensus among political scientists and experts that the macro-level indices for democracy cannot assess, much less measure, the impacts of individual democracy interventions. The focus of democracy interventions funded by the international community is limited in its scope. A typical program focuses on training journalists, or assisting in the establishment of an electoral commission, or training judges for promoting independence of the judiciary. Therefore, even if it is highly successful, its impacts are not significant enough to be captured by aggregated macro-level measures of democracy. As the National Research Council rightly notes, "The committee also finds that all existing measures are severely inadequate in tracking small movements or small differences in levels of democracy between countries or in a single country over time" (2008, p. 72).

Meso-Level Indices

A major development in the measurement of democracy in recent years has been the development of meso-level indices. A need for such indices was found by the program managers and policymakers in democracy promotion agencies who wanted to know the cumulative

> ### Box 3.6 Questionable Validity and Reliability of Macro-Level Indices
>
> "Worries about validity in extant democracy indices are nourished by periodic appraisals focused on specific countries. A recent study by scholars of Central America alleges major flaws in coding for Costa Rica, El Salvador, Honduras, Guatemala, and Nicaragua in three crossnational indices—Polity, Vanhanen, and Mark Gasiorowski—errors that, the authors suspect, also characterize other indices and other countries. . . .
>
> Surprisingly, inter-coder reliability tests are not common practice among democracy indices. Freedom House does not conduct such tests, or at least does not make them public. Polity used to do so, but it required a good deal of hands-on training before coders reached an acceptable level of coding accuracy. This suggests that other coders might not reach the same decisions simply by reading Polity's coding manual. And this, in turn, points to a potential problem of conceptual validity: key concepts may not be well matched to the empirical data. . . .
>
> Defenders of contemporary indices often point out that the extant indices are highly intercorrelated. Indeed, the correlation between Polity II and Political Rights is a respectable 0.88 (Pearson's r). Yet on closer examination consensus across the two dominant indices is largely the product of countries lying at the democratic extreme—Canada, Sweden, the United States, et al. When countries with perfect democracy scores are excluded from the sample the correlation between these two indices drops to 0.78. And when countries with the top two scores on the Freedom House Political Rights scale are eliminated, Pearson's r drops again—to 0.63. This is not an impressive level of agreement. . . .
>
> It follows that differences across indices may produce divergent findings in empirical work where democracy is a key variable. Indeed, Gretchen Casper and Claudiu Tufis show that few explanatory variables (beyond per capita income) have a consistently significant correlation with democracy when different democracy indices are employed. . . .
>
> *We have good reasons to suspect that extant indices suffer problems of validity and reliability and that these problems are consequential.*"
>
> *Source:* Excerpts from Coppedge and Gerring (2011), pp. 251–252; emphasis added.

effects of international assistance on a sector such as elections, the media, or the civil society. For example, USAID officials, who were responsible for providing massive media assistance to Eastern and Central Europe after the collapse of the Soviet Union, were interested to know the effects of assistance programs on the media sector and the sustainability of independent media in recipient countries. They needed an index that could provide an indication of both of these and, therefore, funded the construction of the Media Sustainability Index (MSI) that is now widely used in different parts of the world. The same has been true of the NGO Sustainability Index. Democracy experts and academicians have constructed several sector-level indices; some are widely used while the data for others are yet to be collected. I will mention a few indices below for illustrative purposes.

The Freedom of the Press Index. The Freedom of the Press Index is an annual survey of media independence in 195 countries and territories, and it is at the core of Freedom House's press freedom project. It contains a comprehensive dataset on global media freedom. It assesses the degree of print, broadcast, and Internet freedom; examines the legal, political, and economic environment for media; and analyzes the major media events for each calendar year. The index is based on 23 methodological and 109 substantive questions, and scores are assigned by a team of regional experts and scholars. The ratings are reviewed individually and collectively in a series of regional meetings between analysts and Freedom House staff. Ratings are compared with the previous year's ratings and any major change is subjected to additional scrutiny. The index is used for both designing and evaluating media projects and programs.

The Media Sustainability Index. The MSI, which was developed by the International Research and Exchanges Board (IREX) with USAID support, provides in-depth analyses of the conditions for the functioning of independent media in eighty countries across Africa, Europe, Eurasia, and the Middle East. It assesses media with reference to legal and social norms that protect and promote free speech and access to information; the quality of professional norms followed by journalists; the availability of multiple news sources that provide citizens with reliable, objective news; management of independent media and editorial independence; and the workings of the supporting institutions that serve the professional interest of the media. It uses thirty-eight indicators, which are scored. MSI relies on local experts who are well versed about the media scene.

The Cingranelli-Richards Human Rights Database. The CIRI index contains standards-based quantitative information on a government's adherence to fifteen internationally recognized human rights for 195 countries. It also contains disaggregated measures of specific human rights practices, which can either be analyzed separately or combined into valid and reliable indices, as well as two already aggregated indices. The index describes a wide variety of a government's human rights practices such as torture, workers' rights, and women's rights over a twenty-nine-year period. It is replicable because the detailed coding manual allows anyone to reapply the coding rules to cases included in the dataset. It is also reliable because at least two trained coders evaluate each variable for each country year. Reliability scores are available for each variable.

The index is used by scholars and students who seek to test theories about the causes and consequences of human rights violations as well as by policymakers and analysts who seek to estimate the human rights effects of a wide variety of institutional changes and public policies including democratization, economic aid, military aid, structural adjustment, and humanitarian intervention.

The Civicus Civil Society Index. The World Alliance for Citizen Participation developed the Civil Society Index (CSI) to assess the state of civil society in countries. The index measures five core dimensions of civil society: civic engagement (the extent to which individuals engage in social and policy-related initiatives); level of organization (the degree of institutionalization that characterizes civil society); practice of values (the extent to which civil society practices some core values); perceived impacts (the extent to which civil society is able to impact the social and policy arena); and external environment (socioeconomic, political, and cultural environment within which civil society operates). The CSI is used at the country level and, during 2008–2010, fifty-six countries were engaged in gathering the data. The project pulls together the quantitative research gathered by country partners and complements it with more in-depth analysis from case studies, focus groups and consultations, and the input of advisory committee experts.

The Munck Index of Democratic Elections. Developed by Gerardo Munck (2009), the Index of Democratic Elections can assist in evaluating the entire election process. The index lists four critical aspects of a democratic election (i.e., clean, inclusive, competitive, elected offices) and identifies indicators for each. The methodology enables observers to gather the data before, during, and after the elections, and it is based on expert assessments, polling data, election statistics, and other relevant information. The scoring is disaggregated for each of the indicators. Electoral administration and public perceptions of the elections are not addressed in this methodology. This index has not been used as yet and therefore questions about its reliability remain.

The Elklit and Reynolds Quality of Election Framework. The Elklit and Reynolds framework assesses the quality of elections by focusing on the key elements of the electoral process. Its authors have identified eleven components of the electoral system and developed fifty-four questions to score each of them. Weights are assigned to each of the elements to signify their importance. The weights were developed separately for established democracies and for fledgling democracies, as the authors call them. The methodology relies on country experts to use various sources such as polling data, legislative documents, observer reports, and primary data to score each question in the framework. The main strength of this index is that it covers a broad range of electoral issues and provides the disaggregated data to possible users. No information is available about the use of this index.

Most of the criticisms of macro-level indices that are mentioned above also apply to meso-level indices. There is no consensus about the elements of such indicators. Many of them are based on attitudinal surveys that may be at variance with the empirical reality. Their validity is not always established. Different scholars and experts can assign different weights to different items in the indices. However, as compared to macro-level indicators, they are more relevant to the needs of policy research and evaluation communities. In most cases, the field staff of democracy projects and programs were heavily involved in their construction and, as a result, they cover topics that are of prime interest to program managers and policymakers. They are not simply academic exercises, but are informed by the experience and expertise of the international community. Because their focus is limited to a specific sector, there is not much controversy about the individual items included in them. A few meso-level indices have been used in different political environments and then refined in the light of experience gained.

Evaluators can use these indices in two ways. First, the data generated often provide a relatively accurate picture of the sector. For example, by reading the scores and narratives of a country on the Freedom of the Press Index or the MSI, an evaluator can learn about the state of the media sector as well as the changes that have taken place over time. Second, and more importantly, these indices can be used for identifying evaluation questions, developing questionnaires for surveys, and preparing checklists for structured direct observation in evaluations. For example, both the Munck and Elklit and Reynolds indices contain many critical questions about elections and election systems, on which an evaluation of electoral assistance is likely to focus. Therefore, even if the data are not available, many indices can be helpful to the evaluators.

Despite their usefulness, sector-specific indices generally are not suitable for assessing the impacts of democracy interventions. Often they cannot capture the incremental and subtle changes that take place in a sector. This is illustrated by a USAID evaluation in Albania that I now describe.

Use of Meso-Level Indices in Albania

In 2008, USAID commissioned an evaluation of its Democracy and Governance in Albania (DGA) project with Management Systems International (2008a). DGA was a three-year, $7.2 million project that began in October 2004 and ended in December 2007. It was implemented by a consortium led by the National Democratic Institute with the participation of subgrantee partners. It consolidated under one umbrella three projects that were already being implemented by three organizations. It had five major components: engagement of citizens, political party reform and leadership development, advocacy capacity building, media development, and strengthening of election processes. The overall objective of the evaluation was to examine whether the project had achieved its stated objectives and identify the factors that affected its performance and impacts. A two-person evaluation team reviewed available background information and reports relevant to the DGA program and used primary and secondary statistical information from DGA and other institutional databases. The team also interviewed Albanian government representatives; elected officials; staff of USAID, NGOs, and international agencies; and current and former DGA staff. In addition, the team used three sector-level indices to measure changes in civil society, media, corruption, and election processes. Its findings on these indices are as follows.

First, the team utilized the advocacy component of the NGO Sustainability Index. As Figure 3.1 indicates, advocacy scores in

**Figure 3.1 Albania's Advocacy Scores on the
USAID NGO Sustainability Index**

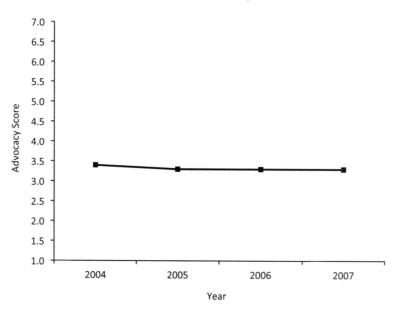

Source: Management Systems International (2008a).

the NGO Sustainability Index for Albania showed a slight improvement from 2004 to 2005 and then the scores were flat, with no discernible progress, through 2007. Thus, the data do not show a consistent pattern.

Second, the team used Transparency International's Corruption Perceptions Index score for Albania, as shown in Figure 3.2. It shows a slight improvement during the project period, as respondents stated that corruption had become less serious—the score increased from 2.5 in 2004 to 2.9 in 2007, with a score of 10 squeaky clean and a score of 0 appallingly corrupt.

Third, the evaluation team analyzed the performance of the project with reference to the IREX Media Sustainability Index. As Figure 3.3 shows, scores on the composite MSI declined during the life of the project. In this index, a score of 0 means that the country does not meet the standards for that element at all and a score of 4 means that it meets the standards well. Thus, the media scene worsened during the life of the project.

**Figure 3.2 Albania's Corruption Scores on
Transparency International's Corruption Perceptions Index**

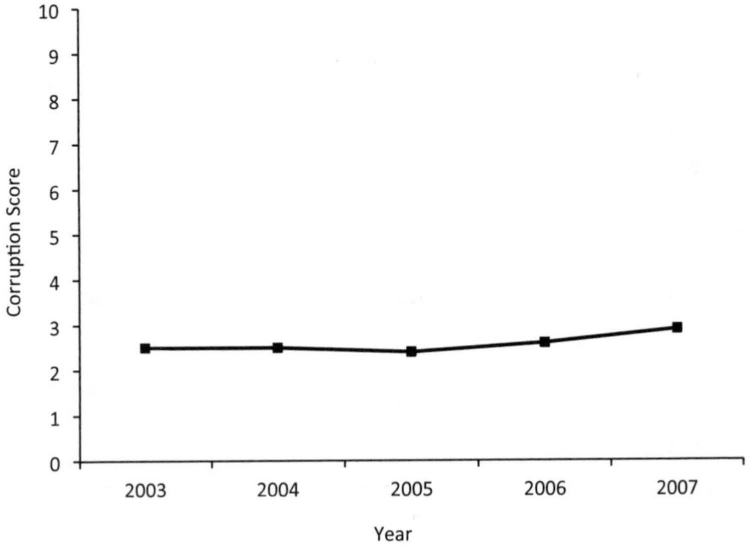

Source: Management Systems International (2008a).

Figure 3.4 presents scores for professional journalism and pluralism of news sources on the Media Sustainability Index. The figure
shows that, while the scores for pluralism remained more or less constant after initial improvement, there was a decline in the score of
professional standards for journalists.

Finally, the team examined the impact of the project with reference to the Freedom House Nations in Transit electoral processes
score, as shown in Figure 3.5. The score is presented negatively (i.e.,
the higher the score, the worse the performance). A score of 7 is the
worst. Figure 3.5 shows that, while the 2006 election did show improvement, there was slippage in 2007.

How should these results be interpreted? It is quite possible that
the project had no consistent effect on the democracy landscape of Albania. However, the data generated by interviews and analysis of project records and documents indicate that the project carried out numerous activities that must have had some impacts. Moreover, even if this
project did not have any impact, there were democracy promotion activities funded by other bilateral and multilateral agencies that might
have positively impacted civil society, the media, and elections.

Figure 3.3 Albania's Scores on the Media Sustainability Index

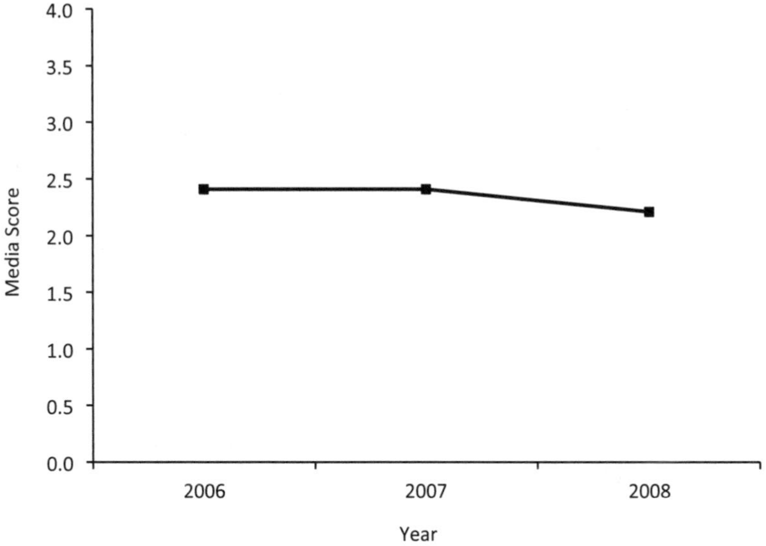

Source: Management Systems International (2008a).

A more plausible explanation is that the sector-level indices used are not able to capture incremental change in a sector. Most sector-specific indices primarily rely on two sources of information: surveys of public opinion and expert judgments. Both of these sources have their own limitations. As mentioned earlier, public perceptions do not always represent reality. Expert opinions can be also subjective. Many experts tend to have strong opinions on democracy issues that may affect their ratings. Moreover, in many cases, experts change each year, which may also affect the ratings because experts tend to use different standards and criteria to make their ratings.

Disaggregating Macro-Level Indices

It is sometimes suggested that, if evaluators disaggregate macro-level democracy indices, they may generate sector-specific data that can be used for monitoring and evaluation purposes. For example, most macro-level democracy indices provide data on elections, media, and even corruption that can be disaggregated and used by evaluators to

Figure 3.4 Albania's Scores on Professional Journalism and Pluralism of News Sources from the Media Sustainability Index

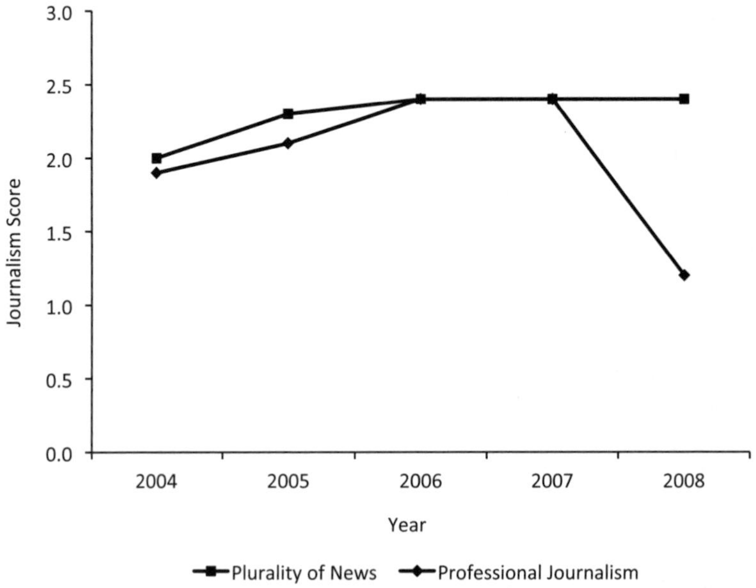

Source: Management Systems International (2008a).

assess the impact of democracy interventions in these areas. USAID's Democracy and Governance Office investigated the feasibility of disaggregating macro-level indices for evaluations.

Preliminary indications were that the disaggregated data will be of limited use in evaluating democracy projects and programs. Many limitations of using sector-level indices also apply to the disaggregated data. Moreover, while most democracy indices focus on different dimensions of democracy, their coverage of each dimension is usually limited. Topics pertaining to human rights, legislative strengthening, judicial independence, civil society organizations, minority rights, and gender are not adequately covered in many macro-level indices. Often disaggregated data are not available because the sponsors of the indices are not willing to provide it or the data are coded in a way that they cannot be disaggregated without considerable recoding.

These limitations can be explained with reference to constructing indicators from macro-level indices for evaluating electoral assistance programs. The election sector has a set of rich output and outcome indicators that can be easily measured. It has "developed a set

**Figure 3.5 Albania's Scores on Electoral Processes
from the Freedom House Nations in Transit Index**

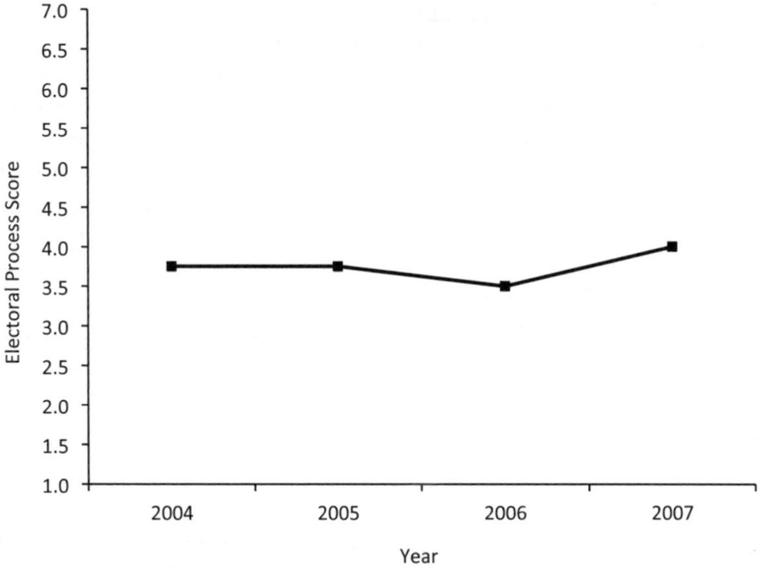

Source: Management Systems International (2008a).

of generally universally recognized key statistics (e.g., voter turnout, percent of ballots spoiled, percent of registered voters, etc.) that enable common frameworks for evaluative purposes" (Sharma 2010, p. 2). Moreover, practically all major indices for democracy invariably focus on elections and electoral processes. For example, the Economist Intelligence Unit's index has two categories that focus on elections: electoral processes and pluralism and political participation. The Freedom in the World Index has several questions on elections that country experts are supposed to answer. Such questions relate to electoral processes. The World Bank's Voice and Accountability index contains several items related to elections. Global Barometer Surveys ask several questions from respondents that include their perception of freeness and fairness of the last elections, whether they voted in the last elections, their interest in politics, their political activities, and their level of media consumption. Under these conditions, one would expect that it would be easier to construct meso-level indices for the electoral sector from the macro indices. Unfortunately, such expectations are not justified.

Rakesh Sharma points to four limitations that restrict the use of macro-level indices for monitoring and evaluation. First, "these (indices) are measures of public perception, and, as such, are limited by the generally incomplete information the public relies on for its perception about the election process and electoral authorities" (2010, p. 8). While public perception is an important element of election processes and public support, rejection, or ambivalence toward election processes can be an important indicator of the general health of the election processes, "they do not provide comprehensive measures for most issues relevant to USAID's result framework" (2010, p. 8).

Second, the indices do not provide disaggregated data about elections or electoral processes. According to Sharma, while these indices generally measure the election processes or their environment through the use of an aggregated construct for which a score or rating is provided, "their analysis (and scores/ratings) of the components or questions is not available to users. Without this disaggregated data, it is difficult for USAID to determine evaluation of specific aspects of the election process and system" (2010, p. 8).

Third, Sharma states that most indices do not provide "weights to signify the importance of specific aspects of the election process. All items are treated equally in the aggregation, a problematic assumption given the realities of election process" (2010, p. 8). For example, while voter education may be an important element in a war-torn society, which has little or no experience in holding elections, it is certainly not as important in societies that have been holding elections for some time. Finally, the indices do not take into consideration all the important elements of an electoral process or system. For example, many indices do not discuss the management and administration of the electoral system.

While Sharma has confined his observations to the election sector, they also apply to other sectors of democracy.

Conclusion

While the construction and use of the above-mentioned three categories of democracy indicators have been a welcome development and experts have made headway in identifying a large number of indicators that can be used to design and monitor democracy interventions, there still is a long way to go before there will be a repertoire of indicators that are reliable, valid, and relevant to the unique characteristics of democracy interventions. The use of indicators, without examining their conceptual and methodological foundations, can be misleading and can confer possibly unwarranted credibility and legitimacy to findings and recommendations. This point is rightly emphasized by Munck, who observes,

> The use of quantitative measures on democracy in the context of democracy promotion activities, however, must be evaluated with considerable caution. Although this development holds the promise of bringing knowledge to bear on politics, many current practices in the use of data are highly questionable. And as a result, the potential for using data to invigorate a democratic agenda is, at the least, curtailed. (2009, pp. 11–12)

[handwritten margin note: in sum: limited so far; needs more development]

4

Designing Realistic
Monitoring Systems

Monitoring should not be regarded as merely a management or
reporting requirement. Rather, it should be regarded as an opportunity to engage beneficiaries so that they feel ownership of
results being achieved and are motivated to sustain them.
—United Nations Development Programme,
Manual on Monitoring and Evaluation

We need effective monitoring systems for democracy programs.
The international community should invest in them.
—An evaluator of a democracy program

For many reasons, most democracy programs in the past did not have
monitoring systems. Often managers did not realize the need for
them and were content with an informal approach to information
gathering about the workings of their program. Even those who ap-
preciated the necessity of monitoring systems lacked technical expertise to institute them. Also, funding agencies did not provide
funds for them, and international NGOs and private sector firms did
not insist on their construction and use. This situation has changed in
recent years, however. There is a growing recognition that well-
designed monitoring systems can promote sound management of democracy programs by enabling managers and stakeholders to track
their progress or lack thereof. They can also promote a culture of accountability. Moreover, they can provide vital data for conducting
rigorous evaluations of democracy programs. As a result, most bilateral and multilateral agencies, and even private foundations, now

demand that their programs institute such a system. Yet the progress has been slow.

I begin this chapter with a brief discussion of the meaning of monitoring and explain how it differs from evaluation. I then discuss the requirements for an effective monitoring system and explain the steps in constructing realistic and responsive monitoring systems. Finally, I suggest that the managers and stakeholders of democracy programs should use monitoring to gain deeper insights into the effectiveness of their democracy programs and the challenges and opportunities they face as well as for critical reflection about the future course of actions.

The Meaning of Monitoring

Simply stated, *monitoring* is systematic collection of data on an intervention's activities, outputs, and, when possible, outcomes. It usually, though not always, involves checking progress against predetermined objectives and targets, which identifies what is happening or is not happening. The OECD has defined *monitoring* as "a continuous function that uses systematic collection of data on specified indicators to provide management and main stakeholders of the ongoing development intervention with indications of the extent of progress and achievement of objectives and in the use of allocated funds" (OECD 2002, pp. 27–28). Three characteristics of monitoring follow from the above definition. First, it is an ongoing activity that begins and also ends with an intervention. Unlike an evaluation, it is not a single event or action. Second, it involves the use of indicators to assess the progress or lack thereof. Systematic and timely data are collected on the selected indicators and the results are communicated to managers and stakeholders. Finally, the purpose of monitoring is to provide feedback to improve the performance and impacts of an intervention. Monitoring, like evaluation, is a learning tool.

The function of monitoring can be explained with a hypothetical example of a program to impart human rights training to security sector personnel in a postconflict society. This three-year program is designed to train fifteen senior officials each quarter, thereby training sixty persons each year. Its monitoring system collects data on a number of performance indicators such as the number of security officials deputed by the government for training each quarter, the number of officials selected for training, the number of officials who completed the training, and the number of attendees who were satisfied with it. It also includes a set of indicators about the utilization of knowledge and skills acquired by the trainees in their official duties. The monitoring requires establishing a deadline for each activity such as the final dates for deputing officials, for completion of their training, and for turning in posttraining surveys about trainees' satisfaction with the program. The analysis of the collected monitoring data will inform the managers and stakeholders about whether the program is working as planned or whether any change is required. For example, if the posttraining surveys of the first batch of trainees show that most of them were not satisfied with the training, the managers need to revisit the course and take suitable corrective action.

In common parlance, monitoring and evaluation (M&E) are often mentioned together. While the two complement each other, they are conceptually and operationally different. *Evaluation* is more comprehensive than monitoring and goes beyond the tracking of progress. It seeks to identify the underlying factors that affect the implementation process, efficiency, sustainability, and effectiveness of an intervention. Evaluations also examine the impacts of an intervention. Box 4.1 clarifies the distinction between monitoring and evaluation.

Box 4.1 Differences Between Monitoring and Evaluation

Monitoring	Evaluation
Continuous/periodic.	Episodic/ad hoc.
Tracks progress against predetermined indicators.	Validity and relevance of indicators open to question.
Focuses mostly on inputs and outputs.	Deals with the issues of effectiveness, efficiency, relevance, impact, and sustainability.
Uses mainly quantitative data.	Uses both quantitative and qualitative data.
Focuses on what and where.	Additionally, focuses on why and how.
Purpose is to improve performance.	Objectives are to promote accountability, informed decisionmaking, and learning.

However, it should be noted that there are exceptions. For example, sometimes evaluations are not episodic (developmental evaluation is a good example). Also monitoring can be outcome focused.

Guiding Principles

In my view, a set of guiding principles should inform the construction and operation of a monitoring system. While these principles are important for all internationally funded programs, they are particularly critical for democracy interventions because of the nature of their activities and the complex political environment in which they are implemented. Unfortunately, they are often overlooked by the designers of monitoring systems.

First, the monitoring system should be developed and maintained with the active participation of key stakeholders. For example, for an intervention designed to support the establishment of a journalism training program at a local university, the designers should consult the concerned university officials, faculty members, and even representatives of the journalists' community to engage them in the implementation of the monitoring system. Participation of the host-country stakeholders promotes local ownership. When these stakeholders are not engaged in determining how the progress of a program will be assessed, what kinds of data need to be gathered and analyzed, and what will be their role in it, they do not develop a sense of ownership. They subsequently tend to perceive the monitoring system as a mechanism of control rather than as a collaborative effort designed to improve the performance and outcomes of the democracy intervention.

Second, the system should be flexible to accommodate changes in both the program and its environment. The overall political environment in which a democracy intervention operates can change rapidly, particularly in transition and postconflict societies. Democracy programs tend to adjust to these changes by adding new activities and dropping the planned ones. Therefore, a monitoring system should be designed in a way that can be easily modified.

Third, as far as possible, the monitoring system should not be based on a simplistic, linear cause-and-effect model. The outputs and outcomes of a democracy intervention depend on many factors and forces that are unforeseen and unforeseeable. Therefore, if the expected outputs or outcomes did not occur, it does not mean that the program failed or vice versa. Those designing and operating a monitoring system should be realistic and recognize its limitations.

Fourth, the system should be designed primarily to serve the decision needs of the management and stakeholders. A common mistake that many designers make is to track a large number of indicators that require collection and analysis of a vast volume of data from primary and secondary sources. Such efforts often result in a waste of time and resources, as most of the gathered data are not used. A monitoring system should not be construed as a research endeavor to satisfy the intellectual curiosity of stakeholders; its only justification is instead to improve the performance and results of a program. The ideal course is to focus on a limited number of variables that are critical to measure the progress, outputs, and outcomes of an intervention. The principle of "less is more" applies well to monitoring.

Fifth, which follows from the fourth principle, a monitoring system should generate timely information so that necessary revisions can be made if and when needed. For example, in the case of a human rights training program, the system should be able to generate and process information about participants' satisfaction with the training prior to the start of the next training course so that, if a significant proportion of participants did not view the training as relevant, corrective actions may be taken. It is also necessary that the monitoring report synchronizes with the budgetary process. If monitoring indicates that the cost of training is higher than originally estimated, this information should be available to managers prior to the finalization of the budget so that additional funds can be allocated for training or other cost-cutting measures can be taken.

Finally, the cost of a monitoring system should be relatively modest. While the cost can vary depending on the size of a program and its components, the nature of information required, and the technical expertise available, it should normally not exceed more than 2 percent to 3 percent of the total cost of a program. A major lesson, which the international community learned from the experience of integrated rural development programs in the early 1970s, is that high-cost monitoring systems are not sustainable. Many monitoring systems for these projects lost legitimacy and support because they involved expenditures that were deemed excessive by managers and stakeholders. The cost of monitoring can be reduced in many ways. The scope of the monitoring can be limited to key variables. The system can be designed in a way that it uses data that are routinely gathered during the implementation phase and the participating organizations can be involved in gathering information. Finally, the existing management staff can be trained to perform monitoring functions, instead of hiring additional staff.

Designing a Monitoring System

Developing a monitoring system is a challenging task that requires imagination and commitment. The resources required to design and operate a system vary depending on the size, activities, and duration of the program. For example, a monitoring system for a small project with a life cycle of one or two years can be designed in a day or two with a few days of expert consultation and can be operated without the hiring of additional staff. On the other hand, more time and effort are required for large programs with a range of activities extending over three to five years. The following steps are usually taken in establishing a monitoring system.

Analyzing the Program

The first step is to understand and analyze the program, its objectives, components, and time frame. Each of these can make a difference in the design. A democracy program that has many components and operates in different sites will have a more complex monitoring system than a smaller project with one or two components. The time frame also makes a difference. A democracy intervention that is designed to support political party building over a span of five years will need a more complex system than an intervention that is planned for one year before the impending national elections.

A systematic review of planning documents can provide the basic information about a program's objectives, focus, and proposed activities; however, it usually will need to be updated. There is a time gap between when an intervention is designed and when it begins, and conditions may change during that interval. Moreover, many democracy interventions are designed with limited or no input from the field, as there is little time to solicit the views of the targeted organizations, other national donor agencies, and local stakeholders. In such cases, the program staff will have to fill many gaps and plan relevant activities.

In addition, designers must carefully review the nature and operations of the organizations and individuals to be assisted as well as the overall political context of the program and its implications for gathering data. For a program to provide assistance to the national election commission for holding elections, the design team will need to review the workings of the commission, the nature of assistance received in the past, and the assistance that other international actors are providing or likely to provide. Such reviews are necessary for developing suitable performance and outcome indicators. Those who design monitoring systems for democracy programs have to pay particular attention to the wider political and institutional environment in which the program will operate.

Finally, designers should consider the available financial resources for monitoring. They also should examine the skills and capabilities of the existing staff to assess their possible roles and responsibilities in the proposed system. This is particularly important for small projects that lack funds for hiring additional full- or part-time staff so that the entire responsibility will fall on the shoulders of existing staff members.

Constructing a Flexible Logic Model Matrix

The second step is to seek a broad consensus among managers and key stakeholders about the inputs, activities, outputs, outcomes, and impacts of a program. In the lexicon of evaluation literature, each of these five constructs has a distinct meaning that can be explained with the example of a hypothetical project on electoral assistance in a transition country. The project, which has a life cycle of two years, has three main components: training local election monitors, strengthening the national election commission, and supporting voter education. The immediate objective of the project is to facilitate the holding of national and regional elections that are scheduled after eighteen months while the ultimate goal is to institutionalize a competitive political system.

Inputs refer to the resources that are expended on a project. For this hypothetical electoral assistance project, these include funds, staff time, and other material resources it is expected to receive during its life.

Activities refer to the services that the project undertakes and the goods it provides to the targeted individuals, organizations, or the general population to achieve its objective. In this hypothetical example, these include the training programs that the project organizes for election monitors; the technical assistance it gives to the national election commission to prepare manuals, guidelines, and election plans; the office equipment it provides to the commission; the meetings and forums it supports for educating voters; and other support activities. These activities are possible because of the initial inputs; thus, there is a causal relationship between them.

(Outputs) are the results of these activities. If a project trains fifty election monitors, this is one of its outputs. So is a strengthened election commission that has received material and technical assistance from the project. Another output is increased understanding among voters of their rights and responsibilities. In theory, outputs are the results of a project's activities but, in many cases, political, cultural, organizational, and even economic factors can affect them.

(Outcomes) are the behavioral changes that result from outputs. If the trained election monitors are able to monitor elections effectively, it is an outcome. If the strengthened election commission organizes relatively freer and fairer elections, it is counted as yet another outcome. In the same fashion, if the voters are able to use the knowledge they acquire for voting, it can be another outcome. In most democracy interventions, it is difficult to attribute the outcomes to outputs. One does not know, for example, if the information that voters gain as a result of voter education programs makes a difference in their voting behavior. Outputs are only one of the contributing factors in the outcomes attributed to democracy interventions.

Finally, impacts are the medium- and long-term changes that outcomes are supposed to cause. In the case of the electoral assistance project, the ultimate goal is to assist in the institutionalization of the norms of competitive elections, which are an essential element of a democratic political order. As indicated in Chapter 6 impacts are most difficult to assess, much less measure. And even if the norms of competitive elections are institutionalized, one cannot be sure that they are the result of the outcomes of a project or program.

The relationship between the five constructs can be presented as

inputs ⟶ activities ⟶ outputs ⟶ outcomes ⟶ impacts

The matrix is not always unambiguous. There often are problems in operationalizing it. People may differ in their views of what are "outputs" and what are "outcomes." Often people treat outcomes as impacts. What is important is that managers and stakeholders develop a shared understanding within the context of the project or program.

Determining Information Needs

The next step is to determine specific information needs of the management and key stakeholders. This can be tricky because managers and stakeholders often are not sure what they really need and seek more information than they can realistically use. When outside experts design monitoring systems without specific guidance, they also tend to be risk aversive and cover more items than are truly necessary. The experience of many democracy programs indicates that, unless care is exercised, the process may result in developing large, complex systems that are not only costly but also difficult to manage. Therefore, it is important to ask the following questions: Who wants the information? Why is the information needed? How will the gathered information be used?

Box 4.2 Information Requirements for Indicators

- Unit of measurement.
- Time frame during which data will be collected.
- Target group to which it will be applied.
- Source of data.
- Reference to a baseline or benchmarks for comparison.
- Take the case of a simple indicator such as "number of journalists trained." The unit of measurement in this case is "trained journalists," which is simple and straightforward. However, to be useful for monitoring purposes, one also needs information about the time frame. Will they be trained in one month or three months or a year? Unless the training is a one-shot affair, a time frame is necessary for comparative analysis. The target groups should also be identified. The hypothetical project on electoral assistance in a transition country, for example, is likely to require that women journalists are included in the training program. Therefore, the indicator will require disaggregated information about the gender composition of the trainees. The source of data should also be mentioned. In this case, the information is likely to be provided by the organizational unit that arranges for training. If the purpose is to make comparisons, a baseline or benchmarks should be established.

Selection of Indicators

The third, and undoubtedly most difficult, task is to select appropriate indicators for monitoring. As discussed in the previous chapter, precise and unambiguous indicators that are not amenable to different interpretations are not always available. Often indicators do not reflect or assess the specific concept that they are supposed to measure. In other words, they lack validity. And many indicators fail to measure incremental change, which is an essential requirement for monitoring. There is no simple solution to this problem. Hopefully, a relatively more valid and reliable inventory of democracy indicators will emerge over time as the democracy community gains more experience and expertise. Meanwhile, those who design monitoring systems will have to exercise extreme caution in identifying indicators. They should clearly explain the limitations of selected indicators to managers and stakeholders and warn against undue reliance on quantitative indicators.

Quantitative indicators can be supplemented by qualitative information. For example, managers of a media assistance program can conduct in-depth interviews with a few journalists trained by the program and write brief notes on these interviews. They also can visit a few training sessions and record their observations. The partnering institutions can be requested to give their assessments about the quality of the training or the problems, if any, they faced in recruiting journalists. In practically all democracy programs, the staff informally gather such information. Such efforts can be formalized and made an integral part of monitoring. Supplementing indicator data by qualitative information makes monitoring more relevant to managers and stakeholders.

Assigning Responsibilities for Information Gathering

The next obvious step is to carefully plan data collection activities and assign individual responsibilities for them. Managers of a program, in consultation with their staff, decide who will gather and analyze data and information, how often, and when. Since many democracy programs tend to have multiple components, the responsibilities can be shared. For an electoral assistance project, the project accountant is the best person to track the costs of various activities while the staff member who supervises training for election monitors is most suited to collect and analyze data for indicators such as the number of people who applied for the training, the number of persons who were selected, and the number of trainees who completed the training. The latter can also supervise surveys about trainees' satisfaction and their utilization of skills and information imparted to them. The staff member in charge of organizing the voter education program can be responsible for gathering information about advertisements and public service announcements on radio and television, public meetings held and the estimated attendance, or the posters distributed. To avoid confusion, the deadline for delivering the data and information should be fixed.

Since partnering organizations usually provide most monitoring data, particular attention should be given to their capacity and willingness to gather it. In an electoral assistance project in a postconflict African country, I found that the project expected the partner institution to manage and conduct minisurveys and focus groups to study people's perceptions and attitudes toward elections. The local partner, however, lacked the technical skills to supervise them and, as a result, the surveys and focus groups were never undertaken. Such situations can be avoided if planners realistically assess the technical and resource capabilities of organizations to be entrusted with the responsibility of gathering data.

Operating a Monitoring System

Only a small proportion of democracy programs can afford a full-time evaluation and monitoring staff. Therefore, a senior manager usually takes the responsibility for operating a monitoring system.

The experience of development programs indicates that many simple measures can contribute to the smooth running of a monitoring system. First, some initial training is necessary for staff who will be engaged in data collection and analysis. When organizations that receive project assistance are expected to provide data, their staff may also be included in the training. For example, a democracy project that assists a national election commission would impart training not only to its own staff but also to an official of the commission, who submits progress reports. The duration of the training may range from a few hours to a few days. Second, most of the data are generated by the program and its partnering organizations without undue reliance on outside experts and organizations. Third, data collection and reporting are standardized and a timetable for the submission of the data and information strictly adhered to. Finally, monitoring reports are simple and succinct. When reports are long, technical managers and stakeholders lose interest and the very purpose of establishing a monitoring system is defeated. The reports may be submitted quarterly or biannually.

Collaborative Critical Reflections

A major limitation of many monitoring systems is lack of critical reflection over the findings by managers and stakeholders. This is rather unfortunate. Managers and stakeholders should discuss the monitoring findings and explore their implications for future activities. Such reflection requires that they focus on four questions on the basis of the gathered data and information: What is happening? Why is it happening? What are its implications for the program? What should we do next?

Thus, managers and stakeholders should go beyond a simple discussion of statistical and qualitative data and critically examine the state of the entire program. Such reflection may even involve questioning the assumptions behind the program or the relevance of many of its activities. They may conclude that no change is needed or vice versa.

This can be explained with a simple illustration. Suppose that a posttraining survey of journalists indicated that a majority of those who took a three-week course on investigative journalism were not satisfied with it. Respondents identified several shortcomings such as the course contents were not suitable to local conditions, the course did not adequately cover topics, trainers used the English language in which trainees were not proficient, and the training material was not provided in time. A collaborative reflection will require a candid discussion of the findings by the managers, trainers who designed and implemented the course, the staff of the organization that provided training, and other stakeholders. Also invited may be a few trainees, if they are willing to articulate their criticism. The objective of the discourse will be to understand the problem, seek sensible solutions, and implement the solutions. Participants may also agree on the future course of action: trainers will revise course contents and provide training material in advance, sponsoring institutions will nominate only those journalists who are proficient in English, and the project manager will delay the next course until necessary revisions can be made.

There are several advantages to a collaborative approach. It facilitates a more comprehensive dialogue because different viewpoints are presented and discussed. It also reduces biases as the data and information are cross-checked by different participants. For example, in the above case, the trainees can elaborate their concerns and even propose solutions that might not have occurred to trainers and managers. Above all, this approach fosters a collective ownership of the follow-up actions. Stakeholders can feel that their viewpoints have been considered and agree on a common set of actions. This in itself is an exercise in promoting democratic norms. Contrast it with a situation where the managers discuss the monitoring report with only the trainers and instruct them to make suitable revisions. In the latter case, neither the trainees nor the sponsoring institutions will feel any stake in the decision.

When should such critical reflections take place? As a rule, a dialogue should take place after a monitoring report is released or when an implementation problem arises. Such meetings may be called by the head of the program or head of the organization providing the training and organizing the course. The meetings should be conducted in a way that facilitates a free flow of ideas and views.

In conclusion, a monitoring system should provide a space where program staff and stakeholders can share their experiences, reflect over them, and make suitable changes if and when necessary to make an intervention more effective and reflective. A monitoring system not only should be a bureaucratic entity to keep records of achievements and failures, but also a forum for brainstorming ideas to improve the intervention.

5

Planning and Managing Evaluations

As I remember, once I was very frustrated with . . . who managed evaluation. He did not understand what is involved in data collection and analysis. . . . Nor did he understand counterfactuals, but he insisted that we measure impacts, when there was no baseline data and even no resources for conducting a survey. It took us a whole afternoon to explain that what he wanted was not possible in the given situation.

—An evaluator of democracy programs

SOWs tend to be overly ambitious and/or . . . insufficient time is budgeted for undertaking rigorous data collection and analysis. This is particularly true in the case of summative evaluations, which examine the impacts of development interventions and the evaluations that are conducted in high-threat environments.

—"Meta-Evaluations of Foreign Assistance Evaluations"

In this chapter, I provide an overview of the planning and managing of democracy evaluations and outline the role of evaluation managers. Most evaluation managers tend to be experienced staff members in bilateral and multilateral donor agencies, foundations, international NGOs, and private sector firms. They define the objectives and scope of evaluations and write the statement of work (SOW) or terms of reference (TOR). They also prepare budgets, select evaluators, facilitate the logistics for fieldwork, and keep in touch with evaluation teams to ensure that the work is done as planned and solve any bottlenecks that might arise. In addition, they communicate with stakeholders, arrange for reviews of evaluation reports, and facilitate discussions of their findings and recommendations. Because of the nature of democracy programming and political sensibilities involved, evaluation managers have to be careful, and even diplomatic, in their interactions. They have to ensure not only that evaluators are able to secure reliable and valid data, but also that the informants are not directly or indirectly harmed by the suspicious political authorities. The edict "do no harm" applies to democracy assistance as much as it does to humanitarian assistance. The roles and responsibilities of evaluation managers can be described with reference to three phases: preevaluation and planning, field research, and review and follow-up.

The Manager's Role During the Planning Phase

Specifying the Objectives and Audience

The first step for an agency or program is to decide if an evaluation is needed and if it will generate findings and recommendations that will be useful to stakeholders. Evaluations undertaken simply to meet bureaucratic reporting requirements are usually a waste of resources. Unfortunately, it is quite common that not until almost the end of a program will its managers realize that there was a provision for evaluation and commission one without much thought about its use. Such situations should be avoided. In the face of shrinking resources, there is no justification for doing an evaluation of a democracy intervention if its findings will not be utilized.

Specification of evaluation objectives can help to sharpen the focus of evaluations and formulate the right questions. It also makes it easier for evaluators to come up with relevant findings and recommendations. To determine the objectives of evaluations, managers may deliberate over such questions as, Who needs evaluation findings and recommendations? Why do they need them? How and when will they use them? The evaluation manager, for example, should have detailed discussions with the supervisor of a civil society program to understand his/her information needs and expectations from the evaluation. Do they want to know about the implementation problems faced by the program? Do they want to find out if the program is likely to meet its targets over time? Do they require information about its sustainability after funding stops? Do they need to find out about its overall impacts? By focusing on these questions, the evaluation manager is able to specify the objectives of the evaluations.

Although many, and perhaps most, managers do not consider the needs of other stakeholders and consult them, it is always prudent to do so. If the headquarters office of an international agency, for example, plans an evaluation of its journalism training project in an African country, the evaluation manager should consult with its implementing partners, staff of the host journalism institutions, and whenever possible a few media outlets at which trainees are employed to solicit their views and suggestions. A major problem with many evaluations conducted by the headquarters of bilateral and multilateral agencies is that host-country stakeholders are not consulted, much less engaged. Evaluation managers located at the headquarters have little time and patience to contact them and, thus, leave this responsibility to their local or regional offices. In many cases, the local stakeholders are informed rather than consulted. I have often heard the complaint from host-country stakeholders that they are treated as a source of information rather than as real stakeholders. This is unfortunate and should change; evaluation managers, whether located at the headquarters or in the field, should seek the inputs from and participation of host-country stakeholders at the planning stage. Even if it causes delays, it is worthwhile because it will make the planned evaluation more relevant to the needs of host countries.

Finally, the evaluation manager decides about the type of evaluation that will be most appropriate. If a program is in its midcycle or is encountering implementation problems, a midterm performance evaluation may be most appropriate. On the other hand, if it is near completion and the operational unit has yet to decide about follow-up, a summative evaluation focusing on sustainability and relevance may be needed. Finally, if the program is highly innovative and breaking new ground, an impact evaluation using experimental and quasi-experimental design may be warranted, if necessary data are available.

Formulating Evaluation Questions

The next, and undoubtedly difficult, step is to draft evaluation questions, which can be classified in three distinct but related categories: descriptive, normative, and cause-and-effect.

Descriptive questions focus on "what is" and shed light on the existing state of the ongoing processes and operations. They answer the questions of who, what, where, when, how, and how many. Examples of descriptive questions are

- How many NGOs received technical assistance from the program to improve their performance?
- What percentage of middle-level journalists, who received overseas training, were able to obtain suitable jobs on their return?
- What proportion of trained election monitors were women?
- Did voter education programs reach the minority groups prior to national elections?

Normative questions evaluate performance with reference to some standards. Sometimes, the targets specified in program documents can serve as benchmarks against which performance is evaluated. In other cases, evaluators establish their own standards. Examples of these questions are

- Did the human rights training for senior government officials serve their needs?
- If not, why not?
- Did the program meet its target of helping fifty community radio stations?
- Was the curriculum developed by the project to train election observers appropriate?

Finally cause-and-effect questions are designed to determine the outcomes and impacts of a democracy program. Examples of such questions are

- Did technical assistance improve the performance of the election commission?
- Did technical assistance contribute to improvements in the financial viability of community radio stations?
- Did the anticorruption program succeed in creating greater awareness about the problem of corruption among citizens?

A single evaluation cannot answer more than a few questions unless the time and resources are abundant, which is rarely the case. Therefore, the number of questions should be limited.

Three criteria are used to select evaluation questions. First, questions need to reflect the priorities of management and stakeholders. If a German foundation, which provides assistance for strengthening political parties in an African country, wants to know if its project will be sustainable after it stops funding it, questions will pertain primarily to sustainability. On the other hand, if the foundation is concerned about its performance, the questions will naturally focus on implementation issues, the problems and challenges that it is encountering, and the steps that can be taken to solve them.

Second, only those questions that require the gathering of fresh data or reanalysis of existing data should be included. Evaluators are supposed to answer questions on the basis of hard evidence (both quantitative and qualitative) and not on their hunches and opinions. Their conclusions should follow from the data and not vice versa.

Third, evaluation questions must be plausible, so that the relevant data and information can be gathered. The feasibility of answering questions should be considered in relation to available time and resources. A major problem with many evaluations of democracy interventions is that evaluation managers tend to list a large number of questions with little regard for time and resource constraints. For example, some democracy evaluations contracted by USAID were expected to answer questions on project performance, sustainability, and impacts, but evaluators were given three weeks to four weeks to gather data and analyze it in a foreign country. Box 5.1 gives an example of a USAID evaluation in Nepal, which had a long list of difficult questions, but evaluators had less than a month to complete it. Such unrealistic expectations undermine the analytical rigor and credibility of evaluations. A sense of realism is needed in compiling questions. If adequate resources cannot be budgeted, questions that require a long time for research should be avoided.

Selection of an Evaluation Design

Evaluation managers also choose appropriate designs for evaluations, taking into consideration the needs of stakeholders, time and resource constraints, and the quality of data and information that can be realistically generated. I discuss the various designs in detail in the next two chapters, but suffice it to mention here that managers can use one of the following designs.

The first, and the most rigorous, category includes experimental and quasi-experimental designs. In experimental and quasi-experimental designs, evaluators compare the results of two groups: one that received treatment (assistance) and the other (control) that did not. The impact is measured by comparing the treatment and non-treatment groups before and after the completion of the project. To

---

Box 5.1 OTI Program Evaluation, Nepal, 2006–2009

Were areas of programmatic focus appropriate and effective for the Office of the Transition Initiative (OTI)? A list of focus areas that should be addressed are geographic, such as which regions and which locations within each region; social strata, youth, nationwide audiences, Kathmandu vs. regions; types of activities such as access to civil society, information dissemination, promoting and diversifying debate; constituent assembly, elections, and linking citizens with the government; style of activities, i.e., short-term, participatory implementation, and locally identified needs; and strategic framework assessing the overarching goal and objectives.

In the Terai, where numerous small-grant activities were supported over an extended period of time, is there evidence of a significant impact related to OTI's overall aims and objectives in Nepal?

Were media—public, private, alternative—activities used appropriately and effectively to further OTI's overall goals and objectives?

What specific recommendations can the evaluation team offer about what elements of OTI's strategy and methods, if any, can support or enhance the USAID/Nepal mission's ability to effectively design and implement future conflict-sensitive programming?

Did the program support US foreign policy objectives? If yes, did it accomplish this by helping local partners advance peace and democracy?

Does the evaluation find significant impact in strengthening democratic processes and increasing momentum for peaceful resolution of conflict?

---

assess the impact of a program designed to expose judiciary officials to human rights issues, evaluators would assign judiciary officials to two groups. The members of the first group (Group A) would be given training while those belonging to the other group (Group B) would be excluded from it. Once the project is completed, participants in the two groups would be tested on their knowledge of and attitudes toward human rights issues. If Group A scores higher than Group B, evaluators would conclude that the higher scores were attributable to the educational program and the project had a positive impact. The difference between experimental and quasi-experimental designs is that in the former participants are randomly assigned in two groups while in the latter members of the control group are selected on the basis of a set of criteria that make them comparable to the treatment group.

The second category of quantitative designs consists of statistical analyses without control groups. Such designs can analyze the data generated by sample surveys, content analyses of documents, and structured observations. One set of designs consists of pre- and post-designs that measure performance before and after an intervention is over. In a variant of this design, time series data are collected at several points in time to smooth over fluctuations. The second set of designs consists of cross-sectional analyses in which outcomes are measured by comparing the varying levels of the exposure to a project's assistance that participants received. For example, the impact of a voter education program funded by an international agency can be measured by correlating the knowledge scores of respondents whose participation in the voter education program varied.

The third category consists of case study designs. A case study examines an intervention it its context, focusing on the dynamic interactions between an intervention, its environment, and the targeted populations. Most information is gathered through reviews of program documents; interviews with program managers, host-country officials, and other stakeholders; focus group discussions; meetings with beneficiaries; and even surveys. All of these designs and their strengths and limitations are discussed in the next two chapters.

Preparing a Statement of Work/Terms of Reference

The next logical step is to prepare an SOW or TOR for the evaluation. An SOW/TOR is a blueprint, a coherent plan of action, and is akin to a research proposal submitted by a researcher. A carefully planned and well-written SOW/TOR will ensure that the evaluation team can meet the information needs of the major stakeholders. Moreover, it reduces possible misunderstandings that may arise between evaluation managers and evaluation teams. Even when internal evaluations are conducted by an agency or organization, it is helpful to prepare an SOW/TOR. Requirements for an SOW/TOR differ from organization to organization; however, a typical SOW/TOR includes the following items.

It begins with a brief description and history of the concerned program, its activities and components, and its implementation to give evaluators an idea of the intervention to be evaluated. It also lists main evaluation questions and indicates the preferred research design. Evaluation managers generally are not experts in evaluation methodology and, therefore, they usually identify the design but leave it to evaluators to propose appropriate details. Only when they possess methodological expertise, do they provide details about the design.

An SOW/TOR also mentions the number of evaluators required and their qualifications and experience. The size of a team may range from one to three or more members including a team leader. The needed qualifications and experience for evaluators is discussed in the section Selection of Evaluators below. A timetable for preliminary research, fieldwork, report writing, and final submission of the report is also included. It should be realistic given the vagaries of data collection in transition and postconflict societies where most democracy interventions are implemented. An SOW/TOR also explains the nature and size of the evaluation report, briefing material, and other documents that are expected from evaluators. If evaluators are expected to make oral presentations to stakeholders, that is also mentioned. The last item is the expected costs. Although the requirements vary, most SOW/TORs mention the expected costs or provide a tentative budget. Box 5.2 shows the elements of a good SOW/TOR.

Assessing Evaluability

In the case of large and complex evaluations, particularly global or regional program evaluations, it is useful to undertake evaluability assessments of an evaluation proposal or SOW/TOR by colleagues or

---

Box 5.2 Elements of a Good Statement of Work

According to USAID, a good SOW usually

- Identifies the activity, results package, or strategy to be evaluated.
- Provides a brief background on implementation.
- Identifies existing performance information sources.
- States the purpose, audience, and use of the evaluation.
- Clarifies the evaluation questions.
- Identifies the evaluation method to answer the questions.
- Discusses evaluation team composition and participation of customers and partners.
- Covers procedures such as schedule and logistics.
- Clarifies requirements for reporting and dissemination.
- Includes a budget.

Source: USAID (2006a).

outside experts. The purpose of such assessments is to have a second look at the evaluation proposal with reference to the following three considerations.

The first consideration concerns whether the evaluation objectives and questions are plausible and relevant data and information can be gathered within the given time and resources. Reviewers may find that the evaluation team will not be able to gain access to the required data. For example, when baseline data are not available, evaluators cannot use experimental or quasi-experimental designs to measure the impacts of voter education programs. Similarly, they may conclude that the required information cannot be gathered in high-threat environments. Many evaluation teams sent by the United States to Afghanistan and Iraq were virtually confined to embassy compounds and could not visit project sites. Had evaluability assessments been undertaken, such situations could have been avoided. Evaluability assessments often administer a dose of realism to evaluation designs.

The second consideration involves the consent and cooperation of stakeholders, particularly of the host country and partnering institutions. The reviewers should be confident that necessary cooperation and participation will be forthcoming. This consideration is particularly important when government officials or ruling elites do not look warmly at democracy interventions or when interventions are being carried out in a highly volatile environment. For example, the reviewers of a human rights evaluation proposal should be confident that the human rights organizations receiving assistance will be willing to share the information and support the evaluation.

Finally, the overall cost of the evaluation should be considered. Ideally, the expected benefits from an evaluation should be at least of equal value to the resources expended on it. While it is not easy to quantify the potential benefits of an evaluation, reviewers may examine the cost-effectiveness of the proposed evaluation and the potential use of its findings.

The Manager's Role During Implementation

Selection of Evaluators

Different bilateral and multilateral donor agencies, international NGOs, and foundations have their own requirements and procedures for recruiting evaluators. Evaluation managers have no option but to scrupulously follow these, even when they may cause delays or entail additional costs. Since the successful conduct of an evaluation depends largely on the quality and capability of evaluators, managers have to be extremely careful about the selection of the evaluators and composition of evaluation teams. The following five criteria may be used for selecting evaluators for large, multiyear programs.

Evaluation skills. Evaluators must possess professional training and experience in evaluation design and methodology. They need to be able to develop appropriate evaluation designs, collect data using various data-gathering methods, establish rapport with stakeholders, and write empirically grounded reports with actionable recommendations. They also should be able to work as a team.

Knowledge of democracy programming. Mere academic knowledge of democracy is not sufficient; evaluators should also have firsthand knowledge of the workings of democracy programs; the problems that they face; the factors and forces that affect them; and, above all, the political context in which they operate.

Country knowledge. Expatriate evaluators must possess knowledge and understanding of the host countries, including their political and social institutions and culture. Other things being equal, preference should be given to evaluators who possess language proficiency, in-country work experience, and a broad understanding of the political context in which a program operates.

Gender mix and gender analysis skills. Gender representation usually aids in data collection. Female evaluators are often more effective in soliciting information and ideas from female respondents, who tend to be more comfortable with them than with male evaluators. The reverse is also true in many traditional societies where men are reluctant to be interviewed by women. When the target population is mixed, evaluation teams should pay particular attention to the gender mix of evaluation teams as well as the team's capacity to undertake gender analysis and data disaggregation by sex if and when necessary.

Host-country representation. Because they better understand the internal dynamics of the society, its power structure, the nature and pace of democratization, and the entire milieu in which a program is implemented, host-country evaluators should be represented in evaluations. Even when highly qualified evaluators are not available, efforts should be made to recruit less-qualified ones so that they can learn from the experience. Box 5.3 shows excerpts about the qualifications

Box 5.3 Qualifications for a Rule of Law Program Evaluation in Liberia in an SOW

Team expertise and composition. The team will be composed of a team leader, senior advisor, a Liberian national consultant, and optional logistical and administrative assistant. *Team leader.* The team leader shall be responsible for coordinating evaluation activities and ensuring the production and completion of the evaluation report. S/he must have substantial experience in managing and leading evaluations of complex democracy and governance and/or justice reform programs as well as in designing and implementing projects, preferably on rule of law. S/he must possess excellent writing and interpersonal skills and be familiar with US government–funded programs, objectives, and reporting requirements. At least twelve years of experience (with at least five years' experience in international development work) managing and/or implementing justice reform programs in Africa or postconflict countries confronting issues similar to those facing Liberia will be highly advantageous. An advanced degree in law or a related field such as court administration, political science, international relations, or public administration is required.

Senior rule of law advisor. The senior advisor must possess a law degree or a master's degree in a law-related field such as criminal law, court administration, human rights law, informal justice systems, political science, public administration, or related area and have at least seven years of professional experience working on issues related to justice reform, legal education, and/or court administration in Africa and experience in international development work. The senior advisor must be familiar with the operation of USAID and/or other international donor programs.

Host-country national consultant. The host-country national consultant must have at least five years of experience working on issues related to justice reform in Africa. Candidates for the consultant position must hold a bachelor's degree in a law-related field, such as criminal law, criminology, political science, sociology, international relations, international development, public administration, human rights, or a related field.

Logistical/administrative support staff. The contractor may add an additional team member for logistical/administrative support, but this is not a requirement.

Source: USAID (2009a).

and experience of evaluators from an SOW for the Evaluation of Rule of Law Programs in Liberia, which was conducted in 2009.

A team of three to four evaluators is usually required for a large multiyear, multicomponent democracy program. For small programs, one democracy expert who has a strong evaluation background may serve the purpose. In such a case, if an expatriate evaluator is employed, it is useful to have a local counterpart.

Support for Data Collection

After evaluators have been selected and necessary preliminary work has been done, the role of the manager shifts. His/her primary responsibility at this phase is to facilitate data collection, ensure the integrity and independence of the evaluation team, and solve logistic or managerial problems. As discussed in detail in Chapter 8, evaluators of democracy programs use a wide variety of data collection methods that include the following:

- Document reviews, using established synthesis techniques to extract and analyze findings and lessons from existing progress reports and other documents.
- Secondary analysis of existing statistical databases, project records, files, and surveys.
- Sample surveys and minisurveys.
- Key informant interviews.
- Focus group discussions.
- Group interviews.
- Structured and nonstructured direct observation.

Evaluation managers do not and should not involve themselves in data collection, but must remain in constant touch with evaluation teams about the nature of data collection methods and the overall quality of data and information they are generating. They should discourage senior project staff from participating in field research as their presence can compromise validity of data collection. When project staff accompany evaluators for key informant interviews, focus group discussions, or direct observation, respondents tend to become cautious in their observations and the evaluation team does not get a realistic picture.

Often, unexpected problems arise during the data collection stage that may require intervention by the manager. For example, an evaluation team member becomes ill and has to leave the team; the evaluators suddenly find that the planned sample surveys cannot be undertaken within the stipulated time; the concerned government officials, who were to be interviewed, have been transferred and the new officials are not familiar with the program; the team members have antagonized senior government officials or political leaders, creating problems for the program itself; or the team has visited areas or organizations that posed security risks. I know of a few cases in which evaluation teams did not follow security restrictions in war-torn societies, creating problems for USAID overseas missions. Sometimes, serious tension occurs within evaluation teams that team leaders are unable to resolve. Good evaluation managers must handle such situations with tact and understanding, keeping in mind the long-term interests of the program and the independence of evaluators.

Inputs in Constructing Sampling

Managers usually leave sampling issues to the discretion of evaluators, and this is a sound practice because constructing a sample requires

---

Box 5.4 Political Insensitivity by an Evaluator

An international agency sent a team to evaluate the workings of a human rights project in an African country that was recovering from civil war. The purpose of the evaluation was to examine the sustainability and effectiveness of the human rights project in a highly charged political environment. A team member, once a trial lawyer by profession, started aggressively questioning senior government officials about the past and present alleged human rights violations. His style of questioning was confrontational and he managed to antagonize senior officials whose cooperation was vital for the survival of the project. The evaluation team leader pleaded with the lawyer, but he did not follow the advice. Thus, the evaluation manager at the headquarters had only two realistic options: either recall the attorney or recall the entire team. To avoid embarrassment to the team member, the manager recalled the entire team on a flimsy pretext. The team wrote the report on the basis of the data that it had already gathered.

technical expertise. However, when nontechnical considerations such as the overall costs, the consent and cooperation of local stakeholders, and the political situation also need to be considered, managers are involved in decisionmaking. There are cases in which some sites or organizations have to be included in the sample for political or strategic considerations. For example, the decision about selection of countries in multicountry evaluations cannot be left entirely to evaluation managers since considerations of the costs of fieldwork as well as strategic considerations can often be important.

The Manager's Role During Review and Follow-Up

Reviewing the Draft Report

It is the responsibility of the evaluation manager to review the draft evaluation report against the requirements stated in the SOW/TOR. After reviewing it, the evaluation manager must share the draft report with colleagues, outside experts, and concerned stakeholders to seek comments and suggestions. Particular attention should be given to the following topics and questions:

- *Data collection.* Are the data and sources of data clearly presented in the main report or as an annex? Were the data collection methods consistent with the approved research design?
- *Quality of data.* What is the quality of data and information gathered by the team? Are there serious questions about their reliability and validity? Does the report mention their relative strengths and weaknesses in a transparent manner?
- *Coverage of evaluation questions.* Are all evaluation questions answered in the report? Are the data and evidence presented clearly? Are alternative explanations of findings explicitly considered and explored?
- *Recommendations.* Do recommendations directly follow from the evaluation's findings and the conclusions? Are they supported by sound analysis and reasoning? Are they "actionable" in the sense that they can be implemented by the commissioning organization and its partners under existing circumstances?
- *Lessons.* Does the report mention lessons that may be used in designing new projects and programs? Are they adequately explained?

Because the evaluation manager may receive conflicting and incompatible comments and suggestions, s/he must consolidate them and communicate them clearly to evaluators. Some evaluation managers also organize workshops to discuss the draft reports.

Dissemination of Evaluation Findings and Recommendations

Evaluation managers are also responsible for disseminating the findings and recommendations among stakeholders. As discussed in detail in Chapter 9, evaluation managers may request three written documents: the entire report, a brief of only one or two pages summarizing the main findings and recommendations, and a six- to eight-page summary that interested stakeholders can easily read and react to. In the past, the practice was to send a printed version of these documents, but now it is usually done electronically to save time and resources.

In addition to distributing reports in written form, evaluation managers encourage oral presentations by evaluation teams. Because they provide an opportunity for personal interaction, such presentations are more effective in communicating evaluation findings and recommendations than are written reports. Stakeholders and technical staff have an opportunity to ask questions about data, findings, and recommendations. Evaluators are able to offer necessary clarifications and give further details about their findings and recommendations. By creating a forum for discussion among managers and decisionmakers, oral briefings often generate momentum for action.

Follow-Up

The role of managers in follow-up differs from organization to organization. While some agencies or organizations expect managers to be actively involved in the implementation of recommendations, others do not encourage such involvement. At a minimum, all evaluation managers should arrange meetings between evaluators and senior program officials to discuss evaluation findings and recommendations and explore their implications. Once such meetings have been completed, it is up to program managers to decide the future course of action. For example, once an evaluation team has completed a midterm evaluation of a legislative strengthening project in a Middle Eastern country, the manager might arrange a meeting between evaluators and senior managers and leave it up to them to take further action. In other cases, the manager might go a step further and play a more active role by assisting senior managers in implementation of recommendations.

To conclude, the job of evaluation managers in a democracy evaluation is critical to its success. To be effective, managers should possess a good understanding of the program being evaluated, the problems and challenges it has faced, the progress it has made, and its intended effects and impacts. Moreover, they should also have a background in social sciences and understand the evaluation process. Above all, they should possess managerial and interpersonal communication skills. During the past decade, the pool of staff in bilateral and multilateral agencies as well as NGOs and foundations who can successfully manage evaluations of democracy programs has expanded rapidly. USAID, for example, has democracy officers in its overseas missions who are qualified to manage evaluations. Many established democracy NGOs such as NDI, IRI, Internews, and IREX have highly trained professional staff to guide the evaluation process. Private sector firms in the United States and Western Europe, which implement democracy projects and programs, are quite proficient in managing evaluations.

6

Experimental and Quasi-Experimental Designs

Since the methods required for quantitative impact evaluations are not in the skill sets of many of those who have worked in impact evaluations, most rigorous evaluations are being done by economists and econometricians, not evaluators. The result is technically competent studies (rigorous impact evaluations) which are often not very good evaluations (they are not quality impact evaluations), with limited thought given to policy relevance. . . . At worst, impact evaluations may focus solely on whether the impact estimate is statistically significant or not—with no discussion of how large it is, whether it varies by group (impact heterogeneity), the cost of achieving it, or the contextual factors which allowed it to happen.

—Howard White

In evaluating the literature on evaluation research methods, we found that randomized experiments are considered appropriate for assessing intervention effectiveness only after an intervention has met minimal requirements for an effective evaluation—that the intervention is important, clearly defined, and well implemented and the evaluation itself is well resourced. Conducting an impact evaluation of a social intervention often requires the expenditure of significant resources to both collect and analyze data on program results and estimate what would have happened in the absence of the program.

—US Government Accounting Office

There is a genuine concern among a segment of political scientists, researchers, and policymakers that, although the international community has been funding a vast array of democracy interventions, there is little or no hard evidence about their net impacts. Only a few impact evaluations have been undertaken by funding agencies or implementing organizations. Often these have been impressionistic, with little or no hard quantitative data. At best, they demonstrate that some expected results have occurred, but they cannot prove that these results can be attributed to programs. In most cases, they do not measure the net impacts of democracy interventions by using counterfactuals. Consequently, the international community has no credible quantitative evidence that their investments in democracy promotion are bearing fruits in consolidating nascent democracies. What is probably worse, according to this view, is that democracy interventions continue to be designed on hunches and impressions rather than on valid findings derived from rigorous evaluation research.

The exponents of this view strongly argue that impact evaluations, using experimental and quasi-experimental designs, should be undertaken to measure the impacts of democracy assistance. Such designs involve the construction of a control or comparison group that enables the evaluator to build a counterfactual case as to what would have happened had the intervention not taken place. As a study commissioned by USAID, "Improving Democracy Assistance: Building Knowledge Through Evaluation and Research," and undertaken by the National Research Council puts it,

> The bottom line is that if there is a strong commitment to answering the question—"Did the resources spent on a given project truly yield positive results?"—the best way to reach the most definitive answer is through an impact evaluation that involves the random selection of units for treatment and the collection of data in both treatment and control groups. . . . Many USAID [democracy and governance] projects that the committee encountered in the field were quite amenable in principle to randomization without changes in design. (National Research Council 2008, pp. 136–137)

Experimental designs, popularly known as randomized control trials (RCTs) that construct treatment and control groups through random sampling and *quasi-experimental designs* that use equivalent comparison groups without random sampling are often labeled as the gold and silver standards for impact evaluation. Both designs have been an integral part of the arsenal of the evaluation community since Donald T. Campbell and Julian C. Stanley published their seminal book *Experimental and Quasi-Experimental Designs for Research* in 1963. In this chapter, I focus on the use of these designs for measuring the impacts of democracy interventions. I explain the logic behind them and outline their defining features. I then briefly discuss the major experimental and quasi-experimental designs for impact evaluations and provide an example. Next, I identify a set of methodological and practical obstacles that make it difficult to use these designs for most democracy interventions. I also present the experience of IRI and NDI in using these designs. I conclude that, while experimental and quasi-experimental designs can generate useful information in many cases, the scope of their application is bound to remain quite limited in democracy interventions.

The Logic Behind Experimental and Quasi-Experimental Designs

The logic behind these designs is simple and can be explained with an illustration. Suppose an international donor agency has been promoting community radio stations in an African country. The purpose of the assistance is to make the stations financially viable. The program trains managers of radio stations on how to raise revenue through various measures such as charging fees for birth, wedding, or social event announcements; soliciting advertisements from local businesses; organizing fund-raising events; and writing proposals to seek outside support for replacing machines and equipment. The program also provides instruction in accounting. Initially, the agency gave technical assistance to 50 out of 200 stations. If the program succeeded in making the assisted stations financially self-sufficient, the agency would like to extend the assistance to the remaining stations in the country.

A simple way to determine this is to measure the change in the balance sheets of the assisted radio stations before and after the technical assistance was provided by the program. Suppose that the evaluators found that at the start of the program ten of fifty selected radio stations were struggling and the remaining forty were facing major losses, but at the end of the program all of the struggling stations had become profitable and twenty of the remaining forty that were incurring major losses had also become more or less self-supporting. Thus, after comparing the baseline (financial conditions of the radio stations before the start of technical assistance) with the postassistance conditions, evaluators might declare that the program is an outstanding success.

The question arises as to how we can be sure that the improvements in the balance sheets of the stations can be attributed to technical assistance. There might be many exogenous factors to explain the observed improvements. For example, it is quite possible that the economic environment has changed for the better. When the program was launched the country was facing a drought and the rural areas were hard-hit, but since then rainfall has increased and resulted in higher agricultural production and incomes. Thus, the radio stations are in a better position to raise funds. It is also possible that the leadership of many radio stations changed. The old managers were replaced by younger and more dynamic leaders who were more business savvy and able to raise income while reducing costs. It is also possible that the government realized the importance of community radio stations and started giving them financial assistance. Unless the influence of such factors can be accounted for, the evaluator cannot be confident that the improvements in the financial conditions of the assisted radio stations can be attributed mostly, if not totally, to the technical assistance provided by the project.

Experimental and quasi-experimental designs enable evaluators to control the effects of exogenous factors by constructing a control or comparison group. In this case, the evaluator will select another group of, say, fifty radio stations that will not receive technical assistance. The treatment group (radio stations that will receive assistance) and control/comparison group (radio stations that will not receive assistance) can be selected in two ways. One approach is to select both groups through random assignment. The alternative is to match them on the basis of some well-defined criteria.

By comparing the performance of assisted radio stations and the nonassisted group, evaluators will be more confident of their inference. They can realistically assume that the other factors such as improvement in economic conditions, change in the leadership, or support from the government have equally affected both groups and, therefore, the observed changes can be attributed to technical assistance. For example, if in the control group only ten of forty stations with negative balance sheets became financially viable, and five of ten struggling stations improved their financial situation, one can be certain that the technical assistance was successful. The evaluator will tabulate the net results of the project as presented in Table 6.1.

Table 6.1 Changes in the Conditions of Treatment and Control Groups (percentage)

Group	Improvement in Stations Incurring Major Losses	Improvement in Struggling Stations
Treatment group	50	100
Control group	25	50
Net gains	25	50

Different Designs

During the past four decades, social scientists have developed and refined several experimental and quasi-experimental designs for research and evaluation. I briefly describe here three most widely used designs, which are of particular relevance to democracy interventions.

Pre- and Posttreatment and Control Groups with Random Assignment

The random assignment design, also known as true experiment, originated in medical research where it is used to test drugs and treatment protocols. A group of patients who have the same disease are selected. The selected patients are randomly assigned to two groups. The patients in the first group are given the new drug while those in the other group take the conventional drug or no drug. Neither the patients nor the medical staff administering the treatment know which drug is administered to which patient. The two groups are tested before and after the treatment, and the differences in their performance are attributed to the medicine. Thus, the treatment group refers to individuals who receive the new drug and the control group to those who do not receive it. The same terminology is now used in project settings.

The experimental design has been widely used in psychology, education, communication, medicine, and related disciplines and has generated rigorous findings and conclusions. However, as Michael Bamberger explains, its use in international development programs has been limited:

> Despite the potential benefits, random assignment has only been
> used in a small proportion of development evaluations for one of the

following reasons: target communities, organizations and individuals are selected according to certain administrative or political criteria (the poorest or most needy or the location where the project is most likely to succeed), subjects are self-selected (individuals and groups make decisions to participate) or political considerations make randomization impractical. (2006, p. 5)

The situation is no better in the case of evaluations of democracy interventions. Although social scientists have conducted experiments to test hypotheses or measure results, and IRI and NDI have started using them in a few of their programs, there are not many examples in which this design has been successfully used to measure the outcomes and impacts, and not mere outputs, of multicomponent, long-term democracy programs.[1] Only occasionally, it has been used to compare the effectiveness of different approaches to delivering assistance. Box 6.1 shows an example in which researchers tested the relative effectiveness of two methods of a civic education program in Sudan.

Some ethicists argue that experimental design poses an ethical problem. Is it fair, they ask, to deny assistance to the members of the control groups? During the green revolution in the 1960s, many agricultural experts raised similar concerns about denying farmers in the control districts access to a high-yielding variety of wheat. This argument can also be applied to democracy interventions. Why should a human rights project, for example, deny technical assistance to human rights organizations in the control group? This criticism is not always justified because resources for democracy assistance are limited and many, if not most, programs cannot provide assistance to all organizations and individuals who need it.

There is no doubt that the experimental design is the most rigorous design in the arsenal of evaluators. Unfortunately, it is probably the most difficult to use because it requires that the outcomes be precisely defined and quantified, that baseline data be collected for both groups before and after the treatment (project activities), and there be no changes in the program after baseline data are collected.

Pre- and Posttreatment and Comparison Groups

When it is not possible to randomly assign individuals, organizations, or other entities into treatment and control groups, quasi-experimental designs are used. Like experimental designs, they involve pre- and posttesting of treatment and control groups, but without random

Box 6.1 The Impact of the *Let's Talk* Civic Education Program

In June 2009, Princeton University and NDI conducted a field experiment to examine the causal impact of *Let's Talk*, a radio-based civic education program used with face-to-face listening and discussion groups. Since 2007, NDI had partnered with Sudan Radio Service to produce a weekly installment of *Let's Talk*. The show contains drama and educational segments about topics like citizenship, democratic participation, elections, and women's role in society, and is broadcast across Sudan on shortwave and local FM stations. NDI's trained corps of civic education officers (CEOs) assembled new or preexisting groups of citizens to listen to and share reactions and questions about episodes of *Let's Talk*. The field experiment examined the impact of the combined radio and discussion program as well as the particular impact of each program component: the drama and educational segments of the radio broadcast, the content of each radio episode, and the CEO-moderated discussion sessions. The study randomly assigned these various program components, the full program, or no programming at all to approximately 700 southern Sudanese citizens in Juba who participated in the study. The radio episodes chosen for the study addressed *Let's Talk's* most popular and important topics: democracy, elections, corruption, women's rights and participation, and citizenship. Outcome measures included recorded discussions of *Let's Talk* episodes, individual surveys, and measurement of actual behaviors, including corruption reporting and participation with civil society organizations. The main findings were as follows:

1. The radio episodes increased citizens' understanding of topics presented, including democracy, elections, corruption, and Sudan's legal framework. Exposure to the half-hour program on democracy, for example, increased the proportion of individuals who could correctly define the concept by 26 percent.

2. The episodes motivated civic participation, specifically volunteering with civil society organizations and reporting incidents of corruption. Of participants who volunteered with civil society organizations (CSOs) following the study, 91 percent had listened to the citizenship program.

3. Compared to the educational segment, the drama segment of the show generated more interest in the politics of southern Sudan and a greater desire to listen to the show again and recommend it to others.

4. CEOs generated more, and more gender-egalitarian, discussions about the *Let's Talk* episodes compared to groups that were left to discuss the show on their own.

(continues)

Box 6.1 continued

5. Discussion increased learning about episode topics and increased civil participation, specifically volunteering with civil society organizations. One hundred percent of those who volunteered with CSOs had participated in a moderated discussion.

6. Discussion increased the perception that radio listening partners agree with the ideas in the radio episode. The perception of partners' agreement, even more than an individual's own personal agreement, was related to learning about episode topics and civic participation.

7. Whereas the radio and discussion programming increased knowledge and motivated behavior, it affected attitudes less frequently and sometimes in unintended ways. Discussion seemed to amplify some attitudes, particularly personally relevant attitudes about gender and corruption, in a direction that was not consistent with radio program messages.

8. Discussion and radio information about democracy and southern Sudan's legal framework increased the extent to which participants linked the legitimacy of their leaders and laws with their performance on behalf of citizens.

Thus, the field experiment found that the *Let's Talk* program was an effective civic education design that could produce measurable increases in civic participation. Its use in combination with NDI discussion moderators was an even more powerful means of imparting knowledge and motivating participatory behavior. The drama segment of *Let's Talk* was successfully raising listeners' interest in the program, but its ability to shape attitudes by engaging citizens on a personally relevant level should be developed further. Future discussion facilitation should strive to emphasize group members' points of agreement with the radio programming since awareness of group members' agreement with the programming was highly influential in the promotion of learning and civic participation.

Source: NDI (2009).

assignment. Instead of random assignment, a comparison group is constructed in a way as to ensure that the two groups match in their characteristics and attributes. Suppose a funding agency wants to evaluate the impact of its assistance to ten of fifty human rights organizations in a postconflict society. The evaluators would form the comparison group by pairing each human rights organization in the treatment group with those to be included in the comparison group. If two organizations in the treatment group are relatively large and the remaining eight are relatively small, evaluators would select two large and eight small organizations for the comparison group.

Although not as rigorous as experimental design, pre- and posttreatment and comparison group design is more widely used than the experimental design in development projects because of the practical difficulties involved in randomization. Moreover, in many cases, the random selection of control groups can result in flawed findings. For example, there are eight women NGOs working for gender equality in a country. Two of these have large memberships while others are relatively small. If we randomly assign these NGOs into project and control groups, it is quite probable that the two large NGOs may fall in the same category, which will distort the findings.

Pre- and Posttreatment Group and a Postcontrol/Comparison Group

In this design, while there are pre- and posttreatment scores for project participants, there is no baseline for a comparison group, which is formed only after the project is complete. For example, for a journalism training project, the evaluators will gather data about the knowledge, skills, and quality of their news stories for the selected journalists before and after the training. In fact, data may be collected sometime after the training so that evaluators can examine its effects on the nature and quality of the journalists' reporting. Evaluators will then also construct a comparison group consisting of journalists who did not receive training. Such data will give evaluators greater confidence in their conclusions. If the pre- and postscores of journalists indicate that the training had positive effects, and this finding is confirmed by comparing the scores for trained journalists with those who did not receive the training, evaluators can assert with confidence that the training had a positive result.

This design is undoubtedly more practical than the earlier two designs because it simplifies data collection for the comparison group. It is easier to form a comparison group at the end of a project than at the beginning and at the end of a project. It reduces the cost of data collection. The obvious limitation of this design is that it may suffer from selection bias.

Methodological and Practical Obstacles

There is little doubt that experimental and quasi-experimental designs are the most rigorous designs to measure impacts. When an intended result can be caused by a multiplicity of factors, as is the case
with democracy interventions, they are undoubtedly the best methodological tools to control the effects of exogenous variables. The problem is that there are many methodological and practical considerations that make it extremely difficult to use them in all but a limited
number of cases. I will briefly explain some of these considerations
here. First, experimental and quasi-experimental designs cannot be
used for programs that cover an entire country or focus on a national
institution or policy simply because control or comparison groups
cannot be constructed in such cases. For example, a comparison/con-
trol group cannot be formed for a program that provides assistance to
fight corruption by mobilizing public opinion and lobbying the national legislature. Because there is only one national election commission that receives international assistance, evaluators cannot use
these designs to measure the impacts of assistance. Similarly, programs designed to change national policies cannot be evaluated. This
severely restricts the potential for the use of these designs because a
significant portion of democracy interventions are designed to influence national organizations and policies.

Second, an essential prerequisite for these designs is that the expected outcomes should be quantified. Program designers not only
need to identify the expected outcomes at the launch of the project,
but they also must quantify them so that they can be measured. For
example, an anticorruption project might have four major components: a training program for judges, technical assistance to the government for strengthening the office of the ombudsman, financial assistance to NGOs that lobby legislatures for enacting anticorruption
measures, and a mass media program to educate the public on corruption problems. The evaluators will have to develop quantitative
indicators for measuring change in each of these components at the
start of the project. They would have to decide, for example, how the
outcome of judges' training will be measured. It will not be enough
to measure change in the knowledge of trained judges because
knowledge is an output and not an outcome. Most likely, they will
settle on behavioral indicators such as the duration of the trial for
corruption cases or the percentage of judgments upheld by the appeals
court. Similarly, they will construct outcome measures for the techni-

cal assistance provided for establishing the ombudsman, support for NGOs, and mass media components.

While it is not always necessary to construct outcome measures for each and every activity of the project, it is important that all major components are covered. The problem arises that the intended outcomes of many components of a complex democracy intervention cannot be quantified without doing justice to the underlying concepts. As repeatedly mentioned in this book, most democracy programs involve institution building or have major institution-building components. The quantitative indicators for measuring institutional changes, which can be directly attributed to a program, are at best questionable. The effects of technical assistance to strengthen the ombudsman, for example, cannot be satisfactorily quantified.

An unintended effect of constructing outcome indicators is that many effects that may be critical for promotion of democracy may be left out. The outcomes for which quantitative measures can be constructed are not necessarily the most important. Moreover, many of the effects of democracy assistance are indirect and even unintended.

Sometimes, it has been suggested that evaluators can use sector-specific (meso-level) indicators for measuring outcomes. For example, instead of focusing on the outcomes for each component of the anticorruption project described above, they focus on indicators such as the World Bank's Voice and Accountability Index or Transparency International's Corruption Perceptions Index. As discussed in Chapter 3, sector-level indicators are not appropriate for measuring program outcomes because changes in a sector are the result of many factors. And even if these measures are used, it is not possible to construct control/comparison groups.

Third, experimental and quasi-experimental designs require that no significant changes be made in the program after baseline information has been collected. If there are major changes, it is quite possible that the baseline information may not remain relevant. The problem arises because democracy programs, like other interventions, evolve in response to changing environments that may offer new opportunities or constraints. Many initially planned activities cannot be carried out while others need to be added. The international community recognizes this and, therefore, provides flexibility to managers to make suitable changes. Although such flexibility is essential for the success of democracy programs, it often makes it difficult, if not impossible, to use experimental and quasi-experimental designs. As Devra C. Moehler notes,

It is difficult (and often impossible) to define an experiment when the objectives, activities and development hypotheses linking the two are not well specified. It can be equally problematic to wait to design the study until after the program parameters are fully clarified; the intense pressure to commence implementation as soon as possible leaves little room for adjustments and baseline data collection, and agreement can be harder to secure after awards are made. The result can be a disjunction between optimal research design and baseline data collected, on the one hand, and the eventual contours of the intervention under investigation, on the other. Measured impact may not reflect real impact due to suboptimal research designs given the actual intervention undertaken. (2010, p. 41)

Fourth, another problem concerns the construction of the control/comparison group. It is rare that treatment and control/comparison groups can randomly be constructed for long-term democracy interventions. Because of the ways in which participants in democracy projects are selected, even the setting up of a comparison, much less control, group remains highly problematic. Most program participants are selected by one of three ways.

One is self-selection, that is, interested individuals and organizations approach a project for assistance. For example, journalists approach a media project for advanced training or resource-starved democracy NGOs seek assistance from a donor-assisted intervention. When individuals and organizations seek assistance, this introduces what researchers call "self-selection bias." For example, the organizations that take the initiative to seek assistance are likely to be different from those that do not. The leaders of these organizations are likely to be more resourceful and familiar with foreign assistance programs and their headquarters are apt to be based in metropolitan areas. It is also likely that some of their officials are proficient in foreign languages and know how to write proposals for assistance. Therefore, it becomes difficult to form equivalent control/comparison groups in such cases.

A second method for selecting participants is to lay down certain criteria and recruit all those who meet them. Most political party assistance projects provide aid to all political parties that meet certain criteria. Likewise, a human rights intervention will assist all NGOs that possess skills and experience to undertake public awareness activities on human rights issues or lobby with the legislative and executive bodies. In such cases, researchers cannot form control/comparison groups. For example, a project may be designed to assist political parties in an African country so that they can effectively compete in national elections. The project is likely to formulate a set of criteria such as the national reach of the party; the commitment of its leaders to democratic competition; the party's willingness to send its officials for training provided by the project; the willingness of its top leaders to participate in high-level dialogue; and, above all, its willingness to accept project assistance. Because all political parties that meet these requirements will be included, evaluators have extreme difficulty in constructing an adequate comparison, much less, control group. If they want to form a comparison group, it is likely to include the dominant ruling parties that do not see the need for assistance, the radical parties that are suspicious of democracy promotion efforts by Western powers, or the very small parties that do not have a national presence. Obviously, the comparison group will not be equivalent to the treatment group, and therefore the findings will be flawed and recommendations misleading. Moreover, it is very unlikely that the parties not receiving assistance will provide evaluators access to their records, documents, and staff.

A third method for selecting participants is to ask sponsoring organizations to nominate individuals for the project's assistance or services. This is often the case with training programs. For example, governments depute judicial officials and legislative bodies nominate their officials for training. Similarly, media organizations nominate their journalists for training. In such cases too, the formation of a viable control/comparison group becomes problematic. The very fact that the trainees are selected or nominated by sponsoring organizations implies that they are different in some respects from the remaining ones.

Fifth, another major obstacle to the use of experimental and quasi-experimental designs is what researchers call "contamination effects." One of the essential requirements of these designs is that the control/comparison group should not be exposed in any way to the information, knowledge, or skills of the treatment/comparison group. For example, the journalists, who received training in investigative journalism, should not share the acquired knowledge and skills with the members of the control group. Or, the law enforcement officials, who learned about their legal responsibilities to enforce human rights, should not disseminate the information to their fellow officials who constitute the control/comparison group. If the past is a guide, this is not a realistic expectation. The experience of development interventions unmistakably shows that information travels fast through formal and informal channels. For example, during the green revolution when an improved variety of wheat seeds was introduced in South Asia, researchers found that, after two years, there was no significant difference in knowledge about the high-yielding variety of wheat seeds between the project farmers who had access to agricultural extension services and those who did not. The obvious explanation was that the nonproject farmers heard about the high-yielding variety through other sources such as radio programs, newspaper reports, and fellow farmers and friends who had seen farms using it. After hearing about the seeds, many had visited the districts in which the program was launched. In a major multicountry evaluation of USAID media assistance, I found that the journalists who received training under the auspices of the project routinely shared the information and skills they acquired with their fellow journalists. Thus, the possibility of contamination is always present.

Sixth, experimental and quasi-experimental designs require that the control/comparison group does not receive similar assistance during the life of the project. For example, if a media assistance project, which has a life cycle of three years, provides technical assistance to twenty-five community radio stations in District A and has formed a control/comparison group of another twenty in District B, the radio stations included in the District B sample should not receive similar assistance from any outside source for the duration of the project. The problem arises because evaluators do not have the authority to prevent outside agencies from assisting radio stations in the comparison/control group. International agencies, NGOs, and foundations are always looking for interesting projects that can make a difference. Thus, it is not unlikely that another organization may decide to assist radio stations included in the control/comparison group in District B. The practice of assisting democracy activists, NGOs, and even governmental agencies that could not get assistance from another source is not uncommon in democracy assistance. As a result, experimental and quasi-experimental designs cannot be realistically applied to evaluate long-term democracy interventions.

Seventh, a basic requirement of experimental and quasi-experimental designs is that the program be effectively implemented. When a program is not implemented well, the use of these designs can produce erroneous results. The analogy of testing a new drug is appropriate here. If members of the treatment group take medicine on an empty stomach when they are supposed to take it after a meal, the results may be misleading. Researchers might then discard a medicine that could have been effective. The same is true with democracy interventions. If a voter education program is not properly implemented, evaluators may not find any significant differences between the knowledge scores of the treatment and comparison/control groups and, thus, wrongly conclude that such programs are not effective. Like all development interventions, all democracy interventions are not always well implemented and, therefore, the use of the two designs may be inappropriate and produce erroneous findings and recommendations.

Eighth, international agencies and organizations often develop programs that complement one another, especially in transition and postconflict societies. To cite an example, following the Dayton Peace Accords in Bosnia, the international community supported initiatives to promote independent media and to counteract the influence of ethnic media. USAID, the European Union, the Organization for Security and Co-operation in Europe, Great Britain, and the Netherlands supported a wide range of media projects to train local journalists, provide technical assistance to nascent media organizations willing to rise above ethnic chauvinism, and develop a legal architecture conducive to the growth of an independent media sector. All of these interventions were interrelated and interdependent and their outcomes could not be examined in isolation from each other. For example, while evaluations showed that the training programs achieved their objectives in terms of the quality of training, most of the trained journalists remained unemployed because media outlets did not have funds to employ them. Thus, when the outcomes of a democracy intervention depend on the successful implementation of a range of programs that are independently designed and implemented by different donors, the focus on net impacts does not make sense. On the other hand, a case study approach would be more suitable to highlight the complex interactions of the evaluated interventions with other programs.

Ninth, most (if not all) democracy interventions do not at present gather baseline information for monitoring and evaluation and are not likely to do it in the near future. In 2010, I reviewed about thirty evaluations of democracy interventions and found only a single evaluation (which was a survey that I describe in Chapter 7) in which baseline data were collected. Although this should not be an excuse for not gathering such information, this is a stark reality that should not be ignored. There are many reasons for this state of affairs. There is no clarity about the outcomes of interventions at the early stage.

Most interventions have general plans for their future activities, but it takes time before they are finalized. Moreover, many projects lack financial resources to design and gather baseline information. This is especially true of small projects managed by NGOs. Even when resources may be provided by a funding agency, programs lack technical expertise to plan and manage baseline data collection.

Tenth, the quest for measuring net results may lead to evaluations that have limited policy relevance. Such investigations do not promote local ownership of evaluations because local partners often do not understand or appreciate their esoteric designs, the drive for quantification that does not answer the how and why questions, and inflexibility. Neither do they promote learning. This point has been noted by Howard White, executive director of the International Initiative for Impact Evaluation, who has suggested that technically rigorous studies are not necessarily sound evaluations (2009).

Finally, the cost of conducting experimental and quasi-experimental designs is very high. Often expatriate evaluators have to be sent to design baselines, construct treatment and control/comparison groups, and provide guidelines for data collection and analysis. They have to train local staff and provide technical advice throughout the project. Conditions are slightly better when local expertise is available. The cost considerations can be a major constraint on many programs.

The International Republican Institute's Experience

Since 2010, IRI has been evaluating democracy assistance programs in two different countries through the use of an experimental evaluation design.[2] The first evaluation measures the impact of an IRI[3] youth civics education training program in Cambodia that provides young people with knowledge on democratic institutions and citizen engagement. The hypothesis of the Cambodia program is that the increased participation of trained Cambodian youth in their communities will lead to improved local government responsiveness to citizens' needs and civic engagement, particularly with youth. The evaluation has been designed to test this hypothesis. The second evaluation measures the impact of two IRI democratic governance programs that focus on changing local citizens' perceptions of democracy in Colombia. The first intervention supports a government office that provides the public with a "one-stop shop" to conduct various public service transactions such as obtaining or applying for social service programs. The second program focuses on an IRI-supported government office that makes available important public sector information and documents and provides support for citizens in their interaction with government (e.g., how to comply with regulations). The evaluation tests the hypothesis that citizens who interact with these new government offices will have an improved level of confidence in democracy as a system of government.

While results of both evaluations were several months away at the time of this writing, IRI's experiences with randomized control trial (RCT) evaluation designs point to a few lessons, which are highlighted below.

Costs Related to Implementing an RCT Evaluation

In IRI's experience, implementing an RCT evaluation has been a costly endeavor. The expertise needed for this evaluation design can be expensive as are the data collection efforts (especially given that baseline and endline data are needed for both treatment and control groups). Indeed, one of IRI's RCT evaluations has exceeded the cost of implementing the program in a given year. In addition, the program staff on the ground had to spend significant time managing various aspects of the evaluation. As such, time spent on the evaluation has meant less time spent on programmatic work. Thus, careful consideration must be given to the cost and time commitment when deciding to implement an RCT evaluation.

Methodological Requirements of an RCT Evaluation

IRI has learned that it should carefully consider if a program is suitable for an RCT evaluation. In Cambodia, for example, only one of eight programs was initially deemed appropriate for various reasons, including the size of the program, the availability of a cohesive control group, and the ability to control for spillover. The youth civic training program was able to provide a large enough sample size and it was deemed feasible to construct control groups; contrast this with a parliamentary governance program, for example, where it is more difficult to construct a control group. However, as IRI gains experience with RCTs, it is better prepared to address some of these challenges with alternate designs, such as sequenced or time-control methods.

Involvement of Stakeholders Early in the Process

To improve the rigor of the evaluative process, it is important to engage key stakeholders in the evaluation from the beginning. In the Colombia evaluation, the actual opening and managing of the governance offices were the responsibility of local government officials; IRI's role was to provide support. The local officials, however, were not as involved in the evaluation design as they could have been at the outset. Thus, they might not have had a full understanding of how programmatic decisions affected the evaluation and, indeed, how the evaluation results might have benefited their work in the future. Given their lack of involvement, the local officials sometimes made programmatic decisions that negatively impacted the evaluation.

Technical Complexity of the Design

RCT evaluation designs are typically quite technical and, therefore, are difficult to understand for nonexperts involved in the evaluation process. Given that much of the evaluation implementation for these two initiatives rested with IRI field staff, significant lead time was needed to ensure that staff appropriately understood the design and methods. In Colombia, the collection of baseline data utilized a data analysis method intended to control for or mitigate some statistical anomalies in the control and treatment groups. IRI staff were not technical experts in this area and had to rely on a consultant. While IRI has no reason to believe that the baseline data were not collected and analyzed according to the strictest methodological standards, this does demonstrate that RCT evaluations can lose the participatory aspect described above—meaning that the design cannot benefit from the full expertise of implementers and other program experts.

Changes in the Composition of Treatment and Control Groups

IRI has learned that evaluators should anticipate design changes before a full rollout of the evaluation. In Cambodia, the pilot phase of the RCT revealed that some training participants involved in the civics education training program were traveling from areas well beyond the treatment regions. The design subsequently was adjusted to capture these participants: if 30 percent or more of the participants came from a nearby region, that region was then added to the treatment pool. This design change introduced new challenges, however, as program staff had to travel to the new treatment regions to obtain the consent of local government officials for access to official data. It is worth noting here that, in some cases, participants came from another region but comprised less than 30 percent of the total number of participants at the training, with the result that their home communes would not be included in the data collection process. In these instances, the activities and community-wide effects of these participants, which might have been evident in data collected from commune officials in their respective communities, would not be captured in the evaluation and lead to a loss of potentially rich data.

Realities on the Ground That Can Negatively Impact RCT Evaluations

Democracy assistance occurs in complex and adapting environments. In contrast, RCTs benefit from programmatic and environmental stability because changes in either can negatively impact an RCT evaluation. In both of IRI's RCT evaluations, changes in the environment have posed challenges for the evaluation. In Colombia, after baseline data were collected, the opening of one of the government offices was significantly delayed due to a variety of factors outside of the program's control. This led to a concern that (1) since time elapsed between baseline data collection and opening of the office, the baseline data might not be as relevant; and (2) because of this delay, there might not be enough time remaining for the program to have impacts that can be captured by endline data collection.

In addition, heavy rains in Colombia in 2011 led to temporary closing of the building that housed one of the new governance offices. The implications of this for the evaluation were unknown at the time of this writing and will depend on how long the office remains closed. However, there was an added concern that citizens who visited the office only to find it closed might feel frustrated, which could have unintended negative consequences for the evaluation (given that impact is measured by public opinion). Weather has also potentially impacted the youth civic education training program in Cambodia. The program noticed a drop in attendance during the rainy season, creating challenges to ensuring that enough participants attended the training sessions to maintain an appropriate sample size for the evaluation. In addition, the composition of the participants differed during the rainy season as many potential participants were involved in planting, and thus could not attend. While this might have affected the consistency of the treatment groups, such information helped the program learn a great deal about different demographics that the program attracts. Thus, one positive result was that the evaluative process has helped IRI staff think about the environmental changes and how they may interact with programs. For example, Cambodian staff began to question the viability of conducting training during the rainy season. In Colombia, staff started considering how the shutting of the government office would impact public opinion, which is important thinking from a program design perspective.

Tension Between Methodological Rigor and Program Flexibility

To ensure methodological rigor, the manner in which a program is implemented should remain consistent across treatment groups and over time. The reality (and, often, a key strength) of democracy assistance, however, is that programs often adapt as implementers learn what is and is not working or due to emergent issues on the ground. An RCT design that is too rigid can hamstring a program due to concerns that program adaptation can compromise findings. In Cambodia, staff often made programmatic changes as the program adapted to changing needs and circumstances on the ground. Due to the RCT design, however, staff initially chose not to undertake new programs in treatment areas in order to preserve the sanctity of the evaluation. Eventually, however, staff allowed new programs to operate within the treatment areas out of concern that youth were being deprived of programs that might benefit them. An overly rigid approach can also constrain knowledge dissemination and replication of program successes to other regions. In Colombia, neighboring municipalities expressed interest in opening governance offices similar to the ones opened in the treatment areas. IRI became concerned, however, that such activities might have negative consequences for the evaluation, as spillover into the treatment area might occur from these other areas. Both of these examples demonstrate the risk of placing too much focus on methodological rigor and allowing the evaluation to take priority over successful programming.

Unexpected Benefits of RCT Evaluations

IRI learned that the very process of implementing the evaluations yielded unexpected benefits that helped improve programs. For example, during the pilot phase of the evaluation, the Cambodia program set out to confirm that the local trainers were implementing the youth civic education training curriculum in a similar fashion across the country, the goal being to ensure consistency of the intervention in treatment groups. During this quality check, program staff realized that trainers in fact were not always adhering to the mandated lesson plan and were sometimes not covering all the material that was expected. Staff came up with a strategy to ensure that all students were receiving the same training topics. In addition, IRI devised a system of providing incentives for trainers to fulfill their new responsibilities for the evaluation. Thus, the evaluative process provided the program with an opportunity to get everyone on the same page with respect to the format of the training program.

Supplementing RCT Data
with Robust Qualitative Research

While it is too early for IRI to conclude how effective the RCT approach has been at measuring net impacts of our interventions, our experience suggests that this approach is not suitable to answer questions related to how and why a program might have had an impact. Was an intervention successful because of its design, sound management, political interest in the host country, or a combination of these factors and forces? From a program perspective, it is often at least as useful to understand the how and why questions as it is the binary question of whether a program has had an impact or not. Furthermore, as is often the case, a program might lead to unintended outcomes that will typically not be noticed in the evaluation (especially given that RCT evaluations overwhelmingly use quantitative research methods such as surveys). Thus, IRI is considering supplementing RCT evaluations with robust qualitative research.

Given that data collection for the two RCT evaluations discussed above was ongoing at the time of writing, IRI believes there is still much to discover about the applicability of RCT evaluations to democracy assistance. However, IRI has found the process of applying RCT methods to democracy and governance program evaluation to have been an enlightening and thought-provoking experience, raising important questions about the process of designing RCT evaluations, the importance of accounting for the need for flexibility in responding to emergent program opportunities and challenges, and considering how to ensure that evaluation findings are best utilized. The lessons learned described above merit consideration when organizations are thinking of undertaking an RCT evalution to measure democracy assistance work.

The National Democratic Institute's Experience

NDI has used experimental designs to evaluate its democracy assistance programs in four countries: South Sudan (2009), Ukraine (2010), Cambodia (2011), and Uganda (2012).[4] Two of these evaluations were at the behest of NDI's donor and two were driven by the desire of NDI staff to better understand the impact of its program innovations. Each of the four random control trials has offered NDI methodological as well as practical lessons on the use of experimental designs for evaluating democracy assistance.

Not surprisingly, NDI has faced challenges with the cost of RCTs, the rigorous methodological requirements, different levels of understanding among program stakeholders, difficulties in randomizing treatment and control groups, constraints on program flexibility, and the need to supplement RCTs with robust qualitative data. For example, in South Sudan, NDI initially hoped to integrate an RCT into a full evaluation of its *Let's Talk* program across the country. However, last-minute changes in program implementation and the risk of a spillover effect required downsizing the original design. The *Let's Talk* program was replicated on a smaller scale and the field experiment was run in Juba only (see Box 6.1). NDI's program in Ukraine designed impact evaluations for two separate programs before settling on NDI's NGO school as an appropriate program for a random control trial. NDI's Constituency Dialogue program in Cambodia was forced to abort its original design once it was discovered that NDI's long-standing program had covered more of the country than originally documented. Finally, in Uganda, NDI has faced ongoing funding challenges that threaten to truncate a complex set of field experiments designed to evaluate a highly innovative pilot program on parliamentary outreach.

However, NDI's experience with RCTs also suggests strategies for mitigating some of the challenges practitioners face in using experimental designs. That is, three of NDI's four experimental designs have been implemented in partnership with academic researchers. These collaborative partnerships have shown much promise, underscoring the value of RCTs for formative rather than summative evaluations of democracy assistance programs. What follows are NDI's emerging lessons, largely illustrated by NDI's current academic-practitioner partnership in Cambodia.

Academic-Practitioner Partnerships for RCTs

As Howard White notes at the beginning of this chapter, international development actors are not often equipped with the skills to design and implement high-quality RCTs. In addition, many researchers do not understand program evaluation, making their efforts rigorous but often less relevant for program and policy decisions. Clearly, both academics and practitioners have much to gain from more effective collaboration.

For academic-practitioner partnerships to be effective, NDI has found that the agreement must be mutually beneficial. Practitioners are motivated by the need for reliable data for decisionmaking, programmatic learning, and donor accountability. Academics are motivated by the need to publish original research that contributes to their disciplines. To ensure that both incentive structures are mutually supportive, NDI agreed to the joint use of data with its academic partners in South Sudan, Uganda, and, most recently, Cambodia. Although there is always a risk that the published research may reflect negatively on a program, NDI finds that the potential benefits of rigorous evaluations greatly outweigh their risk.

Next, academics and practitioners must collaboratively find an overlap between academic research questions and program evaluation questions. This is not a straightforward endeavor and requires both parties to engage in an ongoing creative dialogue, beginning with program design. For example, in 2010, NDI was forced to abort the original experimental design of its multiparty Constituency Dialogue program in Cambodia. The objective of the program was to strengthen accountability by engaging members of the National Assembly from across political parties in dialogues with their constituencies at the local level. However, NDI discovered that it had implemented its long-standing program in more multiparty provinces than previously documented, making it difficult to use villages as the unit of analysis or to randomly assign the intervention across villages. Additionally, an important part of the existing program was that NDI worked with local NGOs to select villages where Constituency Dialogue events would be most useful, making random assignment of the events across all villages untenable. NDI instead focused the RCT on the individual as the unit of analysis and introduced a new innovation into the program. Within each village receiving a Constituency Dialogue event, half of survey respondents were randomly invited to the Constituency Dialogue in a nearby village and half were randomly invited to participate in small deliberative groups one day before the event. The deliberative sessions were held with three to six citizens and a Cambodian facilitator who led a structured process of discussion, debate, and voting on their priority problems and preferred solutions. This program variation helped NDI pose two important evaluation questions: (1) Is participation in the Constituency Dialogue alone necessary and sufficient for changing citizens' attitudes, knowledge, and/or behavior? and (2) Does participation in deliberative sessions before the Constituency Dialogue differentially impact citizens' attitudes, knowledge, and/or behavior?

NDI vetted its revised evaluation design with a network of academic researchers. The researchers suggested that by varying the gender composition of the deliberative sessions and randomly assigning citizens to different subgroups, the RCT could answer additional questions about gender and its influence on citizens' attitudes, knowledge, behavior, and issue priorities. The five additional research questions were (3) How does participation in deliberative sessions before the Constituency Dialogue differentially impact the participants' priorities issue? (4) Does the gender composition of the deliberative sessions differentially impact attitudinal, knowledge, and/or behavioral outcomes of individual participants? (5) Does gender composition of the deliberative sessions differentially impact the priorities of participants? (6) Does the gender of the facilitator of deliberative sessions differentially impact attitudinal, knowledge, and/or behavioral outcomes of individual participants? and (7) Does the gender of the facilitator differentially impact the priorities of participants?

The academic review process also helped NDI identify an academic researcher with complementary interests who could serve as a principal investigator. The principal investigator helped guide the evaluation team in addressing the thorny issues that would inevitably emerge as part of a complex random control trial.

To randomize village selection, the principal investigator suggested allowing local partners to continue to choose villages, but select two prospective villages in each district that were similar according to their criteria. One of these two villages would then be selected to receive the Constituency Dialogue event using a coin toss. The other village would be used as a quasi-control village and receive both a pre- and posttest survey and qualitative follow-up on whether issues had been addressed. The creative dialogue between NDI and the academic researchers not only strengthened the technical rigor of the experimental design, but expanded NDI's menu of evaluation questions and methodological options, making the RCT more meaningful to both practitioners and researchers.

The Mixed-Methods Approach for Answering Complementary Questions

As noted above, RCTs often pose and answer a rather narrow set of questions. However, in the case of Cambodia, NDI faced the opposite challenge. The additional evaluation questions created a more complex evaluation design. The RCT had to be carried out in three provinces over a nine-month period. The program variation required approximately 1,600 pre- and posttest surveys in nine treatment villages and six control villages. Within the 900 treatment surveys, approximately 450 participants were randomly assigned to 90 different deliberative subgroups. The gender composition for each subgroup had to be randomized on the spot. In addition, because of the possibility of a delay in the effect size over time, the pretest and deliberative groups had to be carried out the week before the Constituency Dialogue and the posttest group one week after.

During the pilot phase, the evaluation team worked with a researcher to establish protocols for administering the survey instrument with a local research partner. She also helped the evaluation team explore ways to structure the complementary data collection and analysis. That is, the survey data were supplemented by qualitative data from the deliberation sessions, direct observation of the Constituency Dialogue events, facilitator journals, and long-term issue monitoring. Together, these datasets will provide a much richer picture of the

impact of the intervention on citizens as well as the contextual variables that influence the outcomes of a democracy assistance program.

Support for Integrating RCTs into Live Programs

Although exciting for the evaluation team, the scale and complexity
of the mixed-methods design created additional burdens for NDI's
program staff in Cambodia. Indeed, staff fatigue has been a common
challenge for all four of NDI's impact evaluations. That is, program
managers are engaged in full-time jobs that require ongoing crisis
management, relationship building, and opportunity leveraging as
part of program implementation. Yet without staff cooperation and
engagement, there are countless ways that an experimental design
can go off the rails. To mitigate this risk, NDI outlined clear guidelines for integrating the RCT into the program's implementation plan
and embedded a field researcher in the program itself. The field researcher supported the program by ensuring that protocols for program implementation and data collection were followed for both
qualitative and quantitative data. Importantly, she maintained an ongoing inventory of the surveys and deliberative subgroups to ensure
that NDI met its targeted samples. Finally, the field researcher communicated any emerging challenges to the evaluation team, allowing
them to troubleshoot before they became a crisis.

Program Learning over Accountability

In all of NDI's academic partnerships, RCTs have been used as part
of a formative evaluation—to better understand and improve a program's innovation or implementation. In Sudan, NDI's academic
partnership helped to identify the program components that amplified
the impact of the *Let's Talk* intervention. In Uganda, NDI's partnership with researchers is testing the effectiveness of new technologies
for political communication between members of parliament and
their constituents. In Cambodia, the academic researcher is helping to
understand the impact of introducing innovation into a long-standing
program. In addition, academic incentive structures (including peer
review, human subjects protocols, and the importance of professional
reputations that are tied to individuals) help to ensure the high quality of these collaborative evaluations as well as the objectivity of
findings.

NDI has gained much from these academic partnerships, but does not privilege any one evaluation methodology over another. Evaluation questions should determine the most appropriate evaluation methodology. Indeed, given the high level of effort, cost, and complexity of impact evaluations, RCTs need to be used strategically. However, NDI has found partnerships with academic researchers to be a highly effective strategy in navigating the sometimes perilous cost of experimental design.

Conclusion

I will conclude this section by making the following four observations. First, in view of the methodological and practical problems that I have discussed in this chapter, some of which have been corroborated by the experience of IRI and NDI, the potential for using experimental and quasi-experimental designs for multiyear and multicomponent democracy interventions or the programs that are national in scope is limited. I have discussed the subject with several evaluators with broad experience in evaluating democracy interventions. Most of them were skeptical about the applicability of these designs and invariably took the view that, given the nature of democracy interventions, the actors involved, and the overall circumstances in which they operate, it is difficult to establish control/comparison groups and collect required data. Some also expressed the concern that these designs may stifle innovation and that measuring net impacts may prevent program managers from modifying planned activities or adding new ones. Evaluators also pointed out that democracy interventions, like other development projects, have many unforeseen or unintended effects that cannot be captured by experimental and quasi-experimental designs.

Second, before using experimental and quasi-experimental designs, it is important to make sure that the program has clearly articulated quantitative outcomes that would provide a basis for measuring impacts. Control/comparison groups can be constructed to remain intact and not receive the type of assistance that the treatment groups will receive during the life of the programs. Moreover, there is no chance of contamination in the sense that the skills, information, and knowledge imparted to program beneficiaries will reach the members of the control/comparison groups. Finally, programs have sufficient technical and financial resources to gather baseline and end-line data. These points are clearly stated in a report on program evaluation by the Government Accounting Office (GAO):

> An impact evaluation is more likely to provide useful information about what works when the intervention consists of clearly defined activities and goals and has been well implemented. Having clarity about the nature of intended activities and evidence that critical intervention components were delivered to the intended targets helps strengthen confidence that those activities caused the observed results; it also improves the ability to replicate the result in another study. Confirming that the interventions were carried out as designed helps rule out a common explanation for why programs do not achieve their goals; when done before collecting expensive outcome data, it can also avoid wasting resources. (GAO 2009, p. 21)

Third, while these designs cannot be realistically used for evaluating most multifaceted, long-term interventions or the programs that cover an entire country, they can be fruitfully applied in the following cases.

First, they can be used to measure the impact of short-term interventions or a specific component of a program where impacts can be quantified and for which data can be gathered for treatment and control/comparison groups. For example, evaluators can measure the impacts of a voter education campaign if it does not cover the entire country. They can also measure the effects of various training programs.

Second, these designs can be used to test the effectiveness of different ways of delivering services to the targeted populations. Evaluators can, for example, use them to evaluate the different modes of training election monitors in a postconflict society. They may construct three groups of trainees: one group exclusively trained by expatriate instructors, the other group trained by local experts, and the third group whose members took an online course followed by discussions among the trainees under expert guidance. The differences in the knowledge and performance of the three groups can help the program to identify the most effective ways of training election monitors.

Finally, scholars and democracy experts may use the two designs to test various hypotheses (not the entire programs) that underlie democracy interventions, and their findings may contribute toward developing more effective interventions. In many cases, practitioners and academicians can collaborate, as suggested by NDI's experience.

Fourth, the experience of IRI and NDI suggests some practical measures that can improve the efficacy of these experimental and quasi-experimental designs. For example, whenever possible, evaluations are conducted as collaborative enterprises between the organizations commissioning them and the academic community. The quantitative data obtained through these designs are supplemented by qualitative information gathered through key informant interviews or focus group discussions. Major stakeholders are properly briefed about the nature and requirements of these evaluations.

USAID has launched an initiative to promote the use of experimental and quasi-experimental designs for evaluating its democracy projects. Its democracy and governance office now provides technical and financial assistance to USAID overseas missions to gather baseline and endline data, form comparison/control groups, and analyze the findings. It will take time before USAID analyzes the results of this important effort. However, there is little doubt that the results will enhance our knowledge about the applicability of these designs for democracy programs.

Notes

1. Moehler (2010) cites forty-one completed and ongoing cases of what she calls "field experiments" in three broad areas: elections, community-driven development, and reform in the delivery of the public services.

2. This section was contributed by Jonathan Jones, evaluation officer, and others at IRI.

3. The International Republican Institute is a nonprofit, nonpartisan organization that advances freedom and democracy worldwide by developing political parties, civic institutions, open elections, democratic governance, and the rule of law.

4. This section was contributed by Linda Stern, director of monitoring, evaluation, and learning at NDI.

7

Nonexperimental Designs

I have come to the conclusion that the core of the scientific method is not experimental per se, but the strategy connoted by the "plausible rival hypothesis." The strategy may start its puzzle solving with "evidence" or it may start with hypothesis." Rather than presenting this hypothesis or evidence in the context-independent manner of positivistic "confirmation" (or even of post-positivistic "collaboration"), it is presented instead in extended networks of implications that (while never complete) are nonetheless crucial to its scientific evaluation.

—*Donald T. Campbell*

The methodological gold standard here is *appropriateness*, not any particular method, including randomized control trials, which, in fact, are appropriate for a quite narrow and limited subset of development interventions. . . . Answers emerge from an understanding of the situation. Experts are astute at situation recognition. Appropriate methods, then, are those methods that best fit a particular development assistance situation. . . . That is actually much harder to do than simply advocate the same alleged "gold standard" method for every situation, an example of only having a hammer so everything looks like a nail.

—*Michael Quinn Patton*

In the previous chapter, I discussed the nature, strengths, and limitations of experimental and quasi-experimental designs for evaluating impacts of democracy projects. I concluded that, while these designs

117

are most robust, the scope for their application is limited: they can be used in only a small number of evaluations. In this chapter, I focus on three other categories of evaluation designs that have a greater potential for use and can generate reliable information, insights, and ideas. The first two are statistical designs, pre- and postdesigns and cross-sectional, which do not use a control or comparison group. The third are the case study designs, which are discussed in some detail here because there is considerable confusion about them and most evaluations follow these designs, albeit not always satisfactorily. After discussing these designs, I outline a set of steps that evaluators can take to improve the methodological rigor of evaluations. I suggest that the ideal course is to focus on each evaluation question individually and explore how best it can be answered. The logic of counterfactuals should be applied to evaluations wherever possible. Evaluators should engage host-country evaluators and researchers to provide insiders' perspectives as well as to establish rapport with host-country informants. Finally, evaluators should pay more attention to sampling, and utilize more quantitative data than has been done in the past.

Pre- and Postdesigns

In such pre- and postdesigns, the impact of an intervention is measured by comparing key outcome measures before an intervention began and after it ended. A simple example is that evaluators score the participants in a human rights training program on their knowledge of human rights issues and their roles and responsibilities before and after the training. If there is a significant difference in their scores, one can assume that the training had something to do with it. In long-term interventions, an interrupted time series design, which involves collecting data for multiple time periods, can be used. This design is better than pre- and postdesigns because time series data smooth out the random fluctuations over time. For example, a five-year project undertakes a range of activities to create public awareness about human rights in a postconflict society. Instead of conducting two sample surveys (before and at the end of the project), evaluators annually survey public attitudes, opinions, and perceptions. Inferences based on such data will be more valid and reliable because sudden changes will be smoothed out.

The obvious limitation of these designs is that the influence of exogenous variables is not controlled. For example, the evaluators cannot be sure that the perceived changes in public awareness about human rights are the result of project activities or that they represent a general improvement in human rights situations after the wounds of war have been healed and political normalcy restored. While evaluators can use statistical modeling to control the influence of exogenous variables in programs on health or agriculture, this is not always possible in democracy interventions because we lack sound underlying theory as well as rich past experience on which models can be constructed.

This problem can often be solved by supplementing the data with information gathered from other sources. In the above case, evaluators can also interview the leaders of concerned NGOs, journalists, human rights activists, and other informed people as well as review progress reports of the project and other relevant documents. Thus, if the time series data show that the awareness of human rights issues has increased since the launch of the project, and evidence gathered from other sources indicates that the project played a major part in it, evaluators can reasonably conclude the project has contributed to increased public awareness.

Many requirements of the experimental and quasi-experimental designs also apply to pre- and postdesigns. The project impacts should be such that they can be precisely identified and measured at the beginning of the project. Baseline data are collected before the launch of the project. There are no changes in the original project design and activities over time because, if there are major changes, the baseline information may not remain relevant. Therefore, the political environment in which the project is implemented should not undergo rapid change. Evaluators should consider these factors before using pre- and postdesigns.

Sometimes, time series data that are available from secondary sources can be analyzed to examine the effects of an intervention. For example, the data from public opinion surveys conducted by national or international organizations can help measure changes in public perceptions of corruption or attitudes toward political parties. In a few cases, evaluators can utilize records kept by government agencies for making pre- and postcomparisons. Box 7.1 provides an example of an evaluation of a judicial reform project in Jordan in which evaluators used case management records to examine the impact of reforms on the efficiency of the court system.

Box 7.1 Impact Assessment of Civil Case Management

In 2001, the Ministry of Justice in Jordan launched the Civil Case Management Department (CCMD) as a pilot project designed to improve the managing of court cases. CCMD introduced procedural reforms to prevent unnecessary delays and additional costs to the litigants.

To assess the impact of CCMD, an evaluation was undertaken. The evaluation conducted an analysis of the case management data before and after the establishment of CCMD. It identified and examined the cases that went through the court system before the new system was adopted so that a baseline could be generated for comparison with cases that have been subject to case management. The baseline sample consisted of cases registered in June 2001 before the advent of CCMD (of 460 filed, there were only 7 still pending at the time of the evaluation). The second sample included 460 cases registered between May and June 2004.

The analysis of the data indicated that after the reforms time for notifications was reduced from fifty days to thirty-five days, the number of sessions needed to dispose of cases was reduced from thirty-three sessions to thirty sessions indicating that the hearings are being provided at a faster rate in the more recent years, and the average time from filing to the first hearing before a trial judge was reduced from 135 days to 99 days.

The evaluation concluded that, while significant achievements have been recorded, there could be additional benefits should the reforms cover the full life cycle of the case as opposed to initial intervention as currently adopted.

Source: USAID (2006b).

Cross-Sectional Design

In this design, an intervention's outcomes are measured by examining the varying levels of treatment received by the beneficiaries during the life of a program. For example, suppose the sponsors of a voter education program want to find out its effectiveness in disseminating the information about national elections. The program extensively advertised in newspapers, radio, and television to disseminate its message. The evaluators may undertake a sample survey of the voters. By correlating the knowledge scores of respondents with varying levels of exposure to messages they received in print or electronic media, evaluators would be able to estimate the impacts of the voter education program.

Cross-sectional design has been more widely used in the evaluations of development projects than other quantitative designs and has greater potential for use in democracy evaluations. If supplemented with qualitative data gathered from key informant interviews and focus group discussions, the cross-sectional design can ensure a reasonable degree of methodological rigor. Box 7.2 shows details about an evaluation that used cross-sectional surveys to measure the impacts of a larger civic education program launched by USAID in Kenya.

Cross-sectional designs have an advantage over pre- and post-designs in that evaluators do not depend on the availability of baseline data. Moreover, even if there are major modifications in the programming during the implementation, it does not make any difference as far as the evaluation is concerned. For example, if after launching a voter education program, the project decides to include social media, it will not affect the results because questions about the use of social media can be included in the survey.

Case Study Evaluation Designs

Case study evaluation designs seek to document and analyze democracy interventions in situ, detailing the complexity of actors and factors that contribute to and interact with the phenomenon under study.[1] Evaluators use case studies to examine questions about the complex interactions between multiple variables that often cannot be controlled in experimental or quasi-experimental designs. Instead of testing linear cause-effect relationships between dependent and independent variables, case studies use strategies of thick description, chains of evidence, and iterative techniques of corroboration to empirically document the performance and outcomes of an intervention. Individual case study evaluations use these strategies to uncover the mechanisms of change within a case while comparative case study evaluations answer questions on the similarities and differences between interventions, the contexts in which they took place, or the problems they addressed. Like other evaluation designs, case studies are driven by evaluation questions and require rigor and systematic inquiry for making evidence-based, informed judgments about an intervention.

Box 7.2 Measuring the Impact of the National Civic Education Program in Kenya

USAID/Kenya commissioned a study to assess the impacts of the Kenya National Civic Education Program (NCEP) on individuals' awareness, competence, and engagement in issues related to democracy, human rights, governance, constitutionalism, and nation building. Forty-three Kenyan civil society organizations linked to four larger civil society consortia took part in the program, which ran from April 2006 until September 2007. The program supported approximately 79,000 discrete workshops, poetry or drama events, informal meetings, cultural gatherings, and other public events as well as extensive programming on democracy, governance, and rights-related topics through television, radio, and other mass media outlets. Documents indicate that some 10 million individuals were exposed in some form to face-to-face civic education activities.

The primary source of data for the study was a survey of 3,600 individuals conducted across the country between December 10, 2008 and January 30, 2009. Survey teams from Research International interviewed the treatment group of 1,800 individuals who had been exposed to NCEP face-to-face activities and the control group of 1,800 individuals who were similar to the treatment group but had no NCEP face-to-face exposure. The questions in the survey related to the five general themes of the program: good governance, human rights, democracy, constitutionalism, and nation building.

The study found that the program did have meaningful long-term effects on several important dimensions, notably the cluster of orientations that the authors labeled civic competence and involvement. Individuals in the treatment group were significantly more knowledgeable about politics, more efficacious generally and specifically in regard to the Constituency Development Fund, more participatory at the local level, more aware of how to defend their rights, and more informed about constitutional issues and the desirability of public involvement in the constitutional review process than were individuals in the control group. This suggests the program was successful in achieving at least some of its stated goals. Moreover, there was some influence of the program on variables related to identity and ethnic group relations: program activities led to significant increases in individuals' identification as a Kenyan.

The impact of the program on nearly all other democratic orientations examined in the study was negligible. There were limited effects on a series of variables the authors called democratic values, rights, and responsibilities, and these included such important factors as rejection

(continues)

Box 7.2 continued

of antidemocratic regime alternatives, support for the rule of law, trust in institutions and others, and the acceptance of extensive political responsibilities of citizenship.

The study examined the impact of NCEP mass media coverage. It found that exposure to the programs' mass media initiative augmented the effects of face-to-face activities on several variables in the civic competence and involvement dimension. Yet the media component even on these competence and awareness variables by itself produced relatively little in the way of meaningful impacts. And on virtually all other orientations examined, there were no significant positive impacts registered for media exposure.

The study findings showed that the effects of civic education were influenced strongly by the amount of an individual's exposure to civic education activities, by the kinds of instructional methods used, by the quality of the facilitators, and by the degree to which individuals engaged in discussions about democracy issues after their direct exposure to civic education. Based on the findings, the study made several recommendations for future programs.

Source: Finkel and Horowitz (2009).

Types of Case Studies

Evaluations following case study designs may be explanatory or exploratory in nature.

An explanatory case study answers specific descriptive and normative evaluation questions about a program's performance and impacts within a specific context. For example, evaluators of a parliamentary outreach program might pose questions such as, What were the results of the constituency outreach program compared to its targets, and how was the intervention implemented? What intervention strategies were used and why? How did the problem change over the life of the program and why? To answer these questions, they would review the constituency outreach program's critical assumptions about the context and develop lines of inquiry on relevant actors and factors that may have influenced the program and the changes the program sought to bring about. They would also explore who most influenced the outreach program's processes and outcomes, as well

---

Box 7.3 The GAO's Conceptualization of a Case Study

The US Government Accounting Office has defined the "case study method" as "a method for learning about a complex instance, based on a comprehensive understanding of that instance obtained by extensive description and analysis of that instance taken as a whole and in its context."

The above definition has three main components: "a complex instance," "a comprehensive understanding," and what is "obtained by extensive description and analysis." GAO has clarified them as follows:

> "A complex instance means that input and output cannot be readily or very accurately related. There are several reasons why such a relationship might be difficult. There could be many influences on what is happening and these influences could interact in nonlinear ways such that a unit of change in the input can be associated with quite different changes in the output, sometimes increasing it, sometimes decreasing it, and sometimes having no discernible effect."
>
> A "comprehensive understanding . . . means that the goal of a case study is to obtain as complete a picture as possible of what is going on in an instance, and why."
>
> The third key element, "obtained by extensive description and analysis," has three components. Case studies involve what methodologists call "thick" descriptions: rich, full information that should come from multiple data sources, particularly from firsthand observations. The analysis also is extensive, and the method compares information from different types of data sources through a technique called "triangulation."

Source: GAO (1990), pp. 14–15.

---

as what events occurred during the life of the program, how those events affected the program, and why the events are important.

For an explanatory case study, evaluators gather data, both prospectively and retrospectively. Using a framework for analysis, they would code, review, and analyze the diverse datasets to understand their relationships to each other and offer detailed explanations for the causes of and influences on a program's successes and failures.

Explanatory case study designs can also be used to make comparisons between different kinds of programmatic approaches or to draw comparisons across program sites, again offering judgments on the cases based on the evidence.

Exploratory case study design is relatively more open-ended in nature; evaluators begin with broad research questions about a program and its context and then use the evidence to refine the evaluation design. An exploratory case study of a parliamentary outreach program might begin with basic questions about the program, context, and problems such as, What is the implicit intervention design and its underlying assumptions? How are constituency relationship problems defined? What is happening within the larger context of the parliament or citizenry? Who are the key actors that influence the outreach program? The preliminary answers to these general questions are the starting point for the evaluator who will use them to define the parameters of the case study and to develop a more focused line of inquiry for the evaluation. In exploratory case studies, the data collection and analysis process is inductive, using the findings to iteratively inform and further develop the evaluator's new line of inquiry. In both exploratory and explanatory case studies, the findings may lead to a diagnosis of a program or problem, or they may lead to positing new hypotheses about either or both.

Exploratory case studies can be most useful when democracy interventions evolve in response to a rapidly changing environment, original plans and targets are no longer relevant, programs are new and innovative, or the international community does not have experience and expertise in implementing the intervention. In such cases, evaluations based on an exploratory approach can generate new ideas, insights, hypotheses, and conceptual frameworks.

Whether exploratory or explanatory, all case studies attempt to understand a phenomenon holistically within a larger system or context. For example, if an evaluator visits three polling places in Nigeria to find out whether domestic election monitors have access to the vote tally process, s/he is not using a case study approach. However, if the evaluator collects and analyzes detailed information on the way in which domestic election monitors interact with voters, local officials, political parties, and international observers at one of the polling places on the day of the election, s/he is using a case study approach. In the first instance, the evaluator is documenting compliance with a single, linear dimension of change. In the second instance, the evaluator is documenting the relationship between Nigerian domestic monitors and the complexity of actors within the Nigerian electoral system, using a case to illustrate and explain the dynamic relationships between them.

Unit of Analysis and Sampling

The unit of analysis for a case study may be individuals, a political party, a political system within a country, or a political event. In addition, both explanatory and exploratory case studies can focus on a single case or may select multiple cases for comparison. Whether singular or comparative, a strong case study design will use clear criteria for case selection to purposefully answer the evaluation questions posed.

Purposive (or judgment), nonprobability sampling strategies are most often used in selecting cases to include in an evaluation. *Purposive sampling* is a strategy in which a single or multiple cases are selected based on defined characteristics or criteria of interest. That is, because case studies are inherently unique and may vary in intervention approach, context, problems, or even time scale, selecting comparative case studies should be done purposively; i.e., to answer specific evaluation questions. For example, purposive sampling may be used to select cases at the extremes (or brackets) of a phenomenon in order to understand and explain differences. A case study of a program that promotes women's political participation, for example, may include women candidates who were elected to office as well as those who lost their elections. A *cluster approach* to purposive sampling might select civic education programs implemented within the same province in order to compare similarities and differences within analogous contexts. *Representative cases* of constituency outreach might be chosen as exemplars for their innovative characteristics in addressing citizens' concerns. An election program may select a typical gubernatorial election as a pilot case for monitoring electoral processes. Here, the selected case is used to document in real time the nature of electoral problems and to observe how the election monitoring program interacts within the context. Finally, a *snowball sample* may be used to select cases within a network of difficult to find populations or groups. For example, a member of a clandestine political group within an authoritarian regime might be interviewed and then asked to recommend other cases to include in the study of the network or group.

Data Collection and Analysis

One of the unique features of the case study method is that data collection and analysis are often concurrent. Evaluators collect and analyze

Box 7.4 Narrative Inquiry, Case Study Evaluation, and Democracy Promotion

In Burkina Faso and Guatemala, the National Democratic Institute used an innovative approach called participatory story analysis (PSA) to collect and analyze case study data on rural women's political participation. Challenged in documenting the downstream effects of its programming on rural women, NDI wanted to know the following:

- What was life like for participants before the intervention?
- What were the major challenges participants faced?
- How did the intervention address those challenges?
- What was the long-term transformation?
- What is the emerging vision of democratic change?

Armed with disposable cameras, fourteen indigenous activists from Guatemala and thirty-two councilwomen from three linguistic groups in Burkina Faso returned to their rural communities to answer these questions. Once participants' photos were developed, they reconvened to visually construct and tell their stories. When all the stories were shared, each small group analyzed each element of their stories, identifying common and divergent themes across their group. These themes were then used as part of the groups' meta-analyses and interpretations of the role of women in their countries' emerging democracies. The photos, stories, and analyses contributed to the creation of comparative case studies for each of NDI's programs. While the case studies could not document the scale of the programs' impacts, they illuminated the mechanisms and nature of the programs' impacts on the lives of rural women. In addition, they documented the women's agency in transforming social norms and expanding political space for some of the most marginalized citizens in their counties.

Inspired by photoelicitation (Collier and Collier 1986), most significant change (MSC) stories (Dart 2003), and narrative inquiry (Hymes 1962), PSA was developed by Linda Stern, director of evaluation at NDI, in response to challenges in evaluating democracy interventions that had evolved over time in dynamic political contexts. Because of its focus on oral and visual communication as well as collaborative analysis and interpretation, PSA is a particularly cogent method for capturing the voices of marginalized groups, providing insight into how local actors interpret democracy through their own sociocultural and political lens.

Source: Stern (forthcoming).

data, using the emerging evidence to follow new lines of inquiry and iteratively refine the evaluation questions and framework for analysis. In other words, they follow an ethnographic approach, collecting data in real time to discover the relationships between diverse actors and factors in the context where the program takes place. This is true of both exploratory and explanatory case studies. However, there are many pitfalls that may create bias in the development of a case study and the case study researcher or evaluator will want to take steps to ensure the validity, reliability, accuracy, and precision of the data. To increase confidence in the data collection, analysis, and findings, case studies will generally use three key principles: thick description, triangulation, and chains of evidence.

Clifford Gertz (1973) introduced the concept of "thick description" into anthropology and the social sciences as a method for describing human behavior as well as the larger context and meaning in which it occurs. This ethnographic approach not only entails documenting behavior through techniques of participant observation, but it also attempts to understand the contextual meaning of the behavior. Thick description provides the proverbial "footprints in the snow," then creates an iterative process in which the evaluator will collect data in real time and space, and subsequently review the notes, photographs, videos, or recordings of people and events in order to gain insights on and connections to their sociocultural meaning from the participants' perspectives. For example, the emergence of indigenous Guatemalan women's groups in refugee camps may be interpreted by Western activists as having a feminist origin, ideology, and agenda. However, when examined within the cultural and political context of a collective return movement from exile, the new women's organizations may actually reflect the division of political labor along traditional lines of gender and, therefore, may be an expression of solidarity and not feminist activism. Interpretive in nature, the ongoing examination of descriptive data collected and analyzed in context is a key feature of case studies that helps to ensure construct validity.

The principle of *triangulation* involves the collection and comparison of multiple sources of evidence, using multiple methods. In a case study, triangulation not only serves as a means of corroboration, but also for understanding the mosaic of meanings and interpretations that may exist within a diverse case. For example, female politicians in Burkina Faso may have different explanations and interpretations of the passage of a gender quota law than their male counterparts.

Civil society actors will experience and ascribe meaning to public demonstrations that are different from those of government officials. Marginalized ethnic groups will experience elections differently than mainstream citizens. In order to understand any of these cases—passage of legislation, civic advocacy, national elections—the evaluator collects data and information from different perspectives and sources in order to capture the holistic nature of a phenomenon.

The concept of creating a *chain of evidence* for a case study is used to strengthen the reliability of findings. To construct a chain of evidence, evaluators organize and catalogue all data within a case study database. The evidence should be carefully referenced within the case study report so that if the evidence were provided to another evaluator and examined they would be likely to come to the same conclusions.

Because of the iterative and often inductive nature of case study evaluation, theme coding, matrix categorization, and pattern matching are often used as techniques for structuring and analyzing unstructured information. For example, during the case study design process, the evaluator may identify initial themes relevant to the lines of inquiry or initial assumptions about the program. However, once all data are collected, the evaluator will review each dataset, coding the content when an existing theme is found and coding for new themes as they are identified within the data. The evaluator will use the existing and emerging themes to create a coding frame that organizes the codes into categories and hierarchies that will further aid the analysis. The evaluator may then organize the data in a matrix to compare coded themes with sources of data, attributes of subjects and/or their frequency of occurrence. The matrix analysis will aid the evaluator in identifying patterns that explain results and relationships or generate new hypotheses of change.

Case study designs are particularly suitable for democracy evaluations for three reasons. First, the political context in which democracy programs are implemented is complex and often changing, particularly in transition societies. A case study design can better capture the changing environment and analyze the dynamic interactions that take place between the project, its targeted individuals and organizations, and the political context. Second, in many if not most cases, the underlying conceptual framework for democracy interactions is not clearly spelled out and the intervening variables are not clearly defined. A case study design can clarify and test the underlying assumptions and identify the factors and forces that affect an intervention's implementation and outcomes. Third, as explained in Chapter 1, many impacts of democracy interventions are unforeseen and even unforeseeable and, therefore, cannot be examined by experimental and quasi-experimental designs. Case study designs are eminently suitable to identify them.

Although most evaluations of democracy projects tend to follow a case study design, many suffer from several weaknesses that can undermine the quality of the data and weaken the credibility of findings. Some of the pitfalls include no clear protocols for capturing detailed descriptions of a phenomenon, no corroboration of findings with other sources of data, failure to organize the data into a chain of evidence; not defining purposive sampling strategies, and having no clear framework for analysis. As a result, evaluation reports may look impressionistic based on anecdotal data and, occasionally, give the impression that findings and recommendations are biased.

Steps to Improve Methodological Rigor

While experts may differ about appropriate evaluation designs, most agree that methodological rigor of many evaluations is hardly satisfactory and there is a need to improve their quality and credibility. I mention here a few suggestions that can improve methodological rigor of democracy evaluations. The suggestions are illustrative rather than comprehensive and are mostly based on my reviews of democracy evaluations as well as my own experience.

Focus on Each Evaluation Question

A practical step that evaluators can take is to individually focus on each major question mentioned in an SOW/TOR and reflect over how best it can be answered: What type of data, information, explanations are needed to answer it? How can they be gathered? What time and resources are needed? This will force the evaluators to become rigorous and realistic in data collection and, consequently, their quests will become more specific and sharp. This approach can be illustrated with an example of a summative evaluation of a media assistance project that provides assistance to privately owned media outlets to become financially viable. The evaluation questions are (1) What were the nature, content, and size of technical assistance provided by the project? (2) Did the assistance meet the needs of the targeted media outlets effectively and efficiently? (3) What obstacles did the project face in providing assistance to media outlets? (4) Did the assisted media outlets become or are they likely to become financially self-supporting? (5) Should the funding agency renew the project given its performance and impacts? and (6) What lessons can be drawn from the project?

The evaluation team will discuss each question in detail; explore the nature of data that will be needed to answer them; and develop a sound, practical strategy for data collection. Question 1 is descriptive and necessary information can be gathered from project documents, records of the assisted media outlets, and key informant interviews. Question 2 is normative and will require that evaluators set standards for "efficiently" and "effectively" against which the performance of the project will be judged. The team may tap a variety of sources such as project documents; interviews with the managers of media outlets, project staff, and outside experts; and criteria used by similar projects in the past to develop standards. It may also undertake a survey of assisted media outlets to solicit their views about assistance. Question 3 can be answered on the basis of interviews with the project staff and outside experts while Question 4 will require discussions with the managers of the assisted outlets. Question 5 will require that evaluators explore the subject not only with the managers of the assisted media, but also with the staff media outlets that may be targeted during the next phase. To answer Question 6, the evaluation team might hold a focus group discussion to obtain feedback on its tentative list of lessons learned.

Using Counterfactual Reasoning

Counterfactual logic models seek to answer the question as what would have happened had a particular policy, intervention, or even events not have taken place. Experimental and quasi-experimental designs are the most robust illustrations of counterfactual models, as the differences between the treatment and control/comparison groups enable evaluators to estimate the differences made by a policy or an intervention. As mentioned earlier, the potential for their use in the evaluation of democracy projects is limited. However, pre-, post-, and cross-sectional designs can often provide counterfactual data, albeit weak, that can aid evaluators in assessing impacts.

Even when the quantitative counterfactual models cannot be used, their underlying logic can and should inform democracy evaluators. Before collecting data, evaluators can reflect over the outcomes, identify the factors and forces that may account for the difference between what has happened and what would have happened in the absence of intervention, and come up with hypotheses that can be tested on the basis of available evidence. This can be illustrated by the example of an electoral assistance project in a transition country, which provided services of three expatriate experts to advise the election commission about holding the first postconflict national elections. In addition to focusing on other issues, the evaluation team will consider what would have happened if the three expatriate experts did not advise the election commission. This may lead the team to identify questions such as, Was the election commission in a position to frame rules and regulations without technical assistance? Were there alternative sources of information that might have been tapped? If so, were they adequate? Would its recommendations have carried weight with the interim government in the absence of expatriate advisors? Once the team has prepared questions, it will seek to answer to them during data collection.

Evaluators can follow different strategies to answer counterfactual questions. For example, whenever I posed the question in key informant interviews and focus group discussions as to what would have happened if the concerned project had not been implemented, I have received invaluable insights and perspectives. In an evaluation of a USAID media assistance program in Russia, my colleagues and I visited a few television stations that did not receive foreign assistance (Kumar and Cooper 2003). Although the stations were not systematically selected and their staff was not interviewed on the basis of a questionnaire, these visits gave us some indication of the effectiveness of the program. In some evaluations, the data from other sites, regions, or countries can be used to answer counterfactual issues. Although such efforts are poor substitutes for experimental and quasi-experimental designs, they can improve the methodological rigor of evaluations.

Engaging Host-Country Researchers

The participation of host-country evaluators tends to improve methodological rigor in three ways. First, evaluations become more balanced and objective to the extent to which perspective of insiders is included. Anthropologists have long used emic and etic models to analyze local social and political institutions, culture, beliefs, and behaviors. The *emic model* views local social and political institutions, culture, beliefs, and behaviors in terms of indigenous perspectives and definitions while the *etic model* looks at them from the prism of outsiders. I have observed significant differences in the perceptions, opinions, and judgments of native and expatriate experts in most evaluations. Many interventions that expatriate evaluators viewed as successful were not always judged as successful by host-country evaluators, and vice versa. The truth is that often both are needed to get a balanced picture of an intervention's performance, achievements, and failures. Host-country researchers' understanding of the internal dynamics of their society, its power structure, the nature of political institutions, and pace of democratization contributes to the validity and reliability of evaluation findings.

Second, host-country evaluators can more easily establish rapport with their compatriots than expatriate evaluators. Key informants are usually more candid with host-country evaluators and reveal their views and assessments more freely. Officials of local NGOs are more inclined to reveal the limitations of technical assistance or training programs to a compatriot than to a foreign evaluator. Thus, host-country researchers can often obtain information from their interviews that would never have been revealed to outsiders. Third, local researchers have easy access to data, reports, and studies available in local languages. Only a fraction of the project records, documents, and reports are prepared in the international languages; most are written in local languages. Host-country researchers are able to read these materials, analyze them, and draw necessary conclusions and findings from them.

Greater Attention to Sampling

Sampling has been a problem in democracy evaluations. The basic idea of sampling is to extrapolate from the part to the whole; that is, from the sample to the population. Both probability and nonprobability sampling methods are used in evaluations. In probability sampling, units are randomly selected and have an equal chance of being included in the sample; in nonprobability sampling, units are not selected randomly.

My review of democracy evaluations indicates that most evaluators rely on nonprobability sampling methods for key informant interviews, site visits, or informal surveys of beneficiaries. They do this because such methods are fast, convenient, and inexpensive. However, the problem is that such samples are not always representative of the entire population. And even if they are representative, the readers cannot be sure about them. Therefore, it is necessary that, when using nonprobability sampling, evaluators take every step to ensure that the sample is representative of the entire population. More importantly, they should provide details as to how the sample was constructed and mention its limitations.

While conducting or commissioning surveys, evaluators should pay careful attention to nonsampling errors that arise from many factors such as poor quality of the research instrument, poorly trained enumerators (interviewers), selection bias, nonresponse or response biases, and coding errors. Nonsampling errors tend to pose the greatest threat to the validity of evaluation findings in transition and developing societies, and these cannot be controlled by making the sample larger. Increasing the sample size, which may be beneficial from the perspective of sampling error, can be counterproductive from the perspective of nonsampling errors. Smaller samples are easier to manage and supervise and, therefore, have fewer nonsampling errors. Reducing nonsampling errors requires careful supervision of the research process by skilled evaluators.

Evaluators should also be careful about sample size and not assume that if the population is large, a larger sample size is needed. This is only partially true. The truth is that the larger the size of the population, proportionally a smaller sample size is required. For example, if the population size is 300, a sample of 169 at the 95 percent confidence level with a 5 percent margin of error is sufficient. On the other hand, if the population size is 50,000, a sample of only 381 is needed with the same confidence level and margin of error.[2] The sample size depends on three factors: population size, the variance in the properties of the sampling unit, and the number of characteristics that need to be analyzed.

Greater Use of Quantitative Data

Most democracy evaluations do not use quantitative methods of data collection and rely instead on key informant interviews, informal site visits, and review of project records and documents. There are several reasons for this. Often evaluators do not have time and resources to conduct surveys or censuses. Moreover, many lack expertise in quantitative methods and, therefore, are content with qualitative data collection. Still others do not see the need for quantitative data. Whatever the reason, this imbalance needs to be corrected. Both qualitative and quantitative data are needed for the reliability and validity of the evaluation findings. Moreover, in the absence of quantitative data, evaluations appear anecdotal and impressionistic and are not always credible.

Evaluators can gather quantitative data from three sources: surveys, structured observations, and secondary data. For example, evaluators can conduct surveys of intended beneficiaries (individuals or organizations) to assess the effectiveness and outcomes of an intervention. They can use structured observations in which forms are used for recording observations. When secondary data such as the findings of surveys, opinion polls, or records are available, evaluators can reanalyze them. These methods are discussed in detail in Chapter 8.

A greater use of quantitative methods will enable evaluators to present more precise findings. Instead of noting that a majority of the beneficiary organizations interviewed indicated that the project assistance was helpful to them, evaluators can report that ten of fifteen organizations (nearly 66.5 percent) reported that the project helped them. In the case of election monitoring, for example, evaluators can report that they observed irregularities in only 15 percent of the polling stations they observed rather than that they found only limited instances of irregularities in polling stations.

While I have discussed in this chapter the steps that evaluators can take to improve the rigor of evaluations, it is also important that those commissioning evaluations also create conditions in which rigorous and relevant evaluations can be conducted. For example, they should budget sufficient time and resources for evaluations so that needed data can be gathered and analyzed; they should be careful in selecting evaluators and ensure their independence and integrity of evaluations; and they should ensure that adequate provision for monitoring and evaluation be made at the beginning of a democracy assistance program to ensure that monitoring data are generated for evaluation.

Notes

1. The case study section was contributed by Linda Stern, director of evaluation at the National Democratic Institute.
2. This is explained by Imas, Morra, and Rist (2009), pp. 364–365.

8

Methods for
Data Collection

The choice of methods hinges partly on the evaluation questions to be answered, partly on how well the intervention is understood, and partly on the time and resources available. There is a trade-off between the in-depth understanding that comes from a case study (intensive data collection), for example, and the validity of results yielded from a survey (extensive data collection).
—*Linda Imas, G. Morra, and Ray C. Rist*

I use all social science methods for data collection, but the method which I have found most useful are informal interviews. If you can afford it, take people to lunch or dinner to get inside information.

—*A consultant*

A major problem with democracy evaluations concerns data collection methods. Reviews of democracy evaluations point to less than an encouraging picture. As mentioned in the previous chapter, a few evaluations use surveys, structured direct observation, or secondary analysis of available data. While the scope for using quantitative methods is undoubtedly limited, they certainly can be more widely used than in the past. Moreover, the proper procedures for using qualitative methods such as key informant interviews, focus group discussions, or group interviews are not strictly followed. Interview protocols and focus group discussion guides usually are not included in evaluation reports. Neither are the qualitative data properly coded and analyzed. Therefore, to improve the rigor and credibility of democracy evaluations, it is important that evaluation managers and evaluators pay particular attention to data collection methods.

In this chapter, I focus on various data collection methods that are used for the evaluations of democracy programs. I briefly explain the distinction between qualitative and quantitative methods and then discuss seven specific methods in detail. After describing the steps involved in each of these data methods, I suggest that a multimethod strategy is the most prudent approach to evaluate democracy assistance. The choice of methods depends on the purpose and scope of the evaluation, the time and resources available to evaluators, and the feasibility of using specific methods in the field.

Quantitative and Qualitative Methods

In the popular mind, the obvious distinction between quantitative and qualitative methods is that the findings of the former are expressed numerically and the latter in text. This view is only partially correct. The truth is that the data generated by qualitative methods can also be subjected to rigorous content analysis and then expressed numerically. The responses to questions in key informant interviews, for example, can be numerically coded and tabulated. The evaluator may present the responses in simple tables. On the other hand, quantitative data can be presented in the form of interesting text. Therefore, as Michael Bamberger (2000, pp. 9–12) suggests, the distinction between quantitative and qualitative methods should be understood in the context of the entire research process. He distinguishes the two methods with reference to samples, research protocols, data collection and recording, data analysis, and underlying conceptual framework.

The first difference between quantitative and qualitative methods lies in the selection of individuals, organizations, and communities to be examined by the evaluator. If evaluators are conducting a sample survey, they would invariably use probability sampling so that each subject of the study has an equal and known probability of selection. For example, to examine the effects of journalism training on the careers of journalists, evaluators would select the respondents through a random sampling technique. On the other hand, evaluators using qualitative methods would hardly use random sampling. They would rely instead on purposive, opportunistic, or snowball sampling, taking into consideration the needs of evaluation. On the basis of a set of criteria, they would select key informants who have in-depth knowledge of the media scene and are familiar with the training program funded by the international community. Their focus would be on representative rather than random methods of selection. A key benefit of nonrandom sampling is that qualitative researchers can focus on cases that yield the richest data—in this example, the most successful participants of a journalism training program.

The second difference between the two categories of methods concerns the nature of research protocols. In quantitative research, protocols are precisely defined and should be strictly followed by the evaluator. If an evaluation team is conducting a survey of the leaders of an NGO community to determine their understanding and perceptions of the human rights situation in a country, it would prepare a structured questionnaire, provide precise directions to enumerators as to how to administer the questionnaire, and instruct researchers not to deviate from it. Researchers using qualitative data collection are more flexible. Evaluators interviewing the leaders of democracy NGOs, for example, would follow a list of topics only and frame questions on the spur of the moment. They would pursue the leads and then probe a leader for more details. They would routinely modify their topic lists in light of the information they have already obtained.

The third major difference between quantitative and qualitative methods is in recording. The quantitative data are recorded numerically, which undoubtedly is their principal advantage. On the other hand, qualitative data are most frequently recorded in rich descriptive texts. Evaluators record the responses of key informants, document their observations of informants' nonverbal behavior, and describe the context in which interviews took place. This distinction is a matter of degree, however. Many quantitative surveys include open-ended questions that are recorded as text and many evaluators now use precoded categories to record and classify their qualitative data and information.

The fourth difference between the two methods is that quantitative data are statistically analyzed. Depending on the purpose of evaluation, researchers may calculate means, correlations, regressions, or other measures. In most cases, evaluations of democracy programs do not require sophisticated statistical analysis. The data gathered through qualitative methods are mostly presented as text. Although a part of the data can be presented in numerical form, that does not constitute the core of qualitative methodology. The nuances of focus group discussions, key informant interviews, and informal surveys may be lost when efforts are made to quantify them.

Finally, there is a basic difference in the underlying conceptual framework. Evaluators committed to qualitative research examine a democracy program in the context of the existing social and political environment in which it is designed and implemented. To understand the dynamics of an intervention and the factors and forces that are affecting its performance, evaluators tend to focus on the variables such as existing institutional arrangements, prevailing political values and culture, nature of interactions between program staff and the intended beneficiaries, and stakeholders' perceptions. There is a great deal of subjectivity in their assessment of the program. Evaluators working within the framework of quantitative methods are likely to focus on those variables that can be quantified. They are more likely to emphasize areas such as the number of people, organizations, or communities reached by a program; the number of recipients who are satisfied with the assistance; the perceptions of stakeholders about the effectiveness and impacts of the intervention; and the changes observed in the workings of organizations that received technical and financial assistance from the international community.

I briefly describe below three quantitative methods (surveys, structured direct observation, and secondary data analysis) and four qualitative methods (document reviews, key informant interviews, focus group discussions, and group interviews).

Sample Surveys and Censuses

(other way around)

The difference between a survey and a census is that, in the former, all units in a population are included while, in the latter, only a fraction of the entire population is selected on the basis of probability sampling to draw inferences. Both require collection of information about individuals, organizations, or other units of analysis. Their essential element is a structured questionnaire, which is the basis of data collection. Depending on the scope of evaluation, the respondents may provide information about themselves, others, and/or the organization for which they work.

There are three misconceptions about conducting surveys in developing and transition societies that restricted the use of this powerful research method in evaluating democracy programs. The first misconception is that most surveys in developing countries require personal contacts with respondents; they can not be conducted through the mail, telephone, or Internet. However, conditions have changed considerably in recent years. Cell phones are now widely available, a growing section of people has access to the Internet, and postal services have greatly improved. Most government officials, leaders of NGOs, and academics, particularly those who are stationed in large cities, have access to these services. As a result, evaluators can now use phones, the Internet, and postal services to conduct surveys.

The second misconception is that a large sample is required to draw valid conclusions. But in fact, statistically valid generalizations can be made with a relatively small sample. Most democracy interventions tend to focus on a limited number of governmental and nongovernmental organizations. A small number of judiciary officials are trained, a few democracy NGOs receive assistance for election monitoring, and a limited number of media outlets receive technical and commodity assistance from the international community. Therefore, just a small sample is needed in most cases. A large sample is necessary only when public opinion polls are required for evaluation purposes. Such cases are few. Moreover, secondary data from opinion polls on democracy and political developments are increasingly available in many developing and transition societies and can be used for evaluation purposes.

Finally, there is a perception in some quarters that, to be useful, surveys should include a large number of questions on the workings and outcomes of a democracy intervention. Obviously, this perception is unjustified. The number of questions in a survey questionnaire is determined by the focus and scope of evaluation. In most cases, twelve to thirty questions can generate a wealth of information for a democracy evaluation. Reducing the number of questions in a survey means less investment of time and resources. The fact is that investigators who use the surveys often collect more data than are needed for evaluation purposes.

Well-designed surveys can generate a wealth of data for evaluations of democracy interventions and can improve both their quality and relevance. Surveys involve the following steps.

Focus and Scope

The first step in planning a survey is to determine its focus and scope. The evaluator has to decide which evaluation questions mentioned in an SOW/TOR can be answered by a survey. During the planning stage of an evaluation, there is a temptation to collect more data than are actually needed to answer evaluation questions. Evaluators should resist this temptation in view of the constraints of time and resources that they face. When an evaluation is performed by a visiting expatriate evaluation team, time constraints can be severe; the team usually has only two or three weeks to gather and analyze the survey data and integrate them in the evaluation report. The situation is slightly better when a survey is done by a local research firm. Since the resources for conducting evaluations are usually quite limited, it is important that surveys have a sharp focus and limited scope.

Interview Questions

The second step is to prepare interview questions, keeping in mind the evaluation objectives. This task is not simple; it requires careful consideration because the wording, length, and open and closed nature of questions affect responses. Words used in phrasing survey questions should be simple, be widely understood, and have precise meanings. Slang and colloquialisms must be scrupulously avoided. For the same reason, technical terms should be avoided unless most respondents are experts. Evaluators should not make the mistake of assuming that respondents are familiar with expressions widely used in political science or evaluation research.

Questions should be kept short and succinct. A lengthy question can confuse respondents and cause them to miss the essential point. Indeed, the reliability of responses declines as the length of a question increases. This is particularly true when questions address opinions, judgments, or attitudes. However, when respondents are asked to recall events that happened a long time ago, lengthier questions can be helpful. Such questions provide memory clues and aid recall.

Most questions in surveys or censuses are close-ended questions, which means that response categories are listed and respondents simply identify one or more responses that they consider most appropriate. Response categories for close-ended questions are exhaustive. When a full range of possible answers is not included, the resulting data may be inaccurate. For example, if a question is asked about the sources for funding for civil society organizations, all possible available sources (e.g., government grants, contracts, donations, fees, and rental income) should be listed. This is important because respondents can choose from only the provided categories.

Close-ended questions are easy to ask, still easier to record, and do not require a highly skilled enumerator. Many respondents find them less taxing than open-ended questions because close-ended questions do not require details or contemplation. The listing of the source of information in surveys helps respondents recall the source from which they heard about the issue. The coding of close-ended questions is also simpler, less time consuming, and less likely to contain coding errors. And because the same categories are used, the data are comparable.

Questions should be as specific as possible. Respondents understand and respond better to specific questions than general questions that can be interpreted differently. For example, a general question about the effects of technical and financial assistance provided to a journalism training program run by a university will garner different answers from the respondents. However, if the question is divided and specific questions are asked for the impacts on (1) journalism curriculum, (2) pedagogy, (3) instructional material, (4) recruitment of journalism students, and (5) placement of trained students, the evaluation team is likely to get better answers.

In the evaluation of democracy interventions, evaluators may have to ask sensitive questions about people, organizations, government policies, or corruption. Often out of fear or caution, many respondents may not want to answer them. For example, an informant may not like to answer questions about human rights violations by the government or corruption in high places. Several strategies can be employed to avoid this problem. One common strategy is to ensure that a question conveys the impression that the behavior mentioned is not unusual. For example, a question could be preceded with a statement such as, "Experience indicates that human rights violations are common in most transition societies. Did you hear about any incident involving a human rights violation during the past three months?" Another strategy is to cite the name of an authority trusted

---

Box 8.1 A Survey Tale: Wording of Questions

Two priests were debating whether it was right to smoke during prayers. Both marshaled all kinds of arguments without coming to an agreement. They decided to consult their superiors and meet the next day. When they met, the pro-smoking priest said, "My superior told me that it was right to smoke." "How could it be?" replied the anti-smoking priest. "My superior was emphatic that it was wrong. What did you ask him?" "I asked him if it was all right to smoke while praying," came the reply. "That explains it," said the anti-smoking priest. "I asked whether it was all right to pray while smoking."

by respondents. For example, if there is a respected national newspaper, an evaluator could phrase the question as, "X newspaper has reported many cases of human rights violations. Did you personally hear about a case in which political rights of a person were violated during the past three months?" Still another strategy is to advance reasons for the event or behavior. For example, before asking questions about human rights violations, the evaluator may provide reasons for the prevalence of human rights violations to minimize the sensitivity of questions.

Constructing the Questionnaire

The third step is to construct the questionnaire, which involves arranging the questions in a logical manner, developing a suitable format, and pretesting the questionnaire to identify and resolve problems.

The first question should be simple and nonthreatening, but also important. It should stimulate the respondents' interest in the survey. As a rule, demographic questions should be avoided. If required for analytical purposes, they should be asked at the end.

All relevant questions on a topic should be grouped together. For example, a survey designed to examine the impact of a training project for judges is likely to include questions on the selection of trainees, quality of training, relevance of curriculum, placement of trainees, and contribution of trainees toward improving the performance of judiciary institutions. All of these topics would be separated in the questionnaire and a short statement would be used to facilitate the transition. An example of a transition is, "So far, we talked about the nature of the training program. We would now ask questions about its impact."

All questionnaires should be pretested to identify the problems that need be corrected. In pretesting questions, evaluators examine whether the meaning of questions was clear to respondents, whether they had difficulty answering some questions, and whether the response categories were adequate. Other considerations involve whether the questionnaire retained the attention of the respondents and how much time it took to administer it.

Probability Sampling

The fourth step is to select respondents through probability sampling. The underlying concept behind sampling is that large groups of people, organizations, or other units can be accurately examined by carefully scrutinizing a small number of group members. In probability sampling, each unit in the population has an equal chance of being selected. The selection is carried out by chance procedures and with well-known probabilities for selection. Probability sampling permits the estimation of a sampling error, that is, the probability of error in estimates for a given sample. For example, if the probability sampling is used to estimate the percentage of women who attended voter education meetings, the evaluator can state with confidence that there is only a 5 percent to 10 percent chance that the sampling error will exceed 10 percent of the estimate. Therefore, the data generated by probability sampling are more credible than those in which probability sampling is not used.

Evaluators who examine democracy programs can use four methods of probability sampling. The first method is simple random sampling. A simple random sample can be drawn by lottery. Tags bearing names or identification numbers of all the units in the population are put into a bowl and thoroughly mixed. A predetermined number is then drawn. Although simple, this method is time consuming. A better technique is to number all units and then use random numbers to select the sample. The population unit with the selected numbers is included in the sample.

The second probability sampling method, known as systematic sampling, involves selecting units from a list on the basis of fixed intervals. For example, if a sample of 50 is required for a population of 250 election monitors trained by a democracy project, this means a sample fraction of 50/250, or 1 trainee in every 5 trainees. Therefore, a random number between one and five is used to select the first trained monitor and, thereafter, every fifth trainee will be included in the sample. Systematic sampling is undoubtedly more convenient than simple random sampling. One problem with this method is that an accurate and up-to-date list of the population to be studied is not always available. Therefore, before constructing a sample, available lists should be carefully examined and every effort should be made to check and improve their accuracy.

The third method is stratified sampling in which a population is divided into groups called strata. After strata are determined, independent random samples are drawn from each stratum. Stratification is especially appropriate when a sample is designed to make estimates or comparisons between subgroups of the entire population. For example, to study the effects of assistance provided to community radio stations, the evaluation team may classify the stations in three categories—small, medium, and large—on the basis of the size of the community that they serve. The team would then randomly select community radio stations from each category. There are two types of stratified sampling. The first is proportional, where strata sizes are proportional to their sizes in the population. For example, if the proportion of large community radio stations is 10 percent of the study population, the size of their strata will be 10 percent of the sample. The problem with this method is that sometimes the numbers selected for a small group do not permit satisfactory statistical analysis. Under these conditions, the evaluators may use disproportionate stratified sampling in which different sampling fractions are employed for each stratum.

The fourth probability sampling method is cluster sampling, which does not require a list of the entire population. Cluster sampling is based on the premise that all population units are clustered in one way or another. For example, voters live in villages, towns, or cities; election monitors are affiliated with NGOs; or journalists are employed by media outlets, public relations firms, or the like. While it may be difficult for an evaluation team to prepare an up-to-date list of voters, election monitors, or journalists, it can certainly prepare lists of villages, towns, or cities; democracy NGOs with which election monitors are affiliated; or media outlets and public relations firms where journalists are employed. Cluster sampling is of two types: single-stage sampling and two-stage or multiple-stage sampling. In single-stage sampling, the clusters are randomly selected and every population unit in the selected cluster is included in the sample. In two-stage or multiple-stage cluster sampling, sampling is done in two or more stages. For example, to examine the effects of a voter education program, clusters will first be selected and then a fixed number of voters will be interviewed on the basis of random sampling.

Any of the above four methods of probability sampling can be used by evaluators. The choice should be dictated by the nature and scope of the evaluation and evaluation questions, the availability of lists of the population units, and time and resource constraints.

Mode of Contact

Surveys can be administered in three ways: through mail, telephone, or personal interviews. Surveys administered by mail tend to have poor responses. Unless they are highly motivated, respondents do not take the time to fill out the questionnaire and mail it back. The situation is different when the respondents are connected with the program being evaluated. For example, if an evaluator is conducting a survey to solicit views and suggestions about the strengths and weaknesses of existing technical assistance programs from democracy NGOs that are already receiving technical assistance from an international donor, there is likely to be a good response because the NGOs have a vested interest in communicating their ideas and opinions. Survey questionnaires sent through e-mail tend to have slightly higher response rates in developing and transition countries. As mentioned earlier, a growing majority of government offices, NGOs, and educational institutions now have access to e-mail and they tend to respond quickly. A major limitation of mailed questionnaires is response bias. Some categories of individuals may not like to respond and, as a result, the data generated may not be representative of the entire population. For example, people who are dissatisfied with the democracy assistance may ignore the request.

Telephone interviews are slightly better than mailed questionnaires, as more people are inclined to answer the phone if it is a convenient time for them. Past experience has shown that, when evaluators call on behalf of a program, people respond. Often it is useful to not identify oneself as an evaluator, but as a researcher tasked to examine the workings of a program and its1 effects. Respondents become a bit cautious when they hear the word "evaluation" or "evaluator." Often evaluators are able to gather useful data from the respondents, especially when the number of questions is limited, say ten to fifteen. If the number is larger, respondents can become impatient and not carefully answer questions. Telephone interviews also suffer from response biases.

Albeit costly and time consuming, an individual interview is undoubtedly the most effective way of contacting people. It enables evaluators to record verbal as well as nonverbal behavior of respondents. Interviews should be conducted at a time most convenient to respondents. Evaluators should begin the interview by explaining their background, the objectives of the survey, and the possible uses of the information that respondents will provide. They should read each question slowly and clearly, and use well-established techniques for eliciting fuller and clearer responses, such as repeating the question, pausing for answers, repeating the reply, using neutral comments or questions, and gently asking for clarification.

Recording and Editing

Answers are recorded during the interview. The best time to edit the completed questionnaire is immediately after the interview. Since his/her memory is fresh, the evaluator can correct the responses if they were not recorded properly. Researchers also must pay particular attention to coding, which involves transferring gathered data from questionnaires into categories and translating these categories into numbers. Once the data are coded and cleaned, evaluators use various statistical measures to draw findings and conclusions.

Structured Direct Observation

Another data collection method, which can generate reliable, relevant, and quantitative information, is structured direct observation that involves observing interactions, processes, and behaviors as they occur on the basis of structured observation forms. This method is rarely used in democracy assistance except for election monitoring where monitors occasionally use a checklist to determine the freeness and fairness of elections. However, the structured observation method can be employed in other areas of democracy assistance. For example, evaluators can observe ongoing training sessions for journalists, the organization of public forums by NGOs, or the operations of community radio stations funded by donor agencies. The main strength of direct observation is that an event, institution, facility, or process can be studied in its natural setting, thereby providing a rich understanding of the subject.

The first step in planning structured direct observation is to determine whether direct observation will generate the information that evaluators need. If so, evaluators need to determine the precise focus of the direct observation. For example, suppose an evaluation team is evaluating the activities of a democracy NGO that is organizing public meetings to educate voters about their rights and obligations prior to a national election. If the team has decided to systematically observe such public meetings, it would prepare a list of items to be observed. For example, the team may decide to focus on (1) the initial preparations; (2) the setting of the meeting; (3) the nature and quality of presentations; (4) the nature and frequency of questions asked; and (5) the responses of attendees as evidenced from their verbal and nonverbal behavior.

The next step is to prepare observation forms. Such forms are similar to survey questionnaires except that investigators record their own observations instead of the answers given by respondents. Preparation of forms requires a careful review of concerned events, settings, and participation of the main actors and their behavior. The activities likely to be observed in democracy projects and programs are usually more complex and difficult to specify than in other fields of development assistance such as health and education. For example, while evaluators who observe operations of vaccination clinics can easily prepare observation forms on the basis of available protocols for administering vaccinations, a democracy evaluation team evaluating voter education forums will have to specify each step for holding a public meeting to educate voters. An example of the type of checklist that can be developed for monitoring an election polling station is shown in Box 8.2.

Observation forms should be comprehensive and list every item in a setting, process, and behavior to be observed. This requires consulting local experts and a review of forms used in similar studies. For example, if evaluators are planning to observe public forums on voter education as mentioned above, they will want to know how the meetings are planned and conducted in advance. In many cases, they may observe a meeting and then prepare forms for direct observations. They also must reflect on proper norms for planning and conducting forums based on their previous experience and knowledge.

Most observation forms are checklists that the evaluator marks on-site. For example, evaluators investigating training programs for election monitors will prepare a comprehensive list of the items such as the suitability of the meeting place, seating arrangements, the topics covered in presentations, the quality of presentations, participation of trainees in discussions, and the distribution of any published materials. Although observation forms may have a few open-ended items, most of the items should be close-ended in the sense that answers can be checkmarked. This is necessary to generate quantitative data, which are the defining feature of structured direct observation method.

The observation sites should be carefully selected. If the number is large, the ideal course is to select them through random sampling. For example, an election monitoring team can randomly select 50 sites out of 1,000 polling stations. However, when the number of possible sites is not large, and there are time and resource constraints, evaluators should develop criteria for selecting sites and then consult

---

Box 8.2 A Checklist for Observing an Election Polling Station

A team is conducting an evaluation of electoral assistance and, as a part of the evaluation, it undertakes a structured observation of polling places. The team may send researchers to carefully selected polling stations at 9 a.m., when they open, and use the form for observation purposes, for example.

1. Time of opening the polling station _____
2. Were the polling officials on time?   ☐ Yes   ☐ No
   If not, why? _____
3. Were party representatives present?   ☐ Yes   ☐ No
   If not, why? _____
4. Were election monitors present?   ☐ Yes   ☐ No
   If not, why? _____
5. Were ballots and other relevant materials
   available?   ☐ Yes   ☐ No
   If not, why? _____
6. Was there enough security for voters?   ☐ Yes   ☐ No
7. Did the station provide privacy to voters?   ☐ Yes   ☐ No
8. Did officials try to intimidate any voter?   ☐ Yes   ☐ No
   Please describe the incident _____
   _____
9. Did officials not allow any registered
   voter to vote?   ☐ Yes   ☐ No
   Please give details _____
   _____
10. Were there interruptions in voting?   ☐ Yes   ☐ No
    If yes, please give details _____
    _____
11. How much average time did it take to vote? _____
    (Please take time taken by 5 voters and calculate the average.)
12. Was there any violent incident?   ☐ Yes   ☐ No
    If yes, please give details _____
    _____
13. Were the polling officials impartial?   ☐ Yes   ☐ No
14. Other general observations _____
    _____

---

experts to identify sites that would be most appropriate. For example, an evaluation team examining the operations of community radio stations in an African nation can ask local experts to identify six stations: two highly successful, two moderately successful, and two that are struggling to survive. Timing is also important for direct observation since the observers should be present when an event is occurring. For example, if evaluators are evaluating local programs of community radio stations, they should be present when the various programs are being broadcast.

In most cases, it is necessary to establish some rapport with the concerned staff of the project and organization prior to conducting a direct observation. If evaluators are planning to observe a training program for journalists, they should meet with the trainers in advance to explain the purpose of direct observation and to ease their concerns. Similarly, for observations of public forums on voter education, evaluators should meet with the organizers beforehand. Such preliminary interactions ease possible tensions and allow people to behave more naturally. Evaluators should try to be as inconspicuous as possible. For example, if they are observing a training program, they should sit with the trainees rather than with the trainers.

The presence of outside observers does affect the behavior of those being observed. For example, trainers will make an extra effort to make their presentations interesting or election officials will be more cautious in the presence of outside observers. However, if observers spend sufficient time in the field, people grow accustomed to their presence and behave naturally in their presence. Therefore, it is recommended that, when observing major programs, evaluators should stay at the site longer. If possible, two evaluators should observe together. A team approach can generate better data and minimize individual biases.

As with other data collection methods, after finishing all on-site visits, data should be cleaned and coded. The data from close-ended checklists can be directly coded and analyzed using simple statistics. However, the information from open-ended observations should be written and can be used while preparing the report.

Secondary Analysis of Data

During the past decade, many developing and transition countries have started gathering data on a wide variety of topics concerning democracy and political development. For example, newspapers conduct public opinion polls to gauge public perceptions on a range of public issues. Political parties conduct surveys to understand the orientation of eligible voters and find areas in which their opponents are vulnerable. Research firms and the government also conduct surveys on socioeconomic conditions of their populations. With the growing interest in poverty alleviation, the international community has financed studies that gather data on economic circumstances of the poor and marginalized segments of populations and the strategies that have contributed to their upward mobility. Often these data are stored by the organizations and are available for secondary analysis to answer relevant questions.

The major advantage of using the available datasets is that it saves time and money, which are always in short supply. As explained in Chapter 3, there are several national databases that routinely collect data about democracy, civil and political rights, and human rights that can provide an overall context for democracy interventions and their evaluations. Moreover, there are also a few subsector-level databases that provide data on the media, elections, and civil society. Often these are time series data covering a span of years, which is an added advantage. For example, if evaluators would like to know about people's perceptions of democracy in an African country recovering from a prolonged civil war, they cannot obtain this by conducting a new survey unless they have sufficient time and resources. However, if public opinion surveys about democracy have been done in the past by a research firm, evaluators can use those surveys to gain a historical perspective.

Despite their growing availability, the quality of the available datasets can be problematic. Often the details about the nature of interviews, training of interviewers, coding schemes, and rules for cleaning datasets are not available to outside researchers or evaluators. As a result, they cannot check the accuracy of the data. Therefore, it is important that before using the secondary data, evaluators pay particular attention to two sets of variables. The first set concerns the credibility of the organization holding the database, the professional caliber of the staff who gathered the data, and the availability of the coding scheme and other relevant documents. The second set of variables concerns the accuracy, reliability, and validity of data; the response and missing response rates; and the age of data.

For example, imagine that an evaluation team is examining a political party training program funded by an international donor agency. The purpose is to determine the effectiveness of the training and its effects on the political careers of trained people. At the end of each training session, the project had administered an evaluation form to each trainee and the responses were later coded and utilized. Before using the data, evaluators need to ensure that all responses were coded and recorded (e.g., that officials did not throw away evaluations that were critical of the training), that the coding manual is available, and that the data have not been tampered with. To verify the data, the team may even interview a few respondents. Only when evaluators are reasonably satisfied with these issues, will they undertake secondary data analysis.

Document Reviews

Probably the most widely used source of information for any evaluation are the available records, documents, evaluations, and published and unpublished reports. Past experience has shown that the following categories of documents are of prime importance.

First and the most basic are the documents and reports about the intervention to be evaluated. Often these are provided by the operating unit that commissioned the evaluation. Unfortunately, headquarters of donor agencies or implementing organizations receive only a small proportion of documents prepared at the intervention site. Even when they do obtain them, they often do not have an effective system for storing them and making them accessible to others. Therefore, only when evaluators start visiting the project or program in the field, do they get most documents.

Second, and equally if not more important, are the evaluations conducted about similar interventions. Many agencies routinely put their evaluations on their websites or keep them in their libraries. Often such evaluation reports are easily accessible. Unfortunately, a majority of these evaluations are not shared outside of the office that commissioned them. The past evaluations of similar projects provide valuable information about their performance and outcomes, the data collection methods used, and general findings and recommendations.

Third, there is a growing academic literature in many fields of democracy assistance such as elections, civil society, and political participation. It is often prudent to examine such literature to gain understanding of the subject.

A systematic review of relevant literature can be invaluable for both process and impact evaluations. It provides essential information about the nature, scope, achievements, and challenges facing the intervention to be evaluated. More importantly, it informs evaluators about the findings and recommendations of evaluations of similar projects conducted by other agencies, implementing partners, and research organizations. It thus aids in analyzing the intervention model that underpins the project and program to be evaluated. Above all, it provides tentative answers to the questions that the evaluator will explore in fieldwork. Several steps should be taken for making a systematic review of the literature.

First, once all of the relevant documents, records, and other materials have been collected, it is necessary to take a preliminary look at them and classify them into three categories: most relevant, marginally relevant, and less relevant. This can be easily done by using a few simple criteria for classification. When more than one evaluator is involved, the criteria should be jointly developed so that any relevant item is not excluded. Since the time is limited, such a classification helps in setting priorities.

The second step is to develop a detailed information sheet for the most relevant material and a brief sheet for less relevant material. The information sheet should provide (1) basic information about the document, and (2) substantive information relevant to the evaluation. It is often useful to list substantive material with reference to evaluation questions. For example, imagine that evaluators are evaluating a project that provides technical assistance to independent media outlets in a country to improve their management and marketing practices. The purpose of the evaluation is to help decide about future funding for the next generation of the project. A search of websites and databases identified fifteen evaluations of similar projects in different countries. The team will then prepare an information sheet for each evaluation. Each sheet might answer questions such as

- What was the nature of technical assistance provided to media outlets?
- What was the duration of technical assistance?
- How was the assistance delivered?
- Was the technical assistance combined with commodity assistance?
- What was the training and experience of consultants who provided technical assistance?
- Did the project encounter problems in delivering technical assistance?
- What were the main achievements and limitations of the project?

- What criteria were used to determine success?
- What recommendations did the evaluation team make for the future?

In addition, the information sheet will list reviewers' impressions about the quality of the report, the reliability of the data gathered, and the relevance of the recommendations. While this may sound like considerable work, such an intensive review is extremely useful. When writing their report, the evaluation team can compare its findings with the previous findings. If the findings of earlier evaluations confirm its own findings and conclusions, the team can be confident about the validity of its evaluation. If the findings are inconsistent, it will encourage the team to look back at its data again and examine the factors that shed light on the differences.

The third, and final, step is to present and use the results of the literature review. The results can be even numerically tabulated and presented in the form of tables. For example, if one of the evaluation questions is to find out what kinds of consultant (local or expatriate, managers, or academicians) will be most suitable for the next generation of the project, the team can present the findings of the review in tabular form. It can then compare this information with its own findings. In a few cases, the evaluation report can include a chapter that compares its findings with those of other evaluations.

A mistake that some evaluators of democracy programs make is to cite only those records, documents, and studies that support their findings and recommendations while ignoring others. Such a selective use of the literature is unjustified and even unprofessional. As in social research, evaluators should cite both types of findings—those that confirm their own and those that do not. They should also account for the differences in the findings.

Key Informant Interviews

Simply stated, key informant interviews involve interviewing a select group of individuals who are in a position to provide needed information, ideas, and insights on a particular topic for an evaluation. Two characteristics of key informant interviews are worthy of special mention. First, only a small number of informants are interviewed and they are selected because they possess information or ideas that can be useful to evaluators. Second, key informant interviews are qualitative interviews that involve continually probing the informant. The atmosphere in these interviews is informal, resembling a conversation among new acquaintances. The interviewer subtly takes thorough notes that are elaborated on after the interviews.

Although key informant interviews are conducted widely in the evaluations of democracy projects and programs, the quality and nature of the information that they generate often remain suspect for a variety of reasons: key informants are not carefully selected; interview guides are not prepared in advance; questions are inaptly worded and clumsily asked. The responses are not properly recorded and systematically analyzed. And above all, the findings are not satisfactorily verified. Thus, too often, this potentially useful and versatile method of data collection becomes a poorly planned activity generating information of dubious value and low credibility. However, there are some simple steps that can improve the quality and relevance of the information obtained through such interviews. I mention these briefly below.

First, an interview guide should be prepared that lists the topics and issues to be covered during an interview. Unlike the questionnaire used in survey research, the guide does not list questions. Since the purpose of key informant interviews is to explore an issue in depth, the number of items listed in the guide should be limited, not exceeding ten to fifteen items. Fewer items enable the evaluator to ask follow-up questions depending on the response of informants. Usually, more issues and topics are covered in a session than are identified in an interview guide. This happens because, when informants start to narrate their own experiences or give opinions and information, evaluators are likely to ask more penetrating questions or seek more details. It should be noted that different interview guides may need to be constructed for different categories of key informants. For example, the questions asked of senior political party leaders about electoral assistance are likely to differ from those asked of local election monitors.

Second, key informants should be carefully selected, as the quality of information largely depends on choosing the right informants. Evaluators should identify relevant groups from which the informants will be drawn. For example, to evaluate a project that provides technical assistance to an election commission, an evaluation team may decide to focus on four groups: commission officials, representatives of major political parties, civil society organizations engaged in monitoring elections, and members of the technical assistance teams. The team will select four or five informants from each of the above four groups. As a rule of thumb, fifteen to thirty-five informants are enough for most evaluations. Some additional interviews with senior officials of the government or NGO community may be required strictly for protocol so that they do not feel that their views and opinions were not solicited.

During the interviews, informants may also suggest the names of other persons who can provide useful information and ideas. It is prudent to make provisions for such unplanned interviews at the outset of the study. Sometimes, evaluators have difficulty in identifying key informants at the beginning of their research. In such cases, they can use the "snowball" technique to select the respondents, that is, they will ask respondents for the names of additional persons who should be interviewed.

Third, initial contact is a critical part of the interview during which interviewers must establish rapport with key informants and create an atmosphere of trust so that they are willing to communicate their views and opinions freely. Evaluators should briefly explain their background, the objectives of the interview, and the possible uses of the information and ideas provided by the key informants. They should assure the informants about the confidentiality of information if sensitive issues are to be covered, which is usually the case in democracy evaluations. Evaluators should minimize the use of jargon and technical terms except when they interview experts and academicians. They also should be sensitive to and familiar with local cultural norms and behavior.

If an evaluation team is jointly conducting an interview, it should develop an appropriate procedure so that, without intimidating the respondent, all members will have a chance to ask questions. A simple approach is to designate one evaluator as the primary interviewer and the others as secondary interviewers. After the primary interviewer has covered all of the topics, they will open the interview to the others. This procedure prevents the informant from being subjected to questions from everyone all at once and, thus, allows the interview to proceed smoothly. An alternative is to assign each member specific topics to cover and allocate the time necessary for this.

Fourth, it is a good tactic to begin with factual questions. For example, while interviewing owners and managers of major newspapers, an evaluator could begin with factual questions about their circulation, advertising revenues, or competition between print and electronic media. Questions requiring opinions and judgments should follow factual questions. Examples of the latter include reasons why many newspapers are unable to send their journalists for training, the quality of the training provided by the project, the suitability of training for newspapers, or the cost of training. In phrasing such questions, evaluators should be extremely careful to not make the informant uncomfortable in answering them.

Fifth, questions should be phrased to elicit detailed information. A common mistake is to ask questions that can be answered by a simple yes or no. Although such questions are highly suitable for surveys, they are inappropriate for key informant interviews, which are designed to provide deeper meanings, in-depth descriptions, and thoughtful answers. For example, it is not prudent to ask, "Are you happy with the journalism training provided by the project?" To this, the informant can just say yes or no without providing any details. So the question may be phrased as, "What aspect of the training appealed to you or did not come to your expectations?" Likewise, "What are owners and managers of newspapers saying about the training?" could be asked instead of, "Are media outlets generally satisfied with the training?"

Sixth, it is best to begin with questions about the present and then move to those about the past. Because long-term memory is not always good, replies to questions about the past can be inaccurate. Nevertheless, such questions are necessary because they may provide information that is relevant to the evaluation. One has to be cautious in asking questions about the future. Many informants do not like to speculate about the future with outside researchers.

Seventh, an interview will proceed more smoothly if transitional comments are used to introduce a new topic. To make the interview seem more like a conversation and less like a formal meeting, evaluators can use comments such as, "Your description of the training program was very helpful. Now, I want to ask you a few questions about the utilization of the training by newspapers."

Eighth, skillful probing is essential in seeking elaboration, details, and clarifications. When details are required, both verbal and nonverbal signals can be given to the key informant. Often a nod of the head or a simple yes may be sufficient. The evaluator can then seek additional information by using remarks such as, "This is a crucial subject and I would appreciate if you give me more details," or,

"I am getting the picture, please continue." It is also important that the evaluator take the blame for all failures to communicate instead of giving the impression that the informant is unclear or inarticulate.

Ninth, the evaluator should control conversations without offending the informant. In many cases, respondents will provide long and seemingly irrelevant answers. For example, if the interviewer asks questions about the effects of recent legislation that protects journalists from frivolous lawsuits, the respondent might give a discourse on corruption in the media. In such circumstances, the evaluator should be extremely patient and try to understand what the respondent is really trying to communicate. Some people do not want to speak directly, but rather seek to convey pertinent messages indirectly. For example, it is possible that this respondent is hinting that some journalists and media organizations take undue advantage of the protection granted by the new legislation. Thus, comments that first appear insignificant or irrelevant can often be informative. If the key informant is taking too much time with an irrelevant response, the best course is to use nonverbal communication. When that does not succeed, the interviewer can politely interrupt during a pause with statements such as, "What you said is very enlightening and I understand your point. Now I would like to know. . . ," or, "What you have said prompts me to ask another question. . . ." After that, the evaluator can proceed to a different topic.

Finally, the evaluator should take extensive notes during the interview. Without detailed notes, comments are unduly condensed, details are forgotten, and subtlety is lost. If the informant does not object to being recorded, a tape recorder may be helpful. Experience has shown that, after a few minutes, the interviewee forgets about the recording device. If notes are taken, they should be developed within a few hours; otherwise, a lot of information can be lost unless the evaluator is gifted with a remarkable memory.

Focus Group Discussions

Focus group discussions, which originated as a marketing research tool, are now being used widely in social research. They have become almost indispensable for political operatives who use them to identify issues that voters care about, to test strategies for mobilizing voters around their candidates, and even to find out the areas in which political opponents are vulnerable. Focus groups are also frequently used by evaluators of democracy programs, but their potential is not yet fully utilized. Focus groups can help clarify evaluation questions, shed light on the factors and forces that might explain the performance of an intervention, aid in interpreting the data gathered from different sources, and assist in formulating recommendations for policymakers.

A focus group discussion is essentially a planned dialogue among a small group of people in a naturalistic environment. It involves free and spontaneous discussion on a set of specific topics in which six to twelve people participate with the aid of a moderator. The purpose is to solicit information and ideas from participants. A focus group is not a question and answer session, but a social interaction in which participants stimulate each other's thinking. It is a powerful instrument that, when used properly, can provide an in-depth understanding of a phenomenon, process, or event relating to a democracy intervention. There are several advantages to focus group discussions. First, they are relatively inexpensive. A team evaluating a democracy program can easily organize them with the assistance of local staff. Often experts and informants in developing and transition societies are willing to participate and, thus, will positively respond to invitations. Second, focus groups can be organized quickly, often with a week's notice. Third, and above all, they provide information and ideas that cannot be obtained through other data collection methods such as surveys, secondary data analysis, or even key informant interviews. The following are some of the important steps in conducting focus groups.

First, a succinct list of topics or issues to be discussed must be prepared in advance. Since the discussions are likely to explore a number of ideas surrounding each and every item on the list, the number of topics should be limited to six or eight. For example, initial evaluation findings indicate that journalists trained by a media project are not getting suitable jobs and the purpose of the focus group is to find out the reasons behind it. On the basis of their own expertise and in consultation with other key informants, the evaluator will list a set of possible explanations such as the training does not focus on topics that are in demand; the media outlets have a poor opinion of the training; there is surplus of trained journalists; the trained journalists demand higher wages, which media outlets are not willing to provide; and the media outlets are financially strained because of declining advertising revenues. The evaluator will use this brief list to explore these and other related items in the focus group discussion.

The second step is to select participants. In focus group discussions, it is important that all participants have a more or less similar social or professional status and expertise. Significant differences in the background of participants inhibit free and frank discussion. Participants who are better educated or enjoy higher status tend to dominate the discussion. This is particularly true in traditional and transitional societies where people are not supposed to freely express themselves in the presence of their superiors. I once invited both the chairman of a department and a junior researcher to a focus group in a Southeast Asian country. The researcher did not express his own views even though he was performing the research on the subject. Instead, for every question, he looked at the chairman and reiterated what the chairman said. Evaluators conducting focus group discussions overseas can consult with local informants about possible participants. They must explain that, while they want people with similar backgrounds and experience, they also want participants who have different views and perspectives on the topic to be discussed. Often it is a good strategy to consult with several local informants before making a decision. It is not uncommon that project managers will recommend people who are favorably disposed toward the project.

Experts differ about what information should be shared with participants prior to a focus group discussion. Some suggest that, in order to have spontaneous discussions, it is not prudent to explain to participants in detail about the issues to be discussed. Yet others do not share this view and contend that providing details about questions in advance can contribute to much more focused and informed discussions. In my view, sending advanced information can be quite helpful when the participants are well educated and know about the subject. I often share my findings and tentative recommendations with well-informed participants in advance. The results are generally very useful. The participants come well prepared and raise thoughtful, relevant issues.

Third, venue and time are also important. Focus group discussions should be held in quiet conference rooms and the chairs should be arranged in a way that participants can see each other. The atmosphere should be relaxed and natural. In addition to the moderator, there should be a notetaker who knows the subject and can take fast notes. Recording devices can be used, whenever possible, with the consent of participants. In marketing research, organizers often use a conference room with one-sided glass so that executives can also hear discussions and observe the nonverbal behavior of participants. This is neither possible nor desirable in the case of democracy evaluations because confidentiality is essential. The duration of the focus group may range from sixty to ninety minutes.

Fourth, after the introductions, the moderator (who is the evaluator) should welcome and thank participants and explain the purpose of discussions. Then, the moderator should emphasize some ground rules that are common to all focus groups. Such rules include the following: everyone is expected to speak, each participant's opinion is valuable, there are no correct or incorrect answers to questions, and everyone should confine their remarks to the issues at hand. The moderator should raise one issue at a time in order to keep the discussion focused. During discussions, the moderator can use a flip chart to illustrate the ideas expressed.

In focus group discussions, the role of the moderator is to facilitate discussions in a way that all participants have the opportunity to express themselves, but also to make sure the discussions remain focused. This is indeed a difficult task that requires tact and skills to handle social interactions. In no case should the moderator give the impression of being an expert or respond to any observation. The moderator can clarify the question or issue very briefly. An ideal moderator is an apt listener, demonstrating enthusiasm and interest in what participants are saying. A few tips for moderators are provided in Box 8.3.

At the end of the session, the moderator should summarize major points that were made by participants. If there were differences of opinion on a topic, they should also be mentioned. Participants should be given an opportunity to clarify any point they made. Such a summary helps in the analysis of the information obtained.

The notetaker should record not only the contents of a discussion, but also nonverbal behavior of participants. If a recording device is used, it is best to transcribe the whole discussion, which can be quite time consuming. If sufficient time and resources are not available, evaluators can simply listen to the recorded discussions and take additional notes.

Group Interviews

Unlike focus group interviews, in which participants discuss a subject among themselves, in group interviews investigators ask questions

---

Box 8.3 Tips for a Good Moderator

Ask for clarification: "Can you tell me more about it?"
    Reorient the discussion when it goes off track: "Please wait, how does this relate to . . . ?" or, "Interesting point, but how about . . . ?"
    Use one participant's remark to direct a question to another: "Mrs. U said . . . but what about you, Mrs. Y?"
    Deal with a dominant participant by avoiding eye contact; turning the conversation in a different direction to discourage him/her from speaking; thanking the person and changing the subject.
    Deal with reluctant participants by using the person's name to request an opinion, making frequent eye contact to encourage participation.

Source: Adopted from International Development Research Centre (IDRC), Module C, Focus Group discussion, www.idrc.ca/en/ev-56615-201-DO_TOPIC.html.

---

using a questionnaire. The main interaction is between the interviewers and the respondents. Usually, ten to fifteen participants are invited to group interviews. Evaluators ask all questions included in the questionnaire, discuss the subject, and take votes if participants disagree and faithfully record the responses.

Evaluators who conduct midterm and impact evaluations of democracy programs have often used group interviews. Both the quality and credibility of the findings of group interviews can be vastly improved if investigators follow a set of practical procedures.

First, a structured interview guide should be used. Such a guide facilitates the collection of comparable, systematic data from a series of group interviews. Suppose that five group interviews were held at five sites to understand the reasons for low turnout in a recent national election. If the same questions were posed at each meeting, the evaluator would be able to generate comparable statistical data. A structured guide also keeps the discussions focused. The ideal course is to prepare a structured interview guide, but still to allow evaluators considerable flexibility. The guide should not be used to enforce a rigid course of action. Interviewers should be free to add questions and issues that occur to them during the interview. They should be able to begin with the most relevant questions in the given context.

Only a limited number of questions should be included in a structured guide, and the total number should not exceed fifteen to twenty questions. Each question should be included only after careful consideration. The language should be simple; technical jargon and folksy expressions should be avoided. As in formal surveys, questions that combine two queries should be avoided.

Second, as is the case with focus groups, participants should be carefully selected and should share similar backgrounds. The criteria for selecting participants should be clearly spelled out. Although it is generally not possible to use probability sampling, efforts should be made so that the participants represent the targeted group. For example, if a project funds community radio stations in five districts, the ideal course of action would be to hold group interviews in each of them.

Third, although group interviews can be conducted by one person, a team is preferable for several reasons. It is extremely taxing for one interviewer to ask questions, to probe the respondents, and to take extensive notes. The team approach improves the accuracy of the notes because all the members of the team take notes, which they compare at the end of the interview.

Fourth, as is the case with focus group interviews, evaluators should observe and report nonverbal behavior of respondents. For example, if many respondents demonstrate reluctance in answering a question, it should be noted.

As a mode of data collection, group interviews have many advantages. They can generate both quantitative and qualitative data. They also enable evaluators to gather information rapidly. A group interview with ten to fifteen people can be conducted within an hour or two, which is much less time than it would take to interview each individually. Group participation can sometimes reduce individual inhibitions, thereby providing information that might not otherwise be shared. In some cases, people in groups are willing to share feelings, emotions, and concerns that they would be reluctant to express in more private settings. The obvious reason is that they find a sense of security in the group, which is undoubtedly an important consideration in rural areas where respondents are uncomfortable in the presence of outsiders. For example, the knowledge that other NGOs have the same reservations about the technical support provided by a project can lead a cautious NGO leader to express their own reservations on the subject.

Multimethod Approach

I have briefly discussed a number of quantitative and qualitative methods of data collection above. However, it should be emphasized here that no single method can adequately capture the performance and impacts of democracy interventions. Democracy programs are complex endeavors and their evaluations usually require the employment of more than one method. In my view, a multimethod approach is not only desirable, but usually is necessary for reliable and relevant evaluation findings, conclusions, and recommendations.

Most evaluations of democracy interventions seek to answer a series of questions. Take, for example, an evaluation of a project that provides technical and financial assistance to build and strengthen an independent election commission in a transition society. Here, an evaluation would be expected to answer questions that might include, Did the project materialize as planned? Were there unusual delays? Was the assistance timely? Did the consultants sent by the international community have the skills and expertise necessary to assist in building an electoral commission? Was the training of local staff satisfactory? Is the electoral commission now sufficiently embedded in the national political system so that it will be sustainable? Questions like these cannot be answered on the basis of a single method such as key informant interviews, surveys, or analysis of project documents. A number of methods would be required to generate the needed information.

Another reason for using a mixed-method approach is that often qualitative and quantitative methods complement each other. For example, a survey conducted by an evaluation team found that only 50 percent of the trained judicial officers were satisfied with the training. The survey also documented the trainees' self-reported explanations of why they were not satisfied. Here, key informant interviews and focus group discussions could provide additional and perhaps more nuanced explanations for the lack of satisfaction. The reverse also could be true. Qualitative methods cannot provide data about what percentages of trainees were satisfied or dissatisfied. Only well-designed surveys can answer this question.

Still another reason for using the multimethod approach is that it improves the validity of the findings. When the findings of two different methods support each other, evaluators can be reasonably confident about them. For example, if both surveys' data and key informant

interviews indicate widespread dissatisfaction with the training provided, the evaluator can report with confidence that there were problems with the training and indicate reasons why. If the findings differ,
then the evaluator is likely to further analyze the data and information to seek an explanation for the differences. S/he can also do additional data collection to arrive at findings that are supported by facts.

Finally, there is little doubt that the findings from multimethod
evaluations are more credible and usually more acceptable to stakeholders. The reasons are twofold: first, they have greater validity;
and, second, they satisfy the different methodological orientations of
stakeholders. Some stakeholders put more faith in quantitative methods while others put more in qualitative methods. The use of both
types of methods will satisfy both categories of stakeholders.

9

Communicating Findings and Recommendations

Evaluators should communicate their methods and approaches accurately and in sufficient detail to allow others to understand, interpret and critique their work. They should make clear the limitations of an evaluation and its results. Evaluators should discuss in a contextually appropriate way those values, assumptions, theories, methods, results, and analyses significantly affecting the interpretation of the evaluative findings. These statements apply to all aspects of the evaluation, from its initial conceptualization to the eventual use of findings.

—American Evaluation Association's Guiding Principles

If you want us to read evaluation reports, I have a simple suggestion. Present your findings and recommendations in not more than 4 to 5 pages in plain English and keep all details in annexes.

—A senior official of a bilateral development agency

In this chapter, I focus on communicating the findings and recommendations of democracy evaluations to stakeholders and the public. First, I discuss, albeit briefly, the guiding principles to facilitate effective communication and better utilization of the information generated by evaluations. Next, I explain the three critical elements of an evaluation report (i.e., data and findings, conclusions, and recommendations). I then focus on written communications—evaluation reports, highlights, and briefs—and provide suggestions about their contents and organization. Finally, I discuss oral presentations.

Guiding Principles for Effective Communication

Information Needs of Different Stakeholders

The information needs of different stakeholders of a democracy program are not necessarily the same. Although the situation differs from intervention to intervention, stakeholders can be grouped in four broad categories. The first category consists of the managers and decisionmakers who commission an evaluation. They tend to be the staff of the funding agency, implementing organization, or the intervention itself. The second category consists of the intended target groups such as democracy NGOs, media organizations, journalists, democracy activists, or governmental departments and legislative bodies that an intervention is supposed to aid. The third category consists of the wider democracy communities that are interested in the promotion and institutionalization of democratic cultures. The last category consists of evaluation experts, researchers, and academic scholars interested in democracy and democracy promotion.

Despite their common interest in an evaluation, different stakeholders are not interested in the same information. For example, senior policymakers and decisionmakers in funding agencies have little interest in details about the scope, sources of data, and conduct of evaluations; they are primarily concerned about the main findings and their implications for decisionmaking. A key decisionmaker in a funding agency will be fully content to learn from an evaluation that the agency-funded project to assist in national elections in a transition country performed well, earning plaudits from political parties representing a wide political spectrum. In a few cases, the concerned official may also be interested in critical lessons that can be applied in other situations. The information needs of the democracy NGO, which implemented the project, will be much greater. It will additionally be interested in learning about the factors that contributed to the success of the program, the standards that evaluators used to define success, and the lessons that can be applied in similar interventions. The NGO will also be interested in learning about the overall management of the program and the relationship that the managers had established with functionaries of key political parties in the host country. The leaders of political parties with whom the program worked may want to know about the findings and recommendations pertaining to their political party. Evaluators and researchers working in similar interventions in other countries will want to know about the methodology, the different data collection methods used by evaluators, the conceptual framework that underlined the evaluation, and the findings that can be used to develop further hypotheses for research and theory building.

The implication is that different evaluation products should be targeted to different stakeholders to meet their distinctive needs. For example, a brief of a page or two about main findings and recommendations will be sufficient for senior managers, but a summary and the full report will be required for the implementing NGO. Briefs may be prepared for political parties, emphasizing issues relevant to them. And the evaluation community and concerned scholars will undoubtedly prefer and use the full report with research instruments and other data collection details.

Keeping Key Decisionmakers Informed and Engaged

There is a broad consensus among experts that primary stakeholders (those commissioning evaluations) should not be kept in the dark during the evaluation process. To the contrary, they should be briefed continually as an evaluation progresses. There are many advantages to this course of action: primary stakeholders gain a better appreciation of the findings and conclusions, and how they were derived; they better understand the criteria that evaluators used to determine the success or failure of the intervention; and they obtain advance notice of the recommendations that will logically follow from the findings. If they have serious reservations about the findings or emerging recommendations, they can discuss them with evaluators. They can also provide valuable interpretations for the findings, which might have been overlooked by evaluators. Moreover, they can help the evaluators in formulating more actionable recommendations.

Many exponents of utilization-focused evaluations go a step further and suggest that evaluators should analyze the gathered data and formulate recommendations with the active participation of primary stakeholders. This can be done in two ways. First, a representative of the key stakeholders, most likely the evaluation manager, can attend the meetings in which evaluators review data to draw conclusions and formulate recommendations. Alternatively, the evaluation team can present its preliminary findings at a workshop attended by key stakeholders. My experience with the evaluations conducted by international donor agencies indicates that most evaluators of democracy programs keep in constant touch with evaluation managers and key officials, thereby formally and informally sharing the emerging findings and conclusions. Practically all evaluators share their draft reports before finalizing them, which allows managers and other key stakeholders an opportunity to provide useful inputs.

However, a caveat is necessary here. In many cases, the participation of managers of the concerned program may compromise the independence and integrity of evaluation. Managers have a vested interest in touting the success of their programs to the funding agency or the headquarters of the implementing organization and are naturally concerned that the poor performance of a democracy intervention would reflect poorly on their management capacity. Therefore, some may demand that negative findings be watered down, if not deleted, and even suggest recommendations that favor them. This can occasionally create a major headache for evaluators. There is no easy solution to this problem, but it is important that evaluators do not succumb to the pressure exerted by project managers or other interested key stakeholders.

Paying Attention to Political Context

The growing literature on the politics of evaluations demonstrates the importance of political considerations. We now know that factors such as the political context of evaluations, the conflicting interests of the groups that are likely to be affected by the findings and recommendations of evaluations, and the ideological orientations of decisionmakers are of paramount importance and should not be ignored. The truth is that political factors impinge at each stage of evaluation, beginning from the selection of evaluation questions to the acceptance and implementation of recommendations. Most democracy evaluators understand both political constraints and opportunities, instinctively weigh political factors during the conduct of evaluations, and are careful not to cross the established political boundaries while making recommendations.

In authoritarian and transition countries where democratic norms are not institutionalized, two additional considerations are warranted. First, evaluators should ensure that their reports do not directly or indirectly identify the respondents who might have provided critical information. In such countries, the government often spends more resources on keeping surveillance of its citizens than on education or public health, and democracy activists and NGOs are under constant watch. Therefore, it is quite possible that intelligence services scan the list of key informants listed in the evaluation report of a highly visible human rights program. Even when authorities do not take punitive action against the suspected informants, they add their names to the long list of "subversives" to be constantly watched. Second, evaluators should be careful to present their critical findings in a way that they cannot be used to discredit other democracy programs. While they should point out the shortcomings of the concerned program, they should be careful not to generalize from the limited experience of a single intervention. Many authoritarian governments look for materials that can undermine the credibility of democracy organizations. While I do not know of any case where evaluation findings were used to undermine an ongoing democracy project, I am aware of many cases where the leaders of such organizations were persecuted on flimsy grounds.

Utilizing Different Modes of Communication

As discussed later in this chapter, evaluators should utilize different ways for communicating their findings and recommendations. There are two principal modes of communication that can be explored given the nature of evaluation and the targeted audience. The first is written communication. A well-written evaluation report, which includes data, findings, and recommendations and other documents, is essential and remains the principal vehicle for communication. It is the base from which other reporting formats—summary reports, briefs for senior managers, memorandums, and articles in newsletters or professional journals—can be derived.

Oral communication is also important. Past experience has shown that managers and interested stakeholders often prefer oral reports, which have two distinct advantages. First, there is a greater opportunity for interpersonal interaction. Participants can seek clarifications, ask questions, and explore the implications of findings. Oral reports also provide evaluators with an opportunity to get input about their findings and recommendations. Second, if key managers are present, they can instantly make decisions about follow-up.

The growth of the Internet and electronic media has opened new and unlimited potential for communicating evaluation reports. Evaluators of democracy projects and programs can use chat rooms, teleconferences, videos, and Web conferencing.

Developing a Communication Strategy

Whenever possible, evaluators should develop a communication strategy at the very beginning of the evaluation. The ideal course is for them to discuss with evaluation managers and other key decisionmakers their information needs. Normally, a sound communication strategy covers the following four items:

- Who should receive the needed information?
- What information is needed for different stakeholders?
- When should the information be provided?
- What format is most suitable?

This can be illustrated by the example of an evaluation of a major media project, which provides training, technical assistance, and commodity assistance to emerging independent media outlets in a transition country. First, the evaluators will consult with the evaluation manager and other key officials about communication plans. After these consultations, they may decide to focus on the following audiences: (1) officials who commissioned the evaluation; (2) the project manager stationed in the transition country; (3) the media outlets receiving assistance; and (4) the wider prodemocracy community. The second step is to determine what specific kinds of information each of these audiences needs. Obviously, the key official in the agency and the project manager will want to be continually informed about the progress and outcome of the evaluation while the prodemocracy community will have little interest in learning about the progress of the evaluation. A third and related step is the timing of information sharing. The key official in the agency and the project manager will likely want to be informed and consulted at all stages of evaluation, ranging from finalizing the evaluation design to the formulation of recommendations. Depending on the nature and scope of evaluation, the media outlets receiving assistance also will want to be informed and consulted. The next step is to determine the form of communication. While in the field, the team might use e-mail to communicate with the evaluation manager and hold regular meetings with the project managers and the assisted media outlets. It might also organize a workshop in the transition country to obtain feedback on its findings and recommendations. The essential point is that the evaluation team should map out a sound, practical communication strategy.

Critical Elements of Evaluation Reports

There are three critical elements of an evaluation report, namely, data and findings, conclusions and interpretations, and recommendations. The three are distinct, but organically connected.

Data and Findings

As I suggested in the previous chapter, democracy evaluators tend to use both quantitative and qualitative data. The techniques for analyzing and presenting quantitative data are well known and it is not necessary to discuss them here. A few general suggestions can be made, however. First, the accuracy of the data should be double-checked. Evaluators of democracy projects themselves do not conduct surveys or mine data from other sources such as opinion polls, monitoring records, or governmental statistics. They depend on other researchers for these. Therefore, it is important that they check the data for accuracy. For example, if a commercial organization has conducted a survey of human rights organizations for the evaluation, evaluators are well advised to review the completed questionnaire, coding formats, and the coded data. Often such simple steps can improve both the quality and credibility of gathered data.

Second, statistical analyses should be kept simple. Often elementary descriptive statistics are the best for communicating findings to a broad base of constituencies. Percentages and numerical averages are more effective than analysis of variance or multiple regression tables. The reasons for this are obvious. Evaluation managers and senior officials who supervise democracy assistance are usually not well conversed in complex statistical analyses and they tend to ignore them. The same is true of democracy activists and the leaders of democracy organizations. While larger sets of data may warrant the use of complex statistical techniques, these can still be presented in simpler forms.

Third, tables, graphs, and charts aid stakeholders in understanding the patterns, trends, and relationships that are not always obvious in texts. Line graphs can depict how a variable or a set of variables changes over time. For example, if an evaluation has gathered data about human rights violations in a country, that can be easily depicted as shown in Figure 9.1. Bar graphs are excellent for making comparisons and can provide information about a single variable or

Figure 9.1 Example of a Line Graph Showing Trends in Human Rights Violations

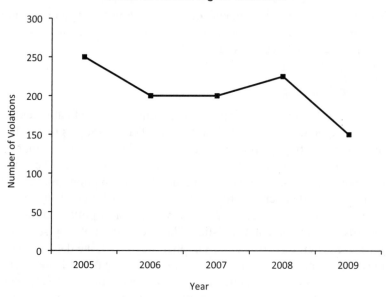

multiple variables. For example, the bar graph in Figure 9.2 compares data about women and men trained as election monitors by a project. Pie charts are also helpful in presenting data. As a rule of thumb, they should not be used when the number of sections in a chart exceeds seven or is fewer than three. The pie chart in Figure 9.3 shows the percentage of three categories of democracy NGOs—those supporting human rights, free and fair elections, and gender equality, which received technical and financial assistance from a project.

As far as possible, graphs and tables should stand alone without the need of text to explain them. They should be clearly labeled and include all the necessary information. They can now be constructed with the aid of word processing programs, spreadsheets, or statistical software.

Evaluators often fail to present qualitative data in a systematic fashion and, as a result, many informative and insightful evaluations of democracy programs lose credibility. A major reason for this failure lies in the fact that, although evaluators take extensive notes, they do not properly code the notes so that they are readily available at the time of report writing. They tend to rely on their memory rather than on a

**Figure 9.2 Example of a Bar Graph Showing
Trained Male and Female Election Monitors**

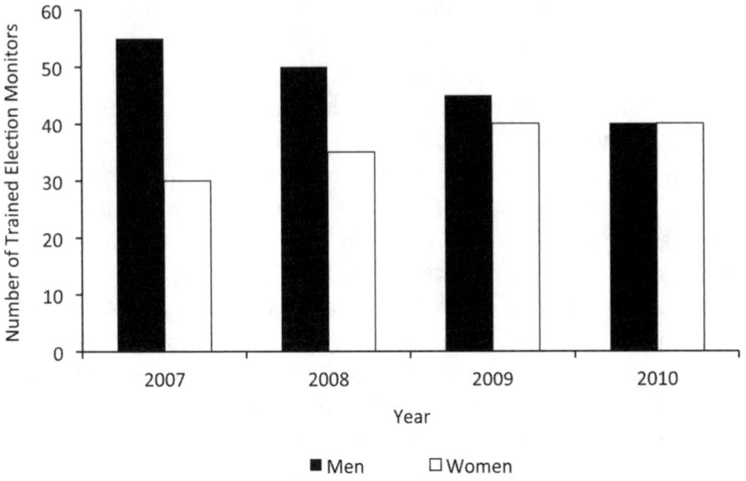

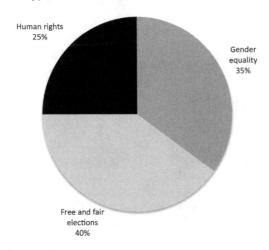

**Figure 9.3 Example of a Pie Graph Showing
What Types of NGOs Receive Assistance from a Project**

Human rights
25%

Gender
equality
35%

Free and fair
elections
40%

review of coded qualitative data. A simple solution is to use descriptive
codes to label the information generated by interviews, site visits, and
focus group discussions. Like numeric codes, descriptive codes can be
organized around relevant ideas, concepts, questions, and themes.

When the data are coded manually, the descriptive codes can be marked in the left margin and a short list can be prepared with page numbers devoted to particular items that will later become subheadings in the text. As an example, a midterm evaluation of a journalism training program is likely to examine many topics, including managerial performance, selection of trainees, participation of female journalists, the suitability of curriculum for the conditions of the host country, and the placement of journalists after the completion of training. For the purposes of descriptive coding, the evaluation team may treat these major topics as separate categories and then develop subcategories. During the past two decades, a number of software packages have been developed to categorize and annotate textual data. Programs such as Ethnograph, QualPro, NVivo 10, and Qualrus allow evaluators to visualize relationships and draw suitable inferences. Computer savvy democracy evaluators can make a judicious use of software programs. Although software packages are available, my own preference is for manual coding as it enables evaluators to go through their notes to conceptualize relationships and findings, revising them if necessary.

Qualitative data can also be presented visually as shown in Box 9.1. The box identifies reasons why an evening journalism training

---

Box 9.1 Reasons for Limited Interest in Journalism Training Program

Male Journalists	Female Journalists
1. Stringent registration requirements	1. Stringent registration requirements
2. Reluctance of employers to sponsor	2. Reluctance of employers to sponsor
3. Lack of proficiency in English	3. Lack of proficiency in English
4. Long duration of the course	4. Long duration of the course
	5. Conflict with domestic responsibilities
	6. Safety concerns about commuting
	7. Limited prospects for promotion after the completion of training

program did not evoke the positive response that the project had expected. It outlines four major reasons for the reluctance of journalists to take advantage of the training: there were stringent registration requirements that took time and effort; employers were reluctant to sponsor journalists for the training for various reasons; the training was conducted in English, which was not the mother tongue of the journalists; and the journalists had to make a three-month commitment. The box also highlights three additional factors that shed light on the reluctance of female journalists in particular: the training was conducted in the evening, when they cooked and shared meals with their families; the journalists were concerned about their physical safety as they had to commute late in the evening; and they thought that they might not be promoted at the completion of the course in a male-dominated society.

Sometimes the findings can be also presented as quotations as shown in Box 9.2, which cites quotations from key informant interviews and focus group discussions. One can list the findings followed by one or more quotes or vice versa.

Finally, qualitative data can also be quantified. For example, Table 9.1 summarizes the suggestions made by key informants for a journalism training program. A few tips for summarizing and presenting qualitative data are provided in Box 9.3.

Most democracy evaluations tend to use more than one data collection method. The question arises as to how to present data gathered from different methods. For example, how should an evaluation team that examined the performance of a human rights program present the data and findings after it has conducted a survey of human rights organizations; interviewed key officials, experts, and activists; and organized focus group discussions? There are two basic approaches.

One approach is to present the data and findings derived from different methods separately. In the case of the human rights program, the evaluation team may first present the findings of the survey, then those of the key informant interviews, and finally those of the focus group. Then, after individually weighing different data sets the team will present its own conclusions. The main advantage of this approach is that it is simple and straightforward. It can often reduce tensions within an evaluation team when its members have different methodological orientations. An evaluator who is more oriented toward using surveys will be able to present the findings, while an evaluator who is an anthropologist will be able to elucidate the findings from key informant interviews and focus group discussions. An

---

Box 9.2 Reasons for Poor Response of Female Journalists

1. Stringent registration requirements:
   To apply for registration is a headache. I had to complete a 10-page application form along with the English translation of a few of my new stories. I won't do it again.
2. Reluctance of employers to sponsor:
   My friend wanted to join the course, but his boss did not allow him. Perhaps, he was afraid that my friend may leave after completing his course.
3. Lack of proficiency in English:
   To be candid with you, most of the journalists speak Spanish. I do not know why the course was offered in English. Most of us do not feel comfortable in English. Next time, you should get Spanish-speaking instructors.
4. Long duration of the course:
   In my view, the major reason why so few people even applied is that it is for three months. How many of us can afford to spend four days every week after a full day of hard work? If the course was for one month, you would have recruited more candidates.
5. Conflicts with domestic responsibilities:
   It was unrealistic to expect that women will attend an evening journalism course. Most of them like to be home with their husband and children in the evening. Only those women journalists who are either single or are rich enough to hire a domestic servant can afford to attend the course.
6. Safety concerns about commuting:
   You know that it is not safe to use public transport after 9 p.m. when the course ends. Journalists cannot afford to have their own transportation and have no alternative but to use local buses, which are not reliable. This must have discouraged many journalists.
7. Concerns about posttraining employment:
   When I asked my friend to apply for the training, she told me that there was no benefit to her. The job market is bad and female journalists have little chance for promotion. The training will only add to their frustration.

---

additional benefit in this course of action is that it provides more details and promotes a better understanding of the findings derived from different data collection methods.

The other approach is to present the data and findings in a triangulated form. The findings from mixed methods are used to inform,

Table 9.1   Recommendations Made by Key Informants

Recommendation	Number of Respondents
Develop need-based training courses	39
Develop objective selection procedures	20
Conduct classes in the local language	19
Provide internship opportunities	19
Plan job placement after training	9
Develop follow-up and refresher courses	6
Give a contract to a local university to run the course	4
Establish an alumni association for the trainees	4

Box 9.3   Tips for Summarizing and Presenting Qualitative Data

1. Look at both the quality and quantity of the answers that mention a specific idea.
2. Be careful to provide a balanced picture. Highlight different perspectives. The most persistent bias in qualitative methods arises from highlighting information and ideas that confirm evaluators' preconceived notions and hypotheses.
3. If possible, have a team of two evaluators to analyze the data and formulate findings.
4. Present findings in a narrative form. Give sufficient details so that the reader understands the findings and how one has arrived at them.
5. Quotes are important in the presentation of qualitative data. They can be either phrases or full sentences.

---

explain, strengthen, and even question each other and are integrated in the text. For example, in the case of the human rights program, the report will first present survey data indicating that a majority of human rights organizations are not satisfied with the assistance offered by the project. However, while discussing the reasons for their dissatisfaction, evaluators will use the data gathered from key informant interviews and focus groups as well. They will provide quotations, illustrations, and insights gathered by these two quantitative methods. The recommendations will most likely be based on the data generated by all these methods. This approach is generally popular with the evaluators of democracy programs for obvious reasons. Such a report is neat and elegant. Interested parties, especially those who have limited time, do not have to read extensive details about individual findings derived from different methods. The methodological battles, if any within the evaluation team, are hidden from the public view.

Conclusions

Findings are different from conclusions. While findings are the empirical facts gathered by an evaluation team, conclusions represent its judgments based on the findings. The general guidance issued by USAID for preparing an evaluation report (USAID 2010, p. 3) compares conclusions "to a court jury's decision to acquit or convict based on the evidence presented" or "a doctor's diagnosis based on the symptoms." In writing reports, democracy evaluators should keep the findings distinct from the conclusions.

A major problem that all evaluators face is to determine whether the program has achieved or is likely to achieve what it was supposed to achieve, that is, whether its performance has been satisfactory, unsatisfactory, or outstanding. The initial program documents are usually not of much help because the expected outcomes, targets, and indicators are at best vaguely stated and rightly so. As mentioned repeatedly in this book, the environment in which democracy intervention operates tends to be fluid. Therefore, even when initial targets and indicators are identified in project planning documents, they are not always sufficient. The planning documents may state that the project should train 100 journalists over the next five years, but it is not likely to mention the quality of training. Evaluators will have to determine if the quality was satisfactory. The truth is that, in most democracy interventions, evaluators have to exercise their own judgment based on the available evidence.

While drawing conclusions, evaluators should clearly spell out the criteria they have used in passing judgments, which may be derived from the program documents, the past experience of similar interventions, and their own substantive knowledge. Making the implicit criteria explicit allows evaluation conclusions to be more transparent and credible. For example, in the case of journalism training, one of the criteria variables can be the percentage of journalists satisfied with the training. The report may state that it has used three categories for determining the success of the five training courses offered by the project: 80 percent or more percent satisfied as outstanding, 50 percent to 79 percent satisfied as successful, and less than 50 percent satisfied as unsatisfactory. The stakeholders may not agree with the criteria used, but they will understand the basis of the conclusions.

Recommendations

Recommendations are undoubtedly one of the most critical elements of evaluations. In fact, they are usually the primary reason for conducting an evaluation. And yet, most evaluators do not give recommendations sufficient thought and reflection. Often they do not think about them until the last stage of writing the report. This is hardly a sound practice. Evaluators should begin to think about recommendations during the data collection stage, even before they perform the data analysis. During interviews with key informants, they can ask about their suggestions for improving the performance of the democracy interventions. For example, while examining the effectiveness of a domestic election monitoring program, evaluators can ask key informants about their suggestions for strengthening the project and reflect over the suggestions they receive. Such reflections will contribute to more practical, experience-based recommendations.

There are two approaches for engaging program managers in formulating recommendations. One approach, often followed in the past, is based on the premise that since recommendations are derived from data and findings, evaluators should formulate them without any inputs from stakeholders. According to this view, by consulting with managers and other stakeholders, evaluators will compromise the integrity of evaluations. Evaluators may embrace their perspective and desist from making recommendations that are not favored by managers and other stakeholders. In sharp contrast, the other view is that the major stakeholders should be involved in developing recommendations, as they are the ones who will ultimately accept and implement them. Recommendations should be developed in workshops attended by evaluators and primary stakeholders. In my view, a middle course should be preferred. While evaluators should keep the managers informed about possible recommendations, they should maintain their independence. Before finalizing their evaluation reports, they should formally and informally share them with primary stakeholders and consider their comments and suggestions, but should not feel bound by them. Such a course of action promotes a better understanding of the rationale and implications of recommendations without compromising their integrity. However, evaluators should exercise caution as to with whom they share their recommendations. For example, if evaluators find that an intervention is poorly managed and therefore will recommend that management staff should change, it might not be prudent to discuss their recommendations with the manager and other senior officials of the project. Rather, they should discuss their recommendations with the headquarters of the NGO or the funding agency that is in charge of the project.

There are certain well-accepted guidelines for formulating recommendations, which can aid evaluators. The first guideline is that all recommendations should logically follow from the data and findings. My review of democracy evaluations indicated that, while most evaluators derived their recommendations from the presented data, some did flout this cardinal norm. In quite a few cases, many recommendations did not derive from the data presented in the report. The obvious explanation is that, while writing reports, evaluators come up with interesting ideas or issues that are important but were not explored earlier. For example, they may realize the need for translating training material in the local language, although they did not ask any questions about it in their survey or key informant interviews. A sensible course is to interview a few key informants about this issue and then mention their responses in the report, which will provide them with a justification to make the recommendation.

Second, recommendations should be practical in the sense that the concerned decisionmakers have the authority and resources to implement them. Making recommendations that cannot be implemented by the decisionmakers is counterproductive; it frustrates those who commission evaluations. For example, it makes little sense for an evaluator of a modest human rights project in an African country to suggest that the funding agency should review its procedures for providing grants to NGOs. While the recommendation may be sensible, the managers of the concerned human rights project would have little influence over the funding agency in such matters. The case would be different if the funding agency had commissioned an evaluation of its procedures for providing grants.

Third, the number of recommendations should be limited. A large number of recommendations undermines the importance of key recommendations. In no case should the recommendation section become what Michael Patton (2008) has aptly called "a laundry list of undifferentiated proposals." Recommendations that pertain to major evaluation questions should not be mixed together with those on the minor and secondary ones. Short-term recommendations may also be separated from long-term recommendations. When an evaluation makes different recommendations for different organizational units, they should be separated. For example, an evaluation of a journalism training program may contain recommendations for the funding agency, managers of the training program, and the university in which the project is housed. Evaluators should distinguish these in the report.

Fourth, as far as possible, recommendations should be specific. It is not enough to say that the project should revise the curricula of its human rights courses; evaluators should also suggest the nature of changes that are required. For example, the evaluators may suggest that the courses should include the new legislation that the country has passed, provide examples of the cases in which human rights were violated by the government, and include the recent activities of human rights organizations. The managers and other stakeholders will feel frustrated if recommendations lack specificity, as they usually know what the problems are. What they often require is information about what needs to be done and how it should be done. However, there are cases where it is prudent not to be too specific and to leave it to the managers to decide what specific courses of action should be taken.

Fifth, sometimes, particularly when major decisions about a project need to be made, evaluators can simply present different options. Suppose a major international agency that has to decide about locating its media training program in a Middle Eastern country has commissioned an evaluation of the program. After reviewing the state of the media and conducting key informant interviews with journalists, media owners, and civil society organizations, the evaluation team might present three options. The training program should (1) continue to be managed by the local office of the agency; (2) be transferred to a local university; or (3) be run by a new training institute. Evaluators would then examine the pros and cons of each option without making any recommendation. The advantage of such a course is that the decisionmakers in the donor agency are able to reflect over the options and decide about the future course of action. Before following such a course, evaluators should consult with the agency to make sure that this is acceptable to it.

Sixth, evaluators should explain the implications of key recommendations when they are not obvious. Most sponsors want such information for their decisionmaking. For example, if an evaluation team recommends that the concerned project should organize a few training workshops for the staff of democracy NGOs to improve their management, it should also explore issues such as the overall cost of the proposed training workshops, the administrative burden it would impose on the project management, and the budgetary approvals that the project would have to seek from the funding agency.

Finally, evaluation experts always emphasize the importance of language. The language should be simple and straightforward, and obtuse expressions should be avoided. Democracy evaluators should be cautious in their choice of language and be sensitive to political and cultural sensitivities. If an evaluation is making recommendations to the host government, it is better to say that "the government may consider giving more authority to the ombudsmen to investigate political corruption" rather than the "government should give more authority. . . ." Although the recommendation may not look powerful, it is likely to be more palatable to the concerned decisionmakers in the host country.

Written Products

Body and Content of the Main Report

Evaluation reports are the primary instruments by which evaluators convey their findings, conclusions, and recommendations to key decisionmakers and stakeholders. Therefore, they should be clear, concise, empirically grounded, and persuasive. They should also be readable and capture the interest of the reader. As far as possible, reports should strike a reasonable balance between depth and length. When reports are lengthy, say over forty pages, readers may be inclined to put them off or only casually read them. On the other hand, if they are too brief, vital information cannot be presented. Probably the best choice is to write a report that is between twenty-five and thirty-five pages in length. Details about research methodology, sampling, or research instruments can be included as annexes so that those who want to go into more depth can find them there. Reports should also make judicious use of quotes, small case studies set in text boxes, and key data displays.

Reports may be structured in two ways. One option is to organize a report around evaluation questions. For each major evaluation question, the report will have a separate section presenting data and findings, conclusions, and recommendations. The second, and more commonly used, option is to present all findings, conclusions, and recommendations in three separate but related sections. The choice should be dictated by the nature of evaluation questions and the information needs of stakeholders. Imas, Morra, and Rist (2009, p. 471) have provided useful tips for preparing evaluation reports that are shown in Box 9.4.

There are no hard-and-fast rules about the contents of an evaluation report. Different agencies, organizations, and firms have their own requirements. However, items that are usually covered are shown in Box 9.5.

Evaluation Briefs for Senior Managers and Policymakers

As indicated earlier, senior managers and policymakers of bilateral and multilateral agencies, international NGOs, or private sector firms

---

Box 9.4 Tips for Preparing Evaluation Reports

1. Keep the purpose of evaluation and stakeholders in mind. Write the report in a way that is best suited to reach them.
2. Use words that are simple, active, positive, familiar, and culturally sensitive. Avoid abbreviations and acronyms to the maximum extent possible.
3. Limit background information to what is needed to introduce the report and its context. Additional information can be included in annexes.
4. Provide sufficient information about the evaluation design and methods so that readers have confidence in the report's credibility, but recognize its limitations.
5. Organize the material into sections that address major themes or answer key evaluation questions.
6. Place major points first in each section, with minor points later.
7. Support conclusions and recommendations with evidence.
8. Place technical information, including the design matrix, research instruments, information about the key informants, and SOW/TOR as annexes.
9. Include an executive summary in the beginning of the report.

Source: Imas, Morra, and Rist (2009), p. 471.

Box 9.5 Outline of an Evaluation Report

1. Executive summary.
2. Introduction.
3. Description of the project or program: description of the project, its objectives, relevant history, and the sociopolitical context in which it was implemented, that is, the underlying theory behind the intervention.
4. Evaluation purpose: evaluation questions; who commissioned the evaluation; what information was expected; and, if possible, how it would be used.
5. Evaluation design and data collection: description of the evaluation design; details about different data collection methods used; strengths and limitations of the collected data; composition of the evaluation team; details about fieldwork.
6. Findings.
7. Conclusions.
8. Recommendations.
9. Lessons, if required.
10. Annexes: statement of work; evaluation design and methodology; research instruments; details about data collection, sites visited, persons interviewed, focus groups conducted, documents reviewed.

---

do not have time to read detailed evaluation reports or even their summaries, but they need to be informed about the key findings and recommendations. The solution lies in preparing evaluation briefs of not more than a page or two. The now defunct Center for Information and Evaluation of USAID successfully used evaluation briefs to inform the senior officials of USAID about the findings and recommendations of its major evaluations. Its briefs proved to be quite popular. Senior officials frequently read them and those interested sought additional information. A major reason for their popularity was that they were succinct, but gave the most essential information to the managers.

A good brief should provide the title of the evaluation, the date, the organizational unit that commissioned it, the name of the project or program, and the country or countries where it was conducted. It should briefly mention the objective and nature of the project and data collection methods. The brief can mention, for example, that the project was designed to create an awareness of the importance of human rights and that the primary sources for information were fifty interviews conducted by evaluators with representatives of human rights organizations, democracy activists, and government officials. The brief should then list key findings. The Center for Development Information and Evaluation (1992) found that the optimal number of findings was five to six. When many more findings were listed in an evaluation brief, the saliency of important findings was lost. When appropriate, short tables or figures can be presented. For example, if the evaluation found that the project has contributed to a gradual decline in the number of human rights violations in the country, it can present a short graph to show the decline. Finally, a brief should mention key recommendations. When findings and recommendations are written in a bulleted form, they usually are more effective than a simple narrative. Senior officials can quickly look at them and even mark those that look important or interesting to them.

Evaluation briefs can be widely shared through e-mail. The entire content of a brief can also be sent in the form of a letter.

Evaluation Highlights

An evaluation highlight falls between an evaluation report and evaluation brief. The concept of evaluation highlights was developed by CDIE (1992) to widely disseminate the findings and recommendations of its evaluations. The underlying premise was that evaluation reports are too long while evaluation briefs are too brief; therefore, another document is needed to serve the needs of technical staff, middle-level managers, host-country stakeholders, and other interested organizations and individuals.

The size of an evaluation highlight can range between eight and twelve pages. In many ways, it is an expanded version of the executive summary of the report. It covers all of the items mentioned in the evaluation report. They are, however, succinct and do not have annexes.

Verbal Communication

Oral Briefings

Oral briefings should be planned in advance, and decisions about substantive (what information will be presented and in what order) and practical planning (who will present and with what audiovisual aids) should be made early. Presenters should carefully select the items that need to be emphasized. The presentations should be flexible to accommodate questions raised by the audience. It is useful to distribute handouts or PowerPoint presentations at the beginning of the briefings.

Although it looks trivial, presenters should be carefully selected. Single presenters are usually more effective. However, when two or more evaluators are involved, it is politically prudent to share the responsibility and coordinate the entire presentation. In its guidelines, USAID suggests that "the presenter should have the dynamism to capture the audience's interest, an effective speaking voice, interpersonal skills to relate to the audience, and confidence and poise to handle distractions" (1992, p. F-5). Unfortunately, most evaluators who give oral briefings are unlikely to possess all of these skills.

Formal presentations should be limited to one-third of the total time allocated for the briefing. Thus, if the total time is limited to one hour, a presentation should not exceed more than twenty minutes, allowing plenty of time for discussion, clarification, and follow-up issues and concerns. Experienced evaluators often anticipate the questions that stakeholders may raise and prepare their responses.

Workshops

Workshops can also be organized to discuss draft findings and recommendations before finalizing evaluation reports. Suppose that an evaluation of a political party assistance program in an African country commissioned by an international donor agency found that (1) the training program for political party functionaries is popular among political parties; (2) women are not adequately represented in the training program; (3) political parties do not send their senior officials to the workshops organized by the project to discuss the sensitive issue of internal democracy within political parties; and (4) the program did not make any headway in persuading political parties to jointly develop a code of conduct. The evaluation has made several recommendations based on these findings. A workshop consisting of primary stakeholders can be organized to discuss them. Participants may question some of the findings, give explanations for others, and even propose recommendations.

Such workshops can be helpful both to evaluators and key stakeholders. While evaluators have an opportunity to gauge reactions to their findings and recommendations, stakeholders are able to offer their comments and suggestions. Moreover, evaluators obtain important feedback that enables them to make suitable revisions. If properly conducted, workshops can also promote a sense of ownership of evaluation among stakeholders.

A word of caution is necessary, however. Sometimes a few participants, who have a vested interest in maintaining the status quo, critique the draft report on flimsy and superficial grounds and are occasionally joined by other participants. Evaluators have to be tactful and explain how data were collected and analyzed as well as how the conclusions and recommendations follow them. When evaluators have solid evidence to back up their findings and conclusions, they can overcome spurious objections and criticisms. In a major multi-country evaluation of assistance provided to women's organizations in war-torn societies, I encountered stiff opposition from a few participants who had not even read the draft summary report. I listed their objections on the board and discussed each of them in detail. In the end, most participants agreed with evaluation findings and recommendations.

A few general steps can improve the outcome of workshops. First, the number of participants should be limited. The ideal size is between ten and fifteen participants who should be carefully selected keeping in view their interest and role in decisionmaking. A summary of the draft report should be shared with the participants in advance. Sending a PowerPoint presentation is not a good substitute for a succinct summary. It is always prudent to know the background of participants so that evaluators can better know their viewpoints. In many democracy evaluations, the key stakeholders in host countries are not always fluent in the English, French, or Spanish languages in which evaluations were conducted. While they understand the language, they are reluctant to express their views. Evaluators should pay special attention to these stakeholders and encourage them to participate in discussions.

Synchronous Communication

Recent advances in electronic communication have opened unprecedented opportunities for face-to-face communication between evaluators and their stakeholders located in different places. Like others, evaluators of democracy programs can take advantage of them. Two kinds of virtual meetings should be particularly mentioned. First are teleconferences in which a single telephone number is given to participants located in different places. Speakerphones are used to communicate. The facilities for teleconferences are easily available in most developing and transition countries. Second are videoconferences, which use audio and video telecommunications to facilitate meetings located at different sites. The only problem is that facilities for videoconferencing are quite limited in developing countries. Although one can get access to them in major cities, they are quite expensive. A cheaper alternative is to use Skype when the participants are located in two sites.

In the end, it is important to reiterate that communicating evaluation findings, recommendations, and lessons should be carefully planned and executed. When appropriate communication strategies are not followed, there is always a risk that they will not be utilized by the stakeholders and evaluation reports will remain only to adorn the bookshelves of the organizations that commissioned the evaluations. Anecdotal evidence indicates that much needs to be done in this area. Evaluation managers of democracy programs should work with evaluation teams in finding ways to effectively communicate evaluation reports in various forms to key decisionmakers in funding and host countries, concerned democracy NGOs, and the academic community as well as to others in the public who value the march of democracy all over the world.

10

Concluding Observations

In this book, I have discussed a wide range of topics, issues, and questions concerning the evaluation of democracy assistance programs. I have also made suggestions for evaluators, evaluation managers, and policymakers in both donor and recipient countries. The purpose of this chapter is to emphasize some recommendations about the future direction of democracy evaluations. These recommendations are not necessarily new and I have discussed most of them in the preceding chapters.

1. *Democracy evaluations should be "utilization focused" in the sense that they generate findings, recommendations, and lessons that can be utilized by the concerned stakeholders.* As Patton, who coined the expression, observes, "Utilization focused evaluation begins with the premise that evaluations should be judged by their utility and actual use; therefore evaluators should facilitate the evaluation process and design any evaluation with careful consideration for how everything that is done, from beginning to end, will affect use" (2008, p. 37). The primary objective of evaluations should be to help managers, policymakers, and other stakeholders in donor and partner countries design and implement effective democracy promotion programs. For example, if an agency commissions a midterm evaluation of a project, which provides technical assistance to the print media, the evaluators should design and conduct the evaluation in a way that their findings and recommendations can be used by the agency and other stakeholders. Evaluations that do not realistically meet the in-

formation needs of the stakeholders are sheer wastes of resources, even when they are conceptually and methodologically sound.

2. *There is a need to improve the methodological rigor of democracy evaluations.* I have reviewed hundreds of democracy evaluations to examine their methodological rigor. Although the quality of democracy evaluations has vastly improved in recent years, many evaluations continue to suffer from serious methodological flaws that undermine their credibility. Often the underlying conceptual framework is not well articulated and a coherent data collection strategy is not followed. Little attempt is made to collect and analyze quantitative data, even when they can easily be gathered. Sometimes proper sampling procedures are not followed. Although most democracy evaluations depend largely on qualitative methods, necessary details about the interview protocols and nonprobability sampling techniques used as well as information about the respondents tend to be missing. As a result, outside experts find it difficult to determine the accuracy of the qualitative data. Therefore, democracy evaluations, like other evaluations, should be based on the data and information that are gathered following the norms of social science research.

Several steps can be undertaken to improve rigor. Evaluators should have strong grounding in social science research methods and possess experience in conducting research in different sociopolitical contexts. They should focus individually on each evaluation question and reflect over how it can best be answered, what type of data are needed to answer it, and how those data can be gathered. Some questions require qualitative data, others require quantitative data, and perhaps most require both. Evaluators should make an effort to use quantitative methods such as surveys, structured direct observations, and analysis of secondary data to generate verifiable findings. They also should carefully select sampling techniques and provide details about data collection methods that they used.

3. *A sense of realism is needed about measuring the impacts of democracy interventions.* Evaluators cannot measure the impacts of a democracy intervention in the way that economists estimate the effects of an agricultural intervention on agricultural production and productivity or the way that health experts measure the effects of a national family planning program on fertility rates. While they can quantify the outputs of specific democracy interventions, they can measure the impacts in only a few cases. For example, while evaluators of a journalism training project can measure the number of journalists trained or

the proportion of trainees who got jobs, they cannot measure the impact of such a training program on the quality of journalism in the country.

As discussed in Chapter 6, the potential for using experimental and quasi-experimental designs to measure the net impacts of democracy interventions is quite limited. Such designs can be used only when the impacts can be quantified, the treatment and control groups can be established before the project begins, and similar assistance can be denied to the members of the control group during the life cycle of the intervention. Moreover, these designs require significant investments in data collection and analysis, which are not always feasible. Finally, democracy interventions evolve in response to changing political circumstances that can make the baseline data less relevant, if not irrelevant. Therefore, experimental and quasi-experimental designs can be used in only a limited number of short-term democracy projects where the goal is to measure immediate outcomes or to test the relative effectiveness of different ways to deliver the goods and services to the targeted individuals and organizations.

The objective of most summative evaluations should be to assess the contributions rather than the net impacts. The contributions can be established by marshaling various kinds of qualitative and quantitative data within in a well-articulated conceptual framework. Although quantitative counterfactual models cannot be used, their underlying logic can be and it should inform summative evaluations. Before collecting data, evaluators must reflect over the outcomes, identify the factors and forces that may account for the differences between what has happened and what would have happened in the absence of the intervention, and come up with hypotheses that can be tested on the basis of the available evidence. They can follow different strategies to answer counterfactual questions. For example, they can pose the question in key informant interviews and focus group discussions as to what would have happened if the concerned project had not been implemented. Often data from other sites, regions, or countries that were not covered by the program can be used to answer counterfactual issues by making comparisons.

4. *Even though democracy evaluators should use indicators, they also should be aware of their limitations.* With the exception of output indicators, the validity and reliability of most performance, meso-level, and macro-level indicators remain questionable. For example, most outcome indicators used or recommended have not been tested

in different social and cultural settings. It will take time before a set of outcome indicators that have solid conceptual and methodological foundations is available to evaluators or policymakers and decision-makers. The construction of meso-level indicators is a work in progress, and it is doubtful that these indicators will ever attain the degree of validity and reliability that the indicators in the health, education, and agriculture sectors have acquired. Political scientists have started to question the validity and reliability of macro-level indicators that are supposed to measure the state of democracy in a country for comparative research. Although meso- and macro-level indicators can provide rich information about the overall context in which democracy programs are designed and implemented and can help evaluators in interpreting their data, they cannot be the basis for assessing, much less measuring, the outcomes and impacts of individual interventions. The use of indicators, without examining their conceptual and methodological foundations, can be misleading and can confer credibility and legitimacy to findings and recommendations that may be totally unwarranted.

5. *Efforts should be made to establish monitoring systems in democracy interventions to track their progress or lack thereof.* The monitoring systems should be simple and based on a limited number of carefully selected indicators, which should be supplemented by qualitative information. They should be cost-effective and supervised by a senior manager. The data and findings of monitoring systems should be reported to all the major stakeholders in a timely fashion. The systems should not merely function as a bureaucratic entity to keep records of achievements and failures, but also should be a forum for brainstorming ideas to improve the intervention. They should provide a space where program staff and stakeholders can share their experiences, reflect over the monitoring data, and make suitable changes if and when necessary.

6. *While all types of evaluations are necessary and should be undertaken, there is a particular need for global or regional program evaluations.* Such evaluations examine the performance and outcomes of democracy assistance in a major sector or subsector such as elections, political party building, rule of law and the judiciary, or human rights. A global evaluation of electoral assistance, for example, is not intended to evaluate the success or failure of individual projects, but to determine the efficacy and outcomes of electoral assistance programs per se. Such evaluations codify past experiences,

lessons, and recommendations in a systematic fashion. Together with metaevaluations, they can generate valuable insights and understandings about the effectiveness and outcomes of democracy assistance, which are very much needed for designing more effective and relevant democracy interventions.

7. *Collaborative evaluations should be promoted to facilitate mutual learning among partnering organizations.* Three categories of collaborative evaluations can be particularly useful. The first category is collaborative evaluations conducted by donor agencies or NGOs of their programs in a country. For example, the International Foundation for Election Systems (IFES), NDI, and IRI undertake a joint evaluation of their electoral assistance programs in Afghanistan. The second category is global or regional evaluations of international assistance in a subsector. These evaluations are similar to those in the first category of evaluations except that they focus on several countries, preferably in all major regions. The countries can be identified on the basis of a set of selected criteria such as the volume of assistance, the nature of political transition, and the feasibility of conducting evaluations. The third category involves evaluations conducted jointly by donor and recipient countries. Such collaboration not only promotes more rigorous evaluations, but it also strengthens cooperation among the different actors engaged in democracy assistance.

8. *There is a need to engage host-country researchers and evaluators in the evaluations.* My analysis of past evaluations indicates that the participation of host-country researchers in evaluations has been limited at best. There are obvious reasons for this. Although the number of trained social scientists who can evaluate democracy interventions is growing, it is still quite small in many transition and postconflict countries. Moreover, the host-country researchers, particularly in authoritarian or semiauthoritarian societies, are susceptible to political pressure; therefore, in many cases, international organizations are reluctant to hire them. Moreover, there is also the problem of language barriers. Therefore, it will take time before host-country evaluators and researchers can themselves conduct evaluations, but it is imperative that they be included in evaluation teams sent by donor agencies. Their participation promotes local ownership. Because they bring to bear insiders' perspectives that are often missed in evaluations exclusively conducted by expatriate staff and consultants, their participation also improves the quality of evaluations. It is encouraging that the international community has become

aware of this problem and is taking steps to engage host-country evaluators and researchers.

9. *Whenever possible, host-country organizations should be encouraged to plan and manage their own evaluations of internationally funded democracy interventions.* Such evaluations will generate useful information, findings, and recommendations that local organizations will be inclined to use. Moreover, they will contribute to strengthening local expertise in evaluations and promoting a better understanding of the advantages and limitations of evaluations. While these evaluations may not always be conceptually or methodologically rigorous, they are worthwhile because they will promote the local ownership of evaluations that is presently missing.

Moreover, international agencies should engage host-country organizations as equal partners and actively involve them in defining the objectives of evaluators; selecting the questions that evaluations should answer; hiring evaluators; reviewing evaluation findings and recommendations; and, finally, utilizing them. In any case, host-country partners should be recognized as major stakeholders. A serious limitation of a majority of democracy evaluations undertaken by bilateral and multilateral agencies is that local partners are not involved in a meaningful way; they are treated as the subject of the evaluations and not as their primary stakeholders.

10. *The international community should take steps to build institutional capacity for democracy evaluations in host countries.* First, it should ensure that the current efforts to strengthen evaluation capacity building should include a distinct focus on democracy assistance. For example, internationally funded evaluation training programs should include trainees who are interested in conducting democracy evaluations. The training should cover the topic of democracy evaluations, draw attention to similarities and differences between the environment and programming of development and democracy assistance, and present case studies of democracy evaluations. Second, modest grants could be given to existing host-country educational and research entities to develop expertise in evaluations of democracy programs. Finally, the funding agencies should support development of e-learning courses on monitoring and evaluation. Such courses could be the most cost-effective way to disseminate the necessary information and skills about democracy evaluations because, once they are developed, the cost of dissemination is almost nothing.

11. *The international community should explore the possibility of establishing an international digital library of democracy evaluations and related studies.* At present, evaluations conducted by bilateral and multilateral organizations, foundations, and private sector firms are not available to evaluators and researchers. This tremendous intellectual loss inhibits the cumulative building of knowledge on democracy evaluations. Therefore, concerted efforts should be made to share evaluations globally so that all those who are interested in democracy assistance can benefit from them.

To accomplish this, the international community could fund the establishment of a digital library for evaluations and related studies. Such a library should be able to store relevant documents in digital format and make them accessible through the Internet. The library could be hosted by an international organization or a research institute and financed by small contributions from a number of agencies that support democracy assistance. Once established, the library could ask bilateral and multilateral agencies, international democracy NGOs, foundations, research institutions, host governments, and evaluators to submit their evaluations and related documents. The costs of establishing and maintaining a digital library would be minimal, particularly if it is attached to an existing digital library. Since the number of evaluations is relatively small, the library would not require many staff.

12. *The international community should promote academic research on the effectiveness and impacts of democracy assistance.* Academicians should be encouraged to test the various assumptions that underlie democracy assistance and examine the relative strengths and limitations of democracy programming, its relationship to other instruments of democracy promotion, the long-term effects of democracy assistance on countries as they march toward democracy, and the factors that explain each of these. For example, it would be interesting to examine whether and, if so, how democracy assistance has contributed to the democratization of countries such as El Salvador, Kenya, and South Africa. Currently, the international community spends between $2 to $3 billion a year to promote democracy. If only one-fifth of 1 percent of this amount were used to promote academic research, it could contribute toward the growth of empirically grounded knowledge, which, together with information generated by evaluations, could assist in developing more effective and relevant programs of democracy assistance.

Appendix 1:
Acronyms

CCMD	Civil Case Management Department
CDIE	Center for Development Information and Evaluation
CEDAW	Convention on the Elimination of Discrimination Against Women
CEOs	civic education officers
CIMA	Center for International Media Assistance
CIRI	Cingranelli-Richards (CIRI) Human Rights index
CSI	Civil Society Index
CSOs	civil society organizations
DAC	Development Assistance Committee
DGA	Democracy and Governance in Albania (DGA) project
GAO	Government Accounting Office
GDP	gross domestic product
GPRA	Government Performance and Results Act
IFES	International Foundation for Election Systems
IREX	International Research and Exchanges Board
IRI	International Republican Institute
MDGs	Millennium Development Goals
M&E	monitoring and evaluation
MSC	most significant change
MSI	Media Sustainability Index
NCEP	National Civic Education Program
NDI	National Democratic Institute for International Affairs
NGOs	nongovernmental organizations
NGOSI	NGO Sustainability Index

OECD	Organisation for Economic Co-operation and Development
OMB	Office of Management and Budget
OTI	Office of the Transition Initiative
PRSP	Poverty Reduction Strategy Plan
PSA	participatory story analysis
RCT	random controlled trial
Sida	Swedish International Development Cooperation Agency
SOW/TOR	statement of work/terms of reference
SSR	security sector reform
UNDP	UN Development Programme
USAID	US Agency for International Development

Appendix 2:
Glossary of
Evaluation Terms

Accountability: Obligation to demonstrate what has been achieved in compliance with agreed rules and standards. This may require a careful, legally defensible demonstration that work is consistent with the contract.

Activity: A specific action or process undertaken over a specific period of time by an organization to convert resources to products or services to achieve results. *See also* Project.

Appraisal: An overall assessment of the relevance, feasibility, and potential sustainability of an intervention or an activity prior to a decision of funding.

Assessment: A synonym for evaluation.

Assumption: A proposition that is taken for granted as if it were true. For project management, assumptions are hypotheses about causal linkages or factors that could affect the progress or success of an intervention.

Attribution: Ascribing a causal link between observed changes and a specific program or intervention(s), taking into account the effects of other interventions and possible confounding factors.

Audit: The systematic examination of records and the investigation of other evidence to determine the propriety, compliance, and adequacy of programs, systems, and operations.

Baseline: Information collected before or at the start of a project or program that provides a basis for planning and/or assessing subsequent progress and impact.

Beneficiaries: The individuals, groups, or organizations that benefit from an intervention, project, or program.

Best practices: Methods, approaches, and tools that have been demonstrated to be effective, useful, and replicable.

Bias: The extent to which a measurement, sampling, or analytic method systematically underestimates or overestimates the true value of a variable or attribute.

Causality: The relationship between one event (the cause) and another event (the effect) that is the direct consequence (result) of the first.

Conclusion: A judgment based on a synthesis of empirical findings and factual statements.

Construct validity: The degree of agreement between a theoretical concept (e.g., peace and security, economic development) and the specific measures (e.g., number of wars, gross domestic product [GDP]) used as indicators of the phenomenon; that is, the extent to which some measure (e.g., number of wars, GDP) adequately reflects the theoretical construct (e.g., peace and security, economic development) to which it is tied.

Content validity: The degree to which a measure or set of measures adequately represents all facets of the phenomena it is meant to describe.

Control group: A selected group that does not receive the services, products, or activities of the program being evaluated.

Cost-benefit analysis: An evaluation of the relationship between program costs and outcomes. Can be used to compare different interventions with the same outcomes to determine efficiency.

Counterfactual: A hypothetical statement of what would have happened (or not happened) had the program not been implemented.

Data: Information collected by a researcher. Data gathered during an evaluation are manipulated and analyzed to yield findings that serve as the basis for conclusions and recommendations.

Data collection methods: Techniques used to identify information sources, collect information, and minimize bias during an evaluation.

Dependent variable: A variable (e.g., output, outcome, response) that is dependent on the independent variable.

Effect: Intended or unintended change due directly or indirectly to an intervention. *See also* Result; Outcome.

Effectiveness: The extent to which an intervention has attained its major relevant objectives.

Efficiency: A measure of how economically resources or inputs (e.g., funds, expertise, time) are used to achieve results.

Evaluability: Extent to which an intervention or project can be evaluated in a reliable and credible fashion.

Evaluability assessment: A study conducted to determine (1) whether the program is at a stage at which progress toward objectives is likely to be observable; (2) whether and how an evaluation would be useful to program managers and/or policymakers; and (3) the feasibility of conducting an evaluation.

Evaluation: A systematic and objective assessment of an ongoing or completed project, program, or policy. Evaluations are undertaken to (1) improve the performance of existing interventions or policies; (2) assess their effects and impacts; and (3) inform decisions about future programming. Evaluations are formal analytical endeavors involving systematic collection and analysis of qualitative and quantitative information.

Evaluation design: The methodology selected for collecting and analyzing data in order to reach defendable conclusions about program or project efficiency and effectiveness.

Experience review: A review that focuses on a limited number of questions and where the data are primarily gathered through the sources such as literature reviews, expert workshops, and key informant interviews.

Experimental design: A methodology in which research subjects are randomly assigned to either a treatment or a control group, data are collected both before and after the intervention, and results for the treatment group are benchmarked against a counterfactual established by results from the control group.

External evaluation: The evaluation of a program conducted by entities or individuals who are not part of the project or program being evaluated.

External validity: The degree to which findings, conclusions, and recommendations produced by an evaluation are applicable to other settings and contexts.

Findings: Factual statements about a project or program that are based on empirical evidence. Findings include statements and visual representations of the data, but not interpretations, judgments, or conclusions about what the findings mean or imply.

Focus group: A group of people convened for the purpose of obtaining perceptions or opinions, suggesting ideas, or recommending actions. A focus group is a method of collecting information for the evaluation process that relies on the particular dynamic of a group setting.

Global or regional program evaluation: Such evaluations examine the performance of major sector or subsector programs to draw general findings, conclusions, and lessons.

Goal: The higher-order objective to which a project, program, or policy is intended to contribute.

Impact: A result or effect that is caused by or attributable to a project or program. Impact is often used to refer to higher-level effects of a program that occur in the medium or long term, and can be intended or unintended and positive or negative.

Impact evaluation: An impact evaluation is designed to assess or measure the outcomes of a project, program, or policy. However, USAID treats it as a subcategory of summative or expost evaluations that uses a control group to measure its precise impact.

Independent evaluation: An evaluation carried out by entities and persons not directly involved in the design or implementation of a project or program. It is characterized by full access to information and by full autonomy in carrying out investigations and reporting findings.

Independent variable: A variable that may influence or predict to some degree, directly or indirectly, the dependent variable. An independent variable may be able to be manipulated by the researcher (e.g., introduction of an intervention in a program) or it may be a factor that cannot be manipulated (e.g., the age of beneficiaries).

Indicator: A quantitative variable that provides reliable means to measure a particular phenomenon or attribute.

Inputs: Resources provided for program implementation (e.g., money, staff, time, facilities, equipment).

Internal evaluation: Evaluation conducted by those who are implementing or managing the intervention or program. *See also* Self-evaluation.

Internal validity: The degree to which conclusions about causal linkages are appropriately supported by the evidence collected.

Intervening variable: A variable that occurs in a causal pathway from an independent to a dependent variable.

Intervention: A project or program.

Joint evaluation: An evaluation in which more than one agency or partner participates. There can be varying levels of collaboration ranging from developing an agreed-upon design and conducting fieldwork independently to pooling resources and undertaking joint research and reporting.

Lessons learned: Generalizations based on evaluation findings that abstract from the specific circumstances to broader situations. Frequently, lessons highlight strengths or weaknesses in preparation, design, and implementation that affect performance, outcome, and impact.

Level of significance: The probability that observed differences did not occur by chance.

Logic model: Often a visual representation that provides a road map showing the sequence of related events connecting the need for a planned program with the program's desired outcomes and results.

Logical framework (logframe): A management tool used to improve the design and evaluation of interventions that is widely used by development agencies. It is a type of logic model that identifies strategic project elements (e.g., inputs, outputs, outcomes, impact) and their causal relationships, indicators, and the assumptions or risks that may influence success and failure. *See also* Results framework.

Metaevaluation: A systematic and objective assessment that aggregates findings and recommendations from a series of evaluations.

Midterm evaluation: Evaluation performed toward the midpoint of program or project implementation.

Mixed-methods approach: Use of both quantitative and qualitative methods of data collection in an evaluation.

Monitoring: Analysis of performance to inform managers and stakeholders about the progress of an ongoing intervention or program, and to detect problems that may be able to be addressed through corrective actions.

Objective: A statement of the condition or state one expects to achieve.

Outcome: A result or effect that is caused by or attributable to the project, program, or policy. *See also* Result; Effect.

Outputs: The products, goods, and services that result from an intervention.

Participatory evaluation: An evaluation in which managers, implementing staff, and beneficiaries work together to choose a research design, collect data, and report findings.

Performance evaluation: An evaluation conducted during the course of project implementation with the aim of improving performance during the implementation phase. *See also* Process evaluation.

Performance indicator: A particular characteristic or dimension used to measure intended changes. Performance indicators are used to observe progress and to measure actual results compared to expected results.

Performance management: Systematic process of collecting and analyzing performance data to track progress toward planned results to improve resource allocation, implementation, and results.

Primary data: Information collected directly by the researcher (or assistants), rather than culled from secondary sources (data collected by others). In program evaluation, it refers to the information gathered directly by an evaluator to inform an evaluation.

Process evaluation: An assessment conducted during the implementation of a program to determine if the program is likely to reach its objectives by assessing whether or not it is reaching its intended beneficiaries (coverage) and providing the intended services using appropriate means (processes).

Program: A set of interventions, activities, or projects that are typically implemented by several parties over a specified period of time and may cut across sectors, themes, or geographic areas.

Project: A discrete activity (or development intervention) implemented by a defined set of implementers and designed to achieve specific objectives within specified resources and implementation schedules. A set of projects make up the portfolio of a program. *See also* Activity; Intervention.

Project appraisal: A comprehensive and systematic review of all aspects of the project (i.e., technical, financial, economic, social, institutional, environmental) to determine whether an investment should go ahead.

Qualitative data: Observations or information expressed using categories (e.g., dichotomous, nominal, ordinal) rather than numerical terms.

Quantitative data: Information that can be expressed in numerical terms, counted, or compared on a scale.

Quasi-experimental design: A methodology in which research subjects are assigned to treatment and comparison groups typically through some sort of matching strategy that attempts to minimize the differences between the two groups in order to approximate random assignment.

Random assignment: The process of assigning research subjects in such a way that each individual is assigned to either a treatment group or a control group entirely by chance. Thus, each research subject has a fair and equal chance of receiving either the intervention being studied (by being placed in the treatment group), or not (by being placed in the control group).

Randomized controlled trials: Evaluations and studies that use an experimental design. *See also* Experimental design.

Rapid appraisal methods: Data collection methods (which fall within the continuum of formal and informal methods of data collection) that can be used to provide decision-related information in development settings relatively quickly. These include key informant interviews, focus group discussions, group interviews, structured observation, and informal surveys.

Recommendations: Proposals based on findings and conclusions that are aimed at enhancing the effectiveness, quality, or efficiency of an intervention.

Reliability: Consistency or dependability of data with reference to the quality of the instruments and procedures used. Data are reliable when the repeated use of the same instrument generates the same results.

Result: The output, outcome, or impact intended (or unintended).

Results framework: A management tool that presents the logic of a project or program in a diagrammatic form. It links higher-level objectives to its intermediate and lower-level objectives. The diagram (and related description) may also indicate main activities, indicators, and strategies used to achieve the objectives. The results framework is used by managers to ensure that their overall program is logically sound and considers all the inputs, activities, and processes needed to achieve the higher-level results.

Risk analysis: An analysis or an assessment of factors (called assumptions in the logframe) that affect, or are likely to affect, the successful achievement of an intervention's objectives. It is a systematic process to provide information regarding undesirable consequences based on quantification of the probabilities and expert judgment.

Sector program evaluation: An evaluation of a cluster of interventions in a sector within one country or across countries, all of which contribute to the achievement of a specific goal.

Self-evaluation: An evaluation by those who are entrusted with the design and implementation of a project or program.

Stakeholders: Entities (e.g., governments, agencies, companies, organizations, communities, individuals) that have a direct or indirect interest in a project, program, or policy and any related evaluation.

Statement of work (SOW): A written description of the objectives, tasks, methods, deliverables, and schedules for an evaluation.

Summative evaluation: Evaluation of an intervention in its later stages or after it has been completed to assess its outcome and impacts. Questions answered include (1) What changes were observed in the targeted populations, organizations, or policies? (2) To what extent can the changes be attributed to the intervention? (3) What factors explain the intended and unintended effects?

Survey: Systematic collection of information from a defined population through interviews or questionnaires.

Sustainability: The degree to which services or processes continue once inputs (e.g., funding, materials, training) provided by the original source(s) decrease or discontinue.

Target: The specified result(s), often expressed by a value of an indicator or indicators, that a project, program, or policy is intended to achieve.

Target group: The specific individuals, groups, or organizations for whose benefit the intervention is undertaken.

Treatment: A project, program, or policy that is the subject of an evaluation.

Validity: The extent to which data measure what they purport to measure and the degree to which those data provide sufficient evidence for the conclusions made by an evaluation.

Variable: An attribute or characteristic in an individual, group, or system that can change or be expressed as more than one value or in more than one category.

Appendix 3:
A Note on Democracy
Assistance Programs

The democracy promotion efforts by Western countries started only after World War II. During the 1950s and 1960s, the United States undertook a few programs to provide news and information to people behind the Iron Curtain. It launched Radio Free Europe and Radio Liberty in 1949 and 1951, respectively, for the people of Europe under communist rule. Both of these radio stations, which were followed by similar ventures in Asia and Cuba, undermined the legitimacy of authoritarian regimes and indirectly supported the notions of freedom, free enterprise, and democracy. While these programs cannot be strictly construed as democracy assistance programs, they were undoubtedly its forerunners.

Democracy assistance came of age during the 1980s and early 1990s. Three factors contributed to its rapid growth and expansion. First, a wave of democracy, called the "third wave" by Samuel Huntington (1993), swept the world transforming its political map. Several authoritarian regimes crumbled, paving the way for electoral democracies in Latin America, Africa, Asia, and Eastern Europe. Second, the Soviet Union disintegrated and its satellite countries and constituents became free to shape their own political destinies. Last but not least, the end of the Cold War contributed to unprecedented cooperation between the two former superpowers for resolving intrastate conflicts. They no longer looked at these conflicts from the prism of the Cold War and, therefore, stopped supporting rival factions. As result, a number of age-old conflicts came to an end in

Africa, Central America, and Asia, creating a favorable environment for peace and democracy.

The United States and European democracies responded to these developments by providing assistance to establish and strengthen institutions and organizations that are essential for a democratic political system. Initially, they gave assistance to hold free and fair elections and strengthen political parties. They also assisted in drafting new constitutions or amending the existing ones to incorporate the norms of human rights, gender equality, and political freedom. Gradually, the international community expanded assistance to the civil society, legislative bodies, judiciary, and independent media. During this period, democracy assistance was fully institutionalized and its legitimacy became firmly established in both donor and recipient organizations.

All major bilateral and multilateral agencies now provide some form of democracy assistance depending on their own priorities. Although the United States and the European Union continue to remain major players, countries such as Germany, the Netherlands, Norway, Denmark, Sweden, and the United Kingdom have not lagged behind and are providing valuable support. The United Nations and its various bodies, which have been long active in democracy promotion, also provide assistance to strengthen democratic institutions and practices. For example, the United Nations Development Programme allocates a substantial part of its budget for projects on human rights, gender equality, and good governance. Several international NGOs such as the International Foundation for Election Systems, International Republican Institute, Internews, National Democratic Institute, Open Society Institute, German political party foundations, and the Netherlands Institute for Multi-Party Democracy have assumed leadership roles in providing or channeling assistance to build and nurture democratic institutions. Most of these organizations now possess valuable expertise and experience in democracy programming and implementation. In addition, many small foundations provide support for projects on independent media, civil society, gender equality, and human rights. Democracy assistance has emerged as a major industry today.

Bilateral and multilateral agencies use various channels for disbursing assistance. In addition to managing their own interventions, they give grants to democracy NGOs mostly located in Europe and North America; contracts to for-profit and nonprofit firms and organizations; and, to a limited extent, direct financial aid to democracy organizations in host countries. There undoubtedly are differences among the major funding agencies. For example, while USAID channels about 50 percent of its democracy assistance through for-profit and nonprofit firms, the European countries channel a relatively larger share of their assistance through democracy NGOs. Private foundations in both the United States and Europe usually run their own programs or directly provide grants to democracy NGOs in host countries. The international community provides assistance in many areas that it considers critical for nurturing and consolidating democracies. I will mention a few programming areas here, but the list is illustrative and not exhaustive.

Electoral Support

During the 1980s, the international community started providing electoral assistance to countries in which authoritarian regimes had collapsed or countries that were recovering from civil wars. Because these countries had little to no experience in free and fair elections, they needed urgent help to elect governments through democratic elections. And the Western countries designed innovative programs of electoral assistance to help them. Electoral assistance helps recipient countries in drafting electoral laws, establishing independent election commissions, preparing voter registries, printing and distributing ballots, establishing polling places, training host-country election monitors, sending international monitors, counting ballots, and preventing fraud and irregularities that can undermine the legitimacy of the electoral process. In recent years, the objective of assistance not only has been to aid in conducting elections, but also to build institutional capacities in recipient countries.

Assistance to Political Parties

While providing electoral assistance, the international community realized that it should be supplemented by support to strengthen and democratize political parties. Political parties in democratizing and fragile countries often lack organizational structures and capacities to perform their roles and responsibilities in a democratic fashion. They also lack ideological cohesion, internal democracy, and sound strategies to contest elections. Frequently, political parties are organized around charismatic leaders who treat the parties as their personal fiefdoms or represent parochial religious, ethnic, and tribal interests. These conditions are worse in postconflict societies where the opposition parties are formed by former politicomilitary movements that have no experience in democratic elections. Consequently, most parties can benefit from some outside help to develop responsive organizational structures, train party cadres, write party manifestos, select candidates for elections, mount election campaigns, and work with civil society organizations. As mentioned above, German party foundations were the first to provide such assistance to fraternal political parties. Later, USAID and its partnering organizations became active, and other bilateral agencies followed suit.

The international community provides financial, commodity, and technical assistance to political parties. It organizes training workshops, meetings, and seminars on topics such as how to recruit party members, how to select candidates for elections, how to write political party manifestos, how to organize public meetings, how to use formal and informal media for publicity purposes, and how to raise funds. International NGOs also encourage political parties to recruit women, ethnic minorities, and marginalized groups and field them as candidates for public office. Commodity and financial assistance has been largely confined to selected war-torn societies. On the whole, the volume of assistance to political parties has been relatively low when compared to electoral assistance because of the political sensibilities involved.

Legislative Strengthening

The international community also provides assistance to strengthen legislative bodies so that they can exercise oversight over the executive branch and perform their legislative functions efficiently and effectively. Such assistance focuses on developing appropriate parliamentary procedures, strengthening the working of parliamentary committees, establishing and supporting research facilities for legislators and their staff, and exposing legislators to the working of legislatures in democratic societies. Many programs organize workshops and seminars on holding public hearings, working with nonprofit organizations, and keeping continuing contacts with the constituents.

Some bilateral agencies also sponsor foreign tours for legislators that involve visiting Western and neighboring democracies. Such visits are quite popular with legislators because it gives them an opportunity to observe the functioning of foreign legislative bodies, meet their counterparts, and do some sightseeing as well. An added advantage is that they promote mutual goodwill between the legislators of democratizing and fragile democracies and their Western counterparts.

The international community also provides limited commodity assistance such as computers, printers, and other equipment. Such assistance has been particularly useful to many postconflict societies where the elected legislators did not have working offices, much less the trained professional staff. Even the modest assistance has helped legislators to perform their duties more effectively in countries such as Cambodia, Liberia, Rwanda, and Ethiopia.

The Rule of Law and the Judiciary

The international community supports a wide range of initiatives to promote the rule of law and strengthen independent judiciary. In the past, it has provided technical support for drafting constitutions in transition and postconflict societies, funded trips of constitutional experts to recipient countries, and even facilitated overseas training for host-country experts to learn about the drafting or amending of constitutions.

The international community also supports strengthening of justice institutions, including the judiciary, ministries of justice, prosecutors' offices, public defenders, ombudsmen's offices, law enforcement agencies, regulatory bodies, law schools, bar associations, and nonstate justice institutions. As early as the 1980s, the United States and European countries provided assistance to reform the judicial and law enforcement agencies in Latin America, which were plagued by human rights abuses and internal corruption, and beholden to political and economic elites. After the fall of the Berlin Wall, Western donors helped newly independent countries in Europe to restructure their judiciaries. The international community now funds rule of law projects and programs in Africa, Asia, and the Near East. More recently, the United States has assisted Iraq and Afghanistan in drafting new constitutions, building courthouses, and training judges and lawyers.

A few agencies have launched some innovative initiatives to promote the rule of law. For example, USAID has initiated a pilot project to test ways to use informal justice institutions and actors in developing countries. It is based on the premise that since customary, traditional, and religious justice systems serve a large percentage of the population in many societies, people's access to justice can be increased by improving and utilizing these. Some international agencies have implemented interventions that enable poor and marginalized groups to have access to the judicial systems.

Security Sector Reforms

Security sector reform (SSR) has emerged as an important core area of democracy and development assistance during the past decade. The earlier focus of SSR was primarily on the demobilization, insertion, and reintegration of former combatants in war-torn societies and, to a limited extent, on training of security forces. With the growth of terrorism in many parts of the world, narcotrafficking across national boundaries, and the perceived need to institutionalize the notions of human rights in security apparatuses, the international community is increasingly engaged in SSR. The focus has shifted from isolated assistance programs to a holistic approach to reform the security sector, which includes institutions, procedures, and practices to ensure internal and external security.

International support for SSR is designed to promote development of legal and policy frameworks consistent with the principles of human rights and the rule of law, improvement in civilian management, oversight and control of the budget for security forces and intelligence agencies, enhancement of cooperation and coordination among security-related and civilian institutions, building of professional security forces, dealing with the past legacies of conflict, improving community security, and demobilization and reintegration of former combatants in the case of postconflict societies.

Independent Media

For the past twenty years, the international community has been providing media assistance to transition and fragile democracies. The purpose of such assistance is to create an enabling environment for independent media, privatize government-owned media enterprises in former authoritarian states, and provide limited assistance to those independent media outlets that are struggling to survive in a hostile political environment. The international community also provides technical assistance to governments for establishing a legal and regulatory architecture for an independent media sector. Such assistance has been critical to those transition countries where the media was earlier controlled, if not owned, by governments so that the necessary legal and regulatory procedures for the functioning of independent media did not exist. Countries in Eastern and Central Europe, postconflict nations in Africa, and a few Middle Eastern countries have benefited from media assistance initiatives. The international community also funds journalism training programs. Such programs support short- and medium-term training for journalists, assist universities in upgrading their journalism departments, and even contribute to the establishment of new journalism training institutions. Bilateral and multilateral donor agencies have assisted and continue to assist community radio stations that serve the needs of local communities and are usually managed by nonprofit organizations.

Many international agencies have also assisted transition and postconflict societies in developing physical and institutional infrastructure for new media, particularly on the Internet. Finally, the international community has provided assistance to galvanize the media for promoting mutual understanding and conflict resolution in wartorn societies.

Human Rights

During the past two decades, the international community has become quite active in providing assistance for promoting human rights. It has supported a wide range of activities. First, it has provided technical assistance for drafting new constitutions or amending the existing ones in transition and postconflict countries. Such assistance has facilitated the incorporation of civil and political rights and safeguards for the rights of women and minorities in these constitutions, although their enforcement remains problematic in many cases.

The international community has provided financial and technical assistance for establishing war tribunals and truth commissions in many postconflict societies. The purpose of these tribunals and commissions is to end the culture of impunity that existed in these countries by bringing to surface past crimes and human rights violations. While tribunals have the authority to award punishment, truth commissions have mainly an educational value, but both have proved to be helpful in healing the wounds of the war and serving as a warning to future oppressors. The international community has also supported human rights monitoring in countries such as Rwanda, Guatemala, Cambodia, and Colombia. Such interventions document human rights violations and bring them to the notice of governments as well as international bodies. Monitoring is mainly done by local organizations with the technical and financial support of the international community.

Finally, a few bilateral agencies and private foundations give assistance to human rights NGOs to raise public awareness about human rights issues, lobby executive and legislative bodies, and support the victims of human rights violations. Unfortunately, the volume of resources has been quite limited when we consider the needs of these organizations. In many authoritarian and semiauthoritarian societies, the international community has also provided modest financial grants to selected human rights activists that have boosted their morale and helped them in carrying on their work.

Civil Society

The international community has been providing technical, commodity, and financial assistance to civil society for nearly three decades. It has particularly focused on three categories of civil society organizations. First are the organizations that are directly engaged in democracy promotion and mobilize support for human rights, social and political justice, and responsive and transparent governmental institutions. While their number is small, they are growing and becoming more vibrant and effective. The second category consists of organizations that, although not directly engaged in democracy promotion, constitute the core of civil society and are essential for the functioning of a democratic system. Examples are labor unions, associations of journalists, professional organizations, business associations, and informal groups such as student movements. At the same time as they promote the interests of their members, they contribute to the growth of a pluralistic political order.

The last category consists of social service organizations that work for the welfare of women, children, youth, indigenous populations, and other groups. International organizations have been awarding contracts to them to implement development interventions. Although not constructed as democracy assistance, such contracts help sustain many voluntary organizations in the developing world. The contracts enable them to charge part of their running expenses to development projects, extend their overreach, and strengthen their organizational capacities. Moreover, contracts often enhance their legitimacy among their peers.

Democratic Governance

Good governance is essential for the consolidation of democracies. Weak government structures that are unable to provide essential services to their citizenry, promote inclusive economic development, or are riddled with corruption can pose serious threats to democracy by undermining its legitimacy. As a result, many bilateral and multilateral agencies include interventions that are designed to improve the functioning of public sector institutions under the heading of "democratic governance."

The international community supports a wide range of interventions to strengthen governmental institutions. It has been providing technical assistance to various governmental departments and agencies to improve their functioning in transition and postconflict countries. International experts have also helped to establish new organizational units at the highest executive levels for policymaking, monitoring, and evaluation. The international community has also organized workshops and training programs via e-learning for governmental officials and managers.

Many bilateral and multilateral agencies fund anticorruption programs to combat the menace of corruption that erodes the legitimacy of democratically elected governments. Such programs have helped governments in framing new rules and regulations, establishing ombudsmen, and instituting organizational reforms. More importantly, these programs have undertaken public education activities to inform people and the civil society about corruption and mobilize their support for anticorruption policies and programs.

Another important area has been the political and administrative decentralization to give citizens and their elected representatives more power in public decisionmaking. Such projects help governments to redistribute authority, responsibility, and financial resources for providing public services among different levels of government. USAID, for example, has undertaken interventions that support the transfer of responsibility for certain public functions from the central government to local and regional elected bodies. The underlying assumption is that decisions made by local authorities will be better informed and more relevant to the diverse interests of the local populace than those made only by national political authorities.

Three general observations about the above-mentioned core areas can be made here. First, the above list is not comprehensive and primarily focuses on what can be regarded as the most important areas of democracy assistance. Second, many interventions cover more than one core area of democracy assistance. For example, electoral assistance programs often include assistance to political parties and vice versa. And media interventions have some components of civil society activities. Finally, while the priorities and focus of democracy assistance to a country differ, a comprehensive strategy for democracy assistance is generally needed because the interventions in core areas are mutually reinforcing.

In addition to the above core areas of democracy assistance, democracy promoters suggest that the norms and values of democracy—participation, transparency, accountability, cooperation, and responsiveness—should inform the design and implementation of development interventions whenever possible. For example, a microenterprise intervention may be designed in a way that promotes the participation of the targeted populations in decisionmaking. Its records and proceedings are well kept and accessible to all who are interested. Its managers are responsible not only to funding agencies, but also to other stakeholders. The leaders of the participating credit groups are democratically elected, and marginalized groups, women, and minorities are well represented in the management. Several multilateral and bilateral agencies have developed such interventions.

References

Alkin, Marvin C., ed. 2004. *Evaluation Roots: Tracing Theorists' Views and Influences*. Thousand Oaks, CA: Sage.

American Evaluation Association, Task Force on Guiding Principles for Evaluators. 1995. "Guiding Principles for Evaluators." *New Directions for Program Evaluation* 66(34): 19–34.

AMEX International and the QED Group. 2011. *Mid-Term Evaluation of USAID's Counter-Extremism Programming in Africa*. Report prepared for USAID, Washington, DC.

Bamberger, Michael. 2000. "Integrating Quantitative and Qualitative Research in Development Projects." Directions in Development, World Bank, Washington DC.

———. 2006. "Conducting Quality Impact Evaluations Under Budget, Time, and Data Constraints." Independent Evaluation Group, World Bank, Washington, DC.

Bamberger, Michael, Jim Rugh, and Linda Mabry. 2006. *Real World Evaluation: Working Under Budget, Time, Data and Political Constraints*. Thousand Oaks, CA: Sage.

Bamberger, Michael, and Howard White. 2007. "Using Strong Evaluation Designs in Developing Countries: Experience and Challenges." *Journal of Multi-Disciplinary Evaluation* 4(8): 58–73.

Barya, John-Jean, Samson James Opolot, and Peter Omurangi Otim. 2004. *The Role of International Assistance in Uganda's Democratic Process*. Assessment report prepared for the Conflict Research Unit, Clingendael Institute. The Hague, Netherlands: Clingendael Institute.

Baum, Matthew, and David Lake. 2003. "The Political Economy of Growth: Democracy and Human Capital." *American Journal of Political Science* 47(2): 333–347.

Becker, Lee B., Tudor Vlad, and Nancy Nusser. 2007. "An Evaluation of Press Freedom Indicators." *International Communication Gazette* 69(1): 5–28.

Beetham, David, Sarah Bracking, Iain Kearton, and Stuart Weir, eds. 2001. *International IDEA Handbook on Democracy Assessment* (The Hague: Kluger Academic Publishers).

Bennett, Claude F. 1982. *Reflective Appraisal of Programs*. Ithaca, NY: Cornell University Media Services.

Berg-Schlosser, Dirk. 2004. "Indicators of Democracy and Good Governance as Measures of the Quality of Democracy in Africa: A Critical Appraisal." *Acta Politica* 39(3) (September): 248–278.

Biddle, C. Stark. 1998. *Evaluation of the USAID Professional Media Program in Central and Eastern Europe*. Report prepared for USAID, Washington, DC.

Birckmayer, Johanna, and Carol H. Weiss. 2000. "Theory-Based Evaluation in Practice: What Do We Learn?" *Evaluation Review* 24(4): 407–431.

Bjorkman, Martina, and Jakob Svensson. 2007. "Power to the People: Evidence from a Randomized Field Experiment of a Community-Based Monitoring Project in Uganda." World Bank Policy Research Paper. Washington, DC: World Bank.

Bjornlund, Eric. 2009. *Evaluation of NIMD' KID Program in Indonesia*. The Hague: Netherlands Institute for Multiparty Democracy.

Blair, Harry. 2008. "Innovations in Participatory Local Governance." In *Participatory Government and the Millennium Development Goals (MDG)*. (New York: United Nations, UN Department of Economic and Social Affairs, Division for Public Administration and Development Management), 77–124.

———. 2011. "Gaining State Support for Social Accountability Mechanisms." In Sina Odugbeni and Taeku Lee, eds., *Accountability Through Public Opinion: From Inertia to Public Action*. Washington, DC: World Bank, 37–52.

Bollen, Kenneth, Pamela Paxton, and Rumi Morishima. 2005. "Assessing International Evaluations: An Example from USAID's Democracy and Governance Program." *American Journal of Evaluation* 26(2): 189–203.

Bruijene, G. A., and M. E. M. Brunings-Stolz. 2008. *Evaluation of NIMD Program on Strengthening Democracy and Policy Development of Political Parties in Suriname*. The Hague: Netherlands Institute of Multiparty Democracy.

Burnell, Peter. 2004. "The Domestic Political Impact of Foreign Aid: Recalibrating the Research Agenda." *European Journal of Development Research* 16(2): 396–416.

———, ed. 2007. *Evaluating Democracy Support Methods and Experiences*. Stockholm: International Institute for Democracy and Electoral Assistance.

Campbell, Donald T. 1999. "The Experimenting Society." In Donald T. Campbell and M. Jean Russo, eds., *Social Experimentation*. Thousand Oaks, CA: Sage, 9–45.

Campbell, Donald T., and Julian C. Stanley. 1963. *Experimental and Quasi-Experimental Designs for Research*. Chicago: Rand McNally.

Carothers, Thomas. 1999. *Aiding Democracy Abroad: The Learning Curve*. Washington, DC: Carnegie Endowment for International Peace.

————. 2006. *Promoting the Rule of Law Abroad: In Search of Knowledge*. Washington, DC: Carnegie Endowment for International Peace.

————. 2007. *U.S. Democracy Promotion During and After Bush*. Washington, DC: Carnegie Endowment for International Peace.

————. 2009a. "Democracy Assistance: Political vs. Developmental?" *Journal of Democracy* 20(1): 5–19.

————. 2009b. "Revitalizing Democracy Assistance." Washington, DC: Carnegie Endowment for International Peace.

Casley, Dennis, and Krishna Kumar. 1986. *Monitoring and Evaluation in Agriculture*. Baltimore: Johns Hopkins University Press, for the World Bank.

————. 1987. *The Collection, Analysis and Use of Monitoring and Evaluation Data*. Baltimore: Johns Hopkins University Press, for the World Bank.

CDIE (Center for Development Information and Evaluation). 1992. *Evaluation Procedures Guidebook for Conducting CDIE Evaluations*. Washington, DC: USAID.

Center for Civic Education. 2008. *"Reconciliation Through Civic Education in Kosovo: Final Evaluation."* Report prepared for USAID, Washington, DC.

Cheechi and Company Consulting, Inc. 2006. *Africa Bureau Anti-Corruption Initiative (ACI): Mid-Term Evaluation*. Report prepared for USAID, Washington, DC.

————. 2008a. *Assessment of Political Party Programming in the Islamic Republic of Afghanistan*. Report prepared for USAID, Washington, DC.

————. 2008b. *Evaluation of the Program on Human Rights and Justice in Cambodia*. Report prepared for USAID, Washington, DC.

————. 2009a. *Local Administration and Reform Project in Cambodia: A Mid-Term Evaluation*. Report prepared for USAID, Washington, DC.

————. 2009b. *Local Governance and Community Development Program in Afghanistan in the Islamic Republic of Afghanistan: An Evaluation*. Report prepared for USAID, Washington, DC.

Chelimsky, Eleanor. 1987. "The Politics of Program Evaluation." In "Evaluation Practice in Review," special issue, *New Directions for Program Evaluation* 34: 5–22.

————. 2006, November 3. "A Clash of Culture: Improving the Fit Between Evaluative Independence and the Political Requirements of a Democratic Society." Presidential keynote address at the annual meeting of the American Evaluation Association, National Conference, Portland, OR.

————. 2007. "Factors Influencing the Choice of Methods in Federal Evaluation Practice Informing Federal Policies on Evaluation Methodology." In "Building the Evidence Base for Method Choice in Government Sponsored Evaluation," special issue, *New Directions for Program Evaluation* 113: 1333.

CIMA (Center for International Media Development). 2007. "Community Radio: Its Impact and Challenges to its Development." www.ned.org/cima.

Cingranelli-Richards Human Rights Database (CIRI). www.ciri.binghamton.edu.

Ciprut, Jose V., ed. 2009. *Democratizations: Comparisons, Confrontations, and Contrasts.* Cambridge: MIT Press.

Civicus Civil Society Index. www.civicus.org.

Collier, John, Jr., and Malcom Collier. 1986. *Visual Anthropology: Photography as a Research Method.* Albuquerque: University of New Mexico Press.

Conway, Francis. 2009. *Local Governance and Citizen Participation Program in Tajikistan: Su-National Government Assessment.* Report prepared for USAID, Washington, DC.

Coppedge, Michael, and John Gerring. 2011. "Conceptualizing and Measuring Democracy: A New Approach." *Perspectives on Politics* 9(2): 247–267.

Crawford, Gordon. 2003. "Promoting Democracy from Without—Learning from Within." *Democratization* 10(2): 1–20.

Dahl, Robert A. 1998. *On Democracy.* New Haven, CT: Yale University Press.

DANIDA (Danish International Development Agency). 2005. *Evaluation Guidelines.* Copenhagen, Denmark: Ministry of Foreign Affairs of Denmark.

Dart, Jessica. 2003. "A Dialogical, Story-Based Evaluation Tool: The Most Significant Change Technique." *American Journal of Evaluation* 24(2): 137–155.

De Luce, Dan. 2003. *Assessment of USAID Media Assistance to Bosnia and Herzegovina 1996–2002.* Report prepared for USAID, Washington, DC.

Democracy International, Inc. 2008. *Liberia Elections and Political Processing Program Evaluation.* Report prepared for USAID, Washington, DC.

Denzin, Norman, and Yvonna S. Lincoln, eds. 2000. *Handbook of Qualitative Research.* 2nd ed. Thousand Oaks, CA: Sage.

de Tollenaere, Marc. 2006. *Democracy Assistance to Post-Conflict Mozambique.* Report prepared for the Conflict Research Unit, Clingendael Institute. The Hague: Clingendael Institute.

de Zeeuw, Jeroen, and Krishna Kumar, eds. 2006. *Promoting Democracy in Postconflict Societies.* Boulder, CO: Lynne Rienner.

Diamond, Larry J. 1995. *Promoting Democracy in the 1990s: Actors and Instruments, Issues and Imperatives.* New York: Carnegie Corporation of New York.

———. 2009. *Developing Democracy: Toward Consolidation.* Baltimore: Johns Hopkins University Press.

Diamond, Larry J., and Leonardo Morlino, eds. 2005. *Assessing the Quality of Democracy.* Baltimore: Johns Hopkins University Press.

Diamond, Larry J., and Marc F. Plattner, eds. 2006. *Electoral Systems and Democracy.* Baltimore: Johns Hopkins University Press.

Donaldson, Stewart I. 2007. *Program Theory-Driven Evaluation Science.* New York: Taylor and Francis.

Doucouliagos, Hristos, and Mehmet Ali Ulubasoglu. 2008. "Democracy and Economic Growth: A Meta-Analysis." *American Journal of Political Science* 52(1): 61–83.

Economist Intelligence Unit. Democracy Index 2008. www.eiu.com/Democracyindex2008.

———. Democracy Index 2011. www.eiu.com/public/DemocracyIndex2011.

EES (European Evaluation Society). 2007. *The Importance of a Methodologically Diverse Approach to Impact Evaluation.* www.europeanevaluation.org.

Elklit, Jørgen, and Andrew Reynolds. 2005. "A Framework for the Systematic Study of Election Quality." *Democratization* 12(2): 147–162.

Evaluation Gap Working Group. 2006. *When Will We Ever Learn? Improving Lives Through Impact Evaluation.* Washington, DC: Center for Global Development. www.cgdev.org.

Finkel, Steven E., and Jeremy Horowitz. 2009, April 23. *The Impact of the Second National Kenya Civic Education Program (NCEP II-URAIA) on Democratic Attitudes, Values and Behavior.* MSI International. Washington DC: USAID.

Fournier, Deborah M. 2005. "Evaluation." In S. Mathison, ed., *Encyclopedia of Evaluation.* Thousand Oaks, CA: Sage.

Freedom House. Freedom in the World 2012. www.freedomhouse.org/report/freedom-world/freedom-world-2012.

———. Freedom of the Press 2012. www.freedomhouse.org/report/freedompress/freedom-press-2012.

Friesen, Ernest. 2006. *Impact of the Civil Case Management Department at Amman First Instance Court.* Report prepared for DPK Consulting and USAID, Washington, DC.

Gamble, Jamie. 2007. *A Developmental Evaluation Primer.* Montreal, Quebec: J. W. McConnell Family Foundation.

GAO (Government Accounting Office). 1990. *Case Study Evaluations.* Washington, DC: GAO.

———. 1992a. *The Evaluation Synthesis.* Washington, DC: GAO.

———. 1992b. *Quantitative Data Analysis.* Washington, DC: GAO.

———. 1995. *Program Evaluation: Improving the Flow of Information to the Congress.* Washington, DC: GAO.

———. 1999. *Case Study Evaluations.* Washington, DC: GAO.

———. 2009. "Program Evaluation: A Variety of Rigorous Methods Can Help Identify Effective Interventions." GAO-10-30. Washington DC: GAO.

Gertler, P., and S. Martinez. 2010. *Impact Evaluation in Practice.* Washington, DC: World Bank.

Gertz, C. 1973. "Description: Toward an Interpretive Theory of Culture." In C. Gertz, ed., *The Interpretation of Culture: Selected Essays.* New York: Basic Books.

Global Barometer Surveys. www.globalbarometers.org.

Green, Andrew T., and Richard D. Kohl. 2007. "Challenges of Evaluating Democracy Assistance: Perspectives from the Donor Side." *Democratization* 14(1): 151–165.

Greene, Jennifer, and Valerie Caracelli, eds. 1997. "Advances in Mixed-Method Evaluation: The Challenges and Benefits of Integrating Diverse Paradigms." *New Directions for Evaluation,* no. 74.

Guba, Egon G. 1989. *Fourth Generation Evaluation.* Newbury Park, CA: Sage.

———, ed. 1990. *The Paradigm Dialog.* Newbury Park, CA: Sage.

Guest, Greg, and Kate MacQueen, eds. 2007. *Handbook for Team-Based Qualitative Research.* New York: Altamira.

Halperin, Morton, Joseph Siegle, and Michael Weinstein. 2005. *The Democracy Advantage: How Democracies Promote Prosperity and Peace.* New York: Routledge.

Hendricks, Michael. 1982. "Oral Policy Briefings." In Nick L. Smith, ed., *Communication Strategies in Evaluation.* Beverly Hills, CA: Sage, 249–258.

———. 1984. "Preparing and Using Briefing Charts." *Evaluation News* 5(3): 19–20.

———. 1994. "Making a Splash: Reporting Evaluation Results Effectively." In J. S. Wholey, H. P. Hatry, and K. E. Newcomer, eds., *Handbook of Practical Program Evaluation.* San Francisco: Jossey-Bass, 549–575.

House, Ernest R. 2005. "Deliberative Democratic Evaluation." In S. Mathison, ed., *Encyclopedia of Evaluation.* Thousand Oaks, CA: Sage, 104–108.

Huntington, Samuel. 1993. *Third Wave of Democratization in the Late Twentieth Century.* Norman: University of Oklahoma Press.

Hymes, D. 1962. "The Ethnography of Speaking." In T. Gladwin and W. C. Sturtevant, eds., *Anthropology and Human Behavior.* Washington, DC: Anthropology Society of Washington.

IBTC (International Business and Technical Consultants). 2007. *Iraq Civil Society Program (ICSP) Final Evaluation.* Report prepared for USAID, Washington, DC.

IDRC (International Development Research Centre). 2007. *Outcome Mapping.* Ottawa, Ontario: IDRC. www.irdc.ca.

Imas, Linda, G. Morra, and Ray C. Rist. 2009. *The Road to Results.* Washington, DC: World Bank.

International IDEA (International Institute for Democracy and Electoral Assistance). 2006. *Assessing the Quality of Democracy Assistance: A Practical Guide.* Stockholm: International IDEA.

———. 2010. *Democracy in Development: Global Consultations on the EU's Role in Democracy Building.* Stockholm: International IDEA.

International Republican Institute (IRI). 2010. *A Comparative Analysis of Political Party Programs at the International Republican Institute.* Washington, DC: IRI.

———. 2011. *Handbook of Monitoring and Evaluation.* Washington, DC: IRI.

Janus, Noreene, and Rick Rock Rockwell. 1998. *The Latin American Journalism Project: Lessons Learned.* Report prepared for USAID, Washington, DC.

Kellogg Foundation. 2001. *Logic Model Development Guide: Logic Models to Bring Together Planning, Evaluation, and Action.* Battle Creek, MI: W. K. Kellogg Foundation.

Kimonyo, Jean-Paul, Noel Twagiramungu, and Christopher Kayumba. 2004. *Supporting the Post-Conflict Transition in Rwanda: The Role of the In-*

ternational Community. Report prepared for the Conflict Research Unit, Clingendael Institute. The Hague, Netherlands: Clingendael, Institute.

King, Jean A. 2007a. "Developing Evaluation Capacity Through Process Use." *New Directions for Evaluation,* no. 116: 45–59.

———. 2007b. "Making Sense of Participatory Evaluation." *New Directions for Evaluation,* no. 114: 83–86.

King, Jean A., Lynn Lyons Morris, and Carol T. Fitz-Gibbon. 1987. *How to Assess Program Implementation.* Newbury Park, CA: Sage.

Kumar, Krishna. 1987a. *Conducting Group Interviews.* Washington, DC: USAID.

———. 1987b. *Rapid, Low Cost Data Collection Methods.* Washington, DC: USAID.

———. 1988a. *Conducting Key Informant Interviews in Developing Countries.* Washington, DC: USAID.

———, ed. 1988b. *Postconflict Elections, Democratization and International Assistance.* Boulder: Lynne Rienner.

———, ed. 1993. *Rapid Appraisal Methods.* Washington, DC: World Bank.

———, ed. 1996. *Rebuilding Societies After Civil Wars.* Boulder: Lynne Rienner.

———. 1998. *Postconflict Elections, Democratization, and International Assistance.* Boulder, CO: Lynne Rienner.

———, ed. 2001. *Women and Civil War: Impact, Organizations and Action.* Boulder: Lynne Rienner.

———. 2004. *USAID Media Assistance: Policy and Programmatic Lessons.* Washington, DC: USAID.

———. 2006a. *Conducting Mini-Surveys in Developing Countries.* Washington, DC: USAID.

———. 2006b. *Promoting Independent Media: Strategies for Democracy Assistance.* Boulder: Lynne Rienner.

Kumar, Krishna, and John Eriksson. 2011. *A Meta-Evaluation of Foreign Assistance Evaluations.* Washington, DC: Office of the Director of Foreign Assistance, Department of State.

Kumar, Krishna, and Marina Ottaway. 1997. *From Bullet to Ballets: Electoral Assistance to Post-Conflict Societies.* Washington, DC: USAID.

Kumar, Krishna, and Laura Randall Cooper. 2003. *Promoting Independent Media in Russia: An Assessment of USAID's Media Assistance.* Report prepared for USAID, Washington, DC.

Lippman, Hal. 2001. *Linking Democracy and Development: An Idea for the Times.* Report prepared for USAID, Washington, DC.

Lipsey, Mark, and David B. Wilson. 2000. *Practical Meta-Analysis.* Thousand Oaks, CA: Sage.

Lockett, Danuta, and Paul Bolton. 2009. *Evaluation of the IRC Gender Based Violence Program in the Democratic Republic of Congo.* Report prepared for USAID, Washington, DC.

Madinane-Morodi Management Information Services. 2005. *Evaluation of Civil Society Capacity Building Initiatives for Interaction with Local Government.* Report prepared for IDASA, PACT, and USAID.

Management Systems International. 2006. *Assessment of the Pre-Electoral Environment: An Evaluation of Support to the Electoral Commission, and Recommendations for Supporting the 2007 Elections.* Report pre-pared for USAID, Washington, DC.

———. 2008a. *Albania DGA Evaluation.* Report prepared for USAID, Washington, DC.

———. 2008b. *Bosnia Justice Sector Development Project Evaluation.* Report prepared for USAID, Washington, DC.

———. 2009. *The Impact of the Second National Kenya Civic Education Program on Democratic Attitudes, Values and Behavior (Final Report).* Report prepared for USAID, Washington, DC.

McClear, Rich, Suzi McClear, and Peter Graves. 2002. *I Called for Help and 100,000 People Came: Media Assistance Program in Serbia—July 1997–June 2002. An Experience Review.* Report prepared for USAID, Washington, DC.

McFaul, Michael. 2010. *Advancing Democracy Abroad: Why We Should and How We Can.* Lanham, MD: Rowman and Littlefield.

Media Sustainability Index (MSI). www.irex.org/msi.

Melia, Tom. 2006. "The Democracy Bureaucracy." *American Interest* 1(4): 122–130.

Mertens, Donna M. 2007. *Transformative Research and Evaluation.* New York: Guilford Press.

Moehler, Devra C. 2010. "Democracy, Governance and Randomized Development Assistance." *The ANNALS of the American Academy of Political and Social Science* 628(1): 30–46.

Morell, Jonathan A. 2005. "Why Are There Unintended Consequences of Program Action, and What Are the Implications for Doing Evaluation?" *American Journal of Evaluation* 26(4): 444–463.

Morris, Daniel. 2002. "The Inclusion of Stakeholders in Evaluation: Benefits and Drawbácks." *Canadian Journal of Evaluation* 17(2): 49–58.

Munck, Gerardo. 2009. *Measuring Democracy: A Bridge Between Scholarships and Politics.* Baltimore: Johns Hopkins University Press.

National Research Council. 2008. *Improving Democracy Assistance: Building Knowledge Through Evaluations and Research.* Washington, DC: National Academies Press.

Natsios, Andrew. 2010. *The Clash of Counter-Bureaucracy and Development.* Washington, DC: Center for Global Development.

NDI (National Democratic Institute). 2009. "Impact Evaluation of the *Let's Talk Civic Education Program.*" Washington, DC: NDI.

OECD (Organisation for Economic Co-operation and Development). 2002. "Glossary of Key Terms for Evaluation and Result-based Management." Paris: OECD/Development Assistance Committee (DAC). www.oecd.org.

———. 2006. *Guidance for Managing Joint Evaluations.* Paris: OECD. www.oecd.org.

Paluck, Elizabeth Levy, and Dan Vexler. 2009. *The Impact of the* Let's Talk *Education Program.* Washington, DC: National Democratic Institute.

Patton, Michael Quinn. 2002. *Qualitative Research and Evaluation Methods.* 3rd ed. Thousand Oaks, CA: Sage.

———. 2008. *Utilization-Focused Evaluation.* 2nd ed. Beverly Hills, CA: Sage.

————. 2010. *Developmental Evaluation*. New York: Guilford Press.

Peou, Sorpono. 2004. *International Assistance for Institution Building in Post-Conflict Cambodia*. Report prepared for the Conflict Research Unit, Clingendael Institute. The Hague, Netherlands: Clingendael Institute.

Polity IV Project. www.systemicpeace.org/polity/polity4.htm.

The QED Group, LLC. 2009. *Evaluation of the Rule of Law Programs in Liberia*. Report prepared for USAID, Washington, DC.

Rahmato, Dessalegen, and Mehert Ayenew. 2004. *Democracy Assistance to Post-Conflict Ethiopia*. Report prepared for the Conflict Research Unit, Clingendael Institute. The Hague, Netherlands: Clingendael Institute.

Reilly, Benjamin, and Per Nordlund, eds. 2008. *Political Parties in Conflict Prone Societies*. Tokyo: United Nations University Press.

Resources for Development Center. 2009. *The International Human Rights Law Outreach Program: A Program Evaluation*. Report prepared for USAID, Washington, DC.

Reynolds, Andrew. 2002. *The Architecture of Democracy: Constitutional Design, Conflict Management, and Democracy*. New York: Oxford University Press.

Rist, Ray C., and Nicoletta Stame, eds. 2006. *From Studies to Streams: Managing Evaluative Systems*. New Brunswick, NJ: Transaction Books.

Rockwell, Rick, and Krishna Kumar. 2003. *Journalism Training and Institution Building in Central American Countries*. Report prepared for USAID, Washington, DC.

Rossi, Peter, Mark Lipsey, and Howard Freeman. 2003. *Evaluation: A Systematic Approach*. 7th ed. Thousand Oaks, CA: Sage.

Rubio-Fabia, Roberto, Antonio Morales, Tomas Carbonell, and Anne Germain Lefevre. 2004. *Democratic Transition in Post-Conflict El Salvador: The Role of the International Community*. Report prepared for the Conflict Research Unit, Clingendael Institute. The Hague, Netherlands: Clingendael Institute.

Rudenshiold, Eric, and Keith Schultz. 2008. *Assessment of the Development and Functioning of the Verkhovna Rada, Ukraine*. Report prepared for USAID, Washington, DC.

Sarles, Margaret J. 2007. "Evaluating the Impact and Effectiveness of USAID's Democracy and Governance Programme." In Peter Burnell, ed., *Evaluating Democracy Support Methods and Experience*. Stockholm: International Institute for Democracy and Electoral Assistance, 47–68.

Scriven, Michael. 2008. "A Summative Evaluation of RCT Methodology: And Some New Entries in the Gold Standards Cup." *Journal of Multi-Disciplinary Evaluation* 5(9): 11–16.

Sharma, Rakesh. 2010. *Electoral Gap Analysis: Electoral Processes Draft*. Draft report prepared for USAID, Washington, DC.

Shultz, Keith, Mohamed Odour, and Andrew G. Mandulbaum. 2009. *End of Project Review and Assessment of the Parliamentary Support Project (PSP) Morocco, 2004–2009*. Report prepared for USAID, Washington, DC.

Sida (Swedish International Development Cooperation Agency). 2008. *Evaluation of NDI's Program on Strengthening Women's Participation in Political and Decentralization Processes in Burkina Faso*. Oslo: COWI.

Smith, Nick, ed. 1992. "Varieties of Investigative Evaluation," special issue, *New Directions for Program Evaluation*, no. 56.

Stake, Robert. 2005. *Multiple Case Study Analysis*. New York: Guilford Press.

Stern, Linda. 2008. *NDI/Uganda—Strengthening Multi-Party Democracy: Internal Mid-Term Review—Preliminary Report on Methodology*. Washington, DC: National Democratic Institute.

———. forthcoming. *Narrative Inquiry, Case Study Evaluation, and Democracy Promotion*. Washington, DC: National Democratic Institute.

Stewart, Susan. 2009. "Democracy Promotion Before and After the 'Colour Revolutions.'" *Democratization* 16(4): 645–660.

Stufflebeam, Daniel, and Anthony Shinkfield. 2007. *Evaluation Theory, Models, and Applications*. San Francisco, CA: Jossey-Bass.

Sundet, Geir, and Max Mmuya. 2009. *Review of Norwegian Support to the National Democratic Institute (NDI) in Kenya*. Oslo: Scanteam.

Taylor, Maureen. 2000. *Final Evaluation of OTI's Programs in Bosnia and Croatia*. Report prepared for USAID, Washington, DC.

Torres, Rosalie, Hallie Preskill, and Mary Piontek. 2004. *Evaluation Strategies for Communicating and Reporting: Enhancing Learning in Organizations*. Thousand Oaks, CA: Sage.

Transparency International Corruption Perceptions Index. www.transparency.org/research/cpi/overview.

UNDP (United Nations Development Programme). 2007. *Handbook on Monitoring and Evaluating for Results*. New York: United Nations.

UNEG (United Nations Evaluation Group). 2007. *Considerations in Strengthening of UN System-Wide Evaluation*. Rome, Italy: United Nations System Chief Executives Board for Coordination.

USAID (US Agency for International Development). 1992. *Evaluation Procedures Guidebook for Conducting CDIE Evaluations*. Washington, DC: USAID.

———. 1996. Monitoring and Evaluation Tip, "Preparing an Evaluation Scope of Work." Washington, DC: USAID.

———. 1998a. Monitoring and Evaluation Tip, "Guidelines for Indicators and Data Quality." Washington, DC: USAID.

———. 1998b. *Handbook of Democracy and Governance Program Indicators*. Technical Publication Series PN-ACC-390. Washington, DC: Center for Democracy and Governance.

———. 2006a. Monitoring and Evaluation Tip, "Constructing an Evaluation Report." Washington, DC: USAID.

———. 2006b. *Impact Assessment of Civil Case Management*. Amman First Instance Court, Rule of Law Project (MASAQ), Amman, Jordan. A report prepared by USAID, Washington, DC.

———. 1998a. Monitoring and Evaluation Tip, "Guidelines for Indicators and Data Quality." Washington: USAID.

————. 1996. Monitoring and Evaluation Tip, "Preparing an Evaluation Scope of Work." Washington, DC: USAID.

————. 1998b. *Handbook of Democracy and Governance Program Indicators.* Technical Publication Series PN-ACC-390. Washington, DC: Center for Democracy and Governance.

————. 2008. *Elections and Political Process in Timore-Leste: Evaluation Report.* USAID: Washington, DC: USAID.

————. 2009a. *Evaluation of Rule of Law Program in Liberia.* Washington DC: USAID.

————. 2009b. *Fostering Justice in Timor-Leste: Rule of Law Program Evaluation.* Washington, DC: USAID.

————. 2010. Monitoring and Evaluation Tip, "Preparing an Evaluation Report." Washington, DC: USAID.

————. 2011. *USAID Evaluation Policy.* Washington, DC: USAID.

Weiss, Carol H. 1998. *Evaluation Research.* 2nd ed. Upper Saddle River, NJ: Prentice Hall.

————. 2007. "Theory-Based Evaluation: Past, Present, and Future." *New Directions for Evaluation,* no. 114: 68–81.

White, Howard. 2009. "Theory Based Impact Evaluation." A Working Paper No. 3IE.

Wholey, Joseph S., Harry P. Hatry, and Kathy E. Newcomer, eds. 2004. *Handbook of Practical Program Evaluation.* 2nd ed. San Francisco, CA: Jossey-Bass.

Whyte, William F., ed. 1991. *Participatory Action Research.* Newbury Park, CA: Sage.

Wollack, Kenneth. 2010. "Assisting Democracy Abroad: American Values and American Interests." *Harvard International Review* (Fall): 20–25.

Wollack, Kenneth, and K. Scott Hubli. 2010. "Getting Convergence Right." *Journal of Democracy* 21(4): 35–42.

World Bank. *Voice and Accountability Index.* www.worldbank.org /governance/wgi/pdf/va.

————. Worldwide Governance Indicators. www.worldbank.org/governance/ wgi/index.

Yin, Robert K. 2002. *Case Study Research: Design and Methods.* 3rd ed. Thousand Oaks, CA: Sage.

Index

Academic research: academic-practitioner partnerships for experimental designs, 109–111; need for research on impacts of democracy assistance, 197

Accountability, 9–10

Activities: meaning in evaluation research, 63–64

Albania: evaluation of democracy and governance program, 48–54

American Evaluation Association, 167

Bamberger, Michael, 91–92, 138–140

Bar graphs, 175

Barnes, Catherine, 35

Burkina Faso: performance evaluation of women's political participation program, 15–16; use of participatory storytelling in evaluation, 127

CDIE. *See* Center for Development Information and Evaluation

Cambodia: International Republican Institute's civic education programs in, 102–108; National Democratic Institute's constituency dialogue program, 108–113

Campbell, Donald T., 88, 117

Case study designs: chain of evidence in case studies, 129; data collection and analysis, 126–129; examples of case study evaluations in Burkina Faso and Guatemala, 127; triangulation of data and evidence, 128–129; types of case studies, 123–125; units of analysis and sampling, 126

Causal relationships in democracy programming: difficulty in establishing, 4, 36–38, 192–193

Cause-and-effect evaluation
    questions, 74
Center for Development
    Information and Evaluation
    (CDIE): evaluation briefs,
    186–187; global evaluation of
    USAID media program, 19–
    20; development of
    methodology for global
    evaluations, 17–18
Center for International Media
    Assistance: experience review
    of community radio stations
    based on an expert meeting,
    22–24
Chain of evidence, 129
Charts and graphs, 173–175
Checklist of form for observing
    polling stations. *See* Form for
    observing polling stations
Cingranelli-Richards Human
    Rights Database, 45–46
Civil society: as core area of
    democracy assistance, 216–
    217
CIVICUS Civil Society Index,
    46
Closed questions. *See* Sample
    surveys
Cluster sampling. *See* Sampling
Collaborative critical reflections
    on monitoring data and
    findings, 68–69
Collaborative (joint) evaluations,
    27–28
Colombia: International
    Republican Institute's
    experience in using
    experimental designs for
    evaluating democratic

governance programs in, 102–
    108
Comparison groups. *See* Quasi-
    experimental designs
Composition of evaluation teams,
    80–81
Construct validity, 37
Content validity, 37
Control groups. *See* Experimental
    designs
Coppedge, Michael, 43–44
Corruption Perceptions Index, 50
Cost-benefit analysis, 12
Cost effectiveness, 12
Counterfactual reasoning for
    democracy evaluations, 131–
    132
Cross-sectional designs, 120–121;
    example of national civic
    education program in Kenya,
    122–123

DAC. *See* Development
    Assistance Committee
DGA. *See* Democracy and
    governance program, Albania
Democratic governance: as core
    area of democracy assistance,
    217–218
Democracy assistance: definition,
    6*n1;* difference between
    democracy assistance and
    development assistance, 2–5;
    growth of democracy
    assistance, 209–211
Democracy assistance, major
    areas of assistance: civil
    society, 216–217; democratic
    governance, 217–218;
    electoral support, 211; human

rights, 215–216; independent media, 214–215; legislative strengthening, 212–213; political parties, 211–212; rule of law and judiciary, 213–214; security sector reforms, 214

Democracy evaluations: obstacles for conducting, 28–30

Democracy evaluations, reasons for conducting: accountability, 9–10; codifying organizational and programming experience, 8–9; improved performance, 8; informed decisionmaking, 8

Democracy evaluations, ways to improve the rigor: engaging host-country researchers, 132–133; focusing on each evaluation question, 130–131; greater attention to sampling, 133–134; greater use of quantitative data, 134–135; using counterfactual reasoning, 131–132

Democracy and governance program (DGA), Albania, 48–51

Democracy promotion: definition, 6*n1*

Descriptive evaluation questions, 73–74

Development Assistance Committee (DAC; of the OECD), 10, 11, 58

Dissemination of evaluation findings, 84

Document reviews: classification of documents for, 153; major documents, preparing information sheet for, 154–155

Economist Intelligence Unit Democracy Index, 39–40; findings for 2008, 41

Electoral assistance: as core area of democracy assistance, 211

Elklit and Reynolds, Quality of Election Framework, 47

Encyclopedia of Evaluation, 10

Engaging host country evaluators and researchers in evaluations, 132–133, 195–196

Equivalency reliability, 37

Ethnograph: software package for organizing textual data, 176

Evaluability assessments considerations, 78–79

Evaluation: briefs, 185–187; definition, 10–11; different from monitoring, 59; external, 25–26; five dimensions of, 11–13; highlights, 187

Evaluation capacity building, in host countries, 196

Evaluation designs. *See* Case study designs; Cross-sectional designs; Experimental designs; Quasi-experimental designs

Evaluation manager's role, in implementing evaluations: inputs in constructing sample, 83–84; selection of evaluators, 79–82; support for data collection, 82–83

Evaluation manager's role, in planning evaluations: assessing evaluability, 78–79; formulating evaluation questions, 73–75; preparing statement of work/terms of reference for evaluations, 77–

78; specifying objectives and audience for evaluation, 72–73

Evaluation manager's role, in reviewing evaluation reports and follow-up, 84–86

Evaluation questions: criteria for selection, 74–75; need for focusing on each question, 130–131; sensitive questions in survey questionnaire, 143–144; types of evaluation questions, 73–74

Evaluation report(s): body and content, 184–185; critical elements of, 173–184; tips for preparing, 185; topics and items to be covered in reviews, 84

Evaluation team: composition of and criteria for selecting team members, 79–82; example of qualifications of team members for a USAID evaluation in Liberia, 81

Experience reviews, 20–22; review based on a meeting on community radio stations, 23–24

Experimental designs (randomized controlled trials): definition, 88–89; and *Let's Talk* civic education program in Sudan, 93–94; logic behind, 89–91

Experimental designs, International Republican Institute's experience: changes in the composition of target groups, 104–105; changes in project environment, 105–106; difficult methodological requirements, 103; early involvement of stakeholders, 104; high cost of designs, 103; supplementing qualitative data, 107–108; technical complexity, 104; tension between methodological rigor and program flexibility, 106; unexpected benefits, 107; methodological and practical obstacles in using designs, 96–102

Experimental designs, National Democratic Institute's experience: academic-practitioner partnership, 109–111; balancing, learning, and accountability, 112–113; mixed-method approach to answering evaluation questions, 111–112

Experimental designs, support for integrating with "live programs," 112; need for realism about using experimental designs in democracy evaluations, 192–193

External validity, 37

Face validity, 37

Focus group discussions: description of, 159–160; facilitating, 162; preparing list of topics to be covered, 160–161; selection of participants, 161; tips for moderator, 163

Follow-up of evaluations, 85–86

Formative evaluation, 13–14

Form for observing polling stations: checklist for, 150

Freedom of the Press Index, 45

Freedom in the World Index, 39

GAO. *See* Government Accounting Office

GPRA. *See* Government Performance and Results Act

Gender mix in evaluation teams, 80

Gerring, John, 43–44

Gertz, Clifford, 128

Global Barometer Surveys, 40–41

Global evaluations, 17–18; of USAID media assistance program, 19; International Republican Institute evaluation of political party assistance program, 21–22; need for more evaluations of democracy programs, 194–195

Government Accounting Office (GAO), 114, 124

GPRA. *See* Government Performance and Results Act

Government Performance and Results Act (GPRA) (1993), 10; Modernization Act (2010), 10

Group interviews: difference from focus group discussions, 162–163; preference of team approach over sole interviewer, 164; preparation of structured interview guide, 163–164

Guatemala: use of participatory storytelling in evaluation, 127

Guiding principles for communicating evaluation findings and recommendations: consideration of information needs of stakeholders, 168–169; developing communication strategy, 172; keeping decisionmakers informed, 169–170; paying attention to political context, 170–171; utilizing different modes of communication, 171

Guiding principles for developing monitoring systems. *See* Monitoring systems for democracy programs, guiding principles for establishing monitoring systems

Human rights: core area of democracy assistance, 215–216

Huntington, Samuelson, 209

Host country evaluator/researchers: engaging in evaluations, 132–133, 195–196

IRI. *See* International Republican Institute

Imas, Linda G. Morra, 137, 185

Impact/summative or ex-post evaluations, 14–17

Impacts: meaning in evaluation, 12, 63

Independent media: core area of democracy assistance, 214–215

Indicator: definition, 31–32

Inputs: meaning in evaluation research, 63

Institutional capacity building for evaluation, 196
Instrumental validity, 37
Integrating randomized controlled trials into live programs, 112
Internal evaluations, 24–25
International digital library for democracy evaluations, 197
International Republican Institute (IRI): evaluation of political party assistance program, 21; experience with experimental designs, 102–107
Internal validity, 37
Inter-rater reliability, 37
Interview guide for key informant interviews, 156

Jones, Jonathan, 22, 115
Jordan: impact assessment of civil case management project, 120

Kenya: impact evaluation of national civic education program, 122–123
Key informant interviews: definition, 155–156
Key informant interviews, steps in conducting: beginning with factual questions, 157–158: choosing informants, 156–157; constructing interview guide, 156; control of conversations, 159; phrasing of questions, 158; probing, 158–159; rapport with informants, 181

Legislative strengthening, 212–213

Let's Talk civic education program, 93–94
Liberia: qualifications for evaluators for a rule-of-law program, 81
Logic behind experimental and quasi-experimental designs, 89–91
Logic model matrix, 63–64

McFaul, Michael, 28–29
Macro-level democracy indices: disaggregation of macro-level indices, 51–54; major macro-level indices used in research and evaluations, 39–41; meaning, 38–39; uses and limitations, 41–43
Media Sustainability Index, 45, 51–52
Meso-level democracy indicators: description, 43–45; major meso-level indices used in research and evaluation, 45–47; use of meso-level indicators in an evaluation of democracy and governance project in Albania, 48–54
Micro-level democracy indicators, 32–38
Mixed-method approach to answer questions in randomized controlled trial evaluations, 111–112
Moehler, Devra C., 97–98
Monitoring: definition, 58–59; different from evaluation, 59
Monitoring systems operations, 81–82
Monitoring systems for

democracy programs:
collaborating critical
reflections, 68–69
Monitoring systems for
democracy programs, guiding
principles for establishing
monitoring systems: active
participation of stakeholders,
60; flexibility to accommodate
changes in program and
environment, 60; generating
timely information, 61;
keeping costs modest, 61–62;
not based on simplistic, linear
cause-effect model, 60–61;
serving the decision needs of
managers and stakeholders, 61;
operating a monitoring system,
67–68
Monitoring systems for
democracy programs, steps in
designing monitoring systems:
analyzing program, 62–63;
assigning responsibilities for
information gathering, 66–67;
constructing flexible logic
model matrix, 63–64;
determining information needs,
65; selecting suitable
indicators, 66
Morell, Jonathan, 4
Multimethod approach to data
collection for evaluations,
165–166
Munck, Geraldo L., 55
Munck Index of Democratic
Elections, 46–47

NGOSI. *See* NGO Sustainability
Index

NDI. *See* National Democratic
Institute
National Democratic Institute
(NDI): evaluation of program
to strengthen women's
political participation in
Burkina Faso and Guatemala,
127; experience with
experimental designs,
108–113; impact evaluation
of *Let's Talk* civic education
program in Sudan,
93–94
National Research Council
Report, 7; concern about the
state of democracy evaluation,
88; criticism of macro-level
indicators, 41–43
Natsios, Andrew, 31
NGO Sustainability Index
(NGOSI), 48–49
Nonprobability sampling, 126
Normative evaluation questions,
74
NVivo: software program for
organizing textual data, 176

OTI. *See* Office of the Transition
Initiative
Obstacles to conducting
evaluations of democracy
programs, 28–30
Office of the Transition Initiative
(OTI; of USAID): program
evaluation in Nepal, 76
Oral briefings on evaluation
findings and
recommendations, 187–188
Outcome level democracy
indicators, 34–38

Outcomes: meaning in evaluation research, 64
Outputs: meaning in evaluation research, 64

Participatory evaluations, 26–27
Participatory Story Analysis, 127
Patton, Michael Quinn, 26, 117, 182, 191
Performance indicators for democracy programs, 33–34
Performance/process evaluations, 13–14; performance evaluation of women's political participation program in Burkina Faso, 15–16
Pie charts, 175
Planning evaluations. *See* Steps in planning evaluations
Political party assistance: as core area of democracy assistance, 211–212; International Republic Institute global evaluation, 21
Polity IV, 40
Pre- and postdesigns, 118–120; example of a USAID evaluation using this design in Jordan, 120
Pre- and posttreatment and control groups with random assignment. *See* Experimental designs
Pre- and posttreatment and comparison groups. *See* Quasi-experimental designs
Probability sampling, 144–146
Probing. *See* Key informant interviews

Promoting evaluations by host country organizations, 196
Purposive sampling. *See* Nonprobability sampling

Qualitative data: collection methods, 138–140; presentation of, 174–178
Quantitative data: collection methods, 138–140; need for greater use in democracy evaluations, 134–135; presentation of, 173–174
Qualpro: software program for organizing textual data, 176
Qualrus: software program for organizing textual data, 176
Quasi-experimental designs: different from experimental designs, 88; logic behind, 89–91; methodological and practical obstacles in using, 96–102; pre- and posttreatment group and a postcomparison group, 92–95
Questionnaires. *See* Sample surveys

Randomized controlled trials (RCTs). *See* Experimental designs
Random sampling. *See* Probability sampling
Recommendations: approaches to engaging program managers in formulating, 181–182; guidelines for formulating, 182–184
Relevance: meaning in evaluation research, 13

Reliability: definition, 37
Re-test reliability, 37
Reviewing evaluation reports. *See* Evaluation reports
Rist, Ray C., 137, 185
Rule of law and judiciary: core area of democracy assistance, 213–214

Sample surveys: difference between surveys and censuses, 140; focus and scope, 141–142; interview questions, 142–144; misconceptions about in developing and transition countries, 141–142; mode of contact, 146–147; recording and editing, 148; selection of probability sampling method, 144–146; steps in conducting surveys, constructing questionnaire, 144
Sampling: evaluation manager's inputs in, 83–84; need for greater attention to sampling in democracy evaluations, 133–134; nonrandom sampling for case studies, 126; nonsampling errors, 14; probability sampling, 144–146; sample size, 134;
Secondary analysis of data, 174–176
Security sector reform as a core area of democracy assistance, 214
Selection of evaluators, 79–80; examples of qualifications for evaluators in a rule-of-law evaluation in Liberia, 81

SIDA. *See* Swedish Agency for International Development Cooperation
Single-stage sampling. *See* Probability sampling
SOW. *See* Statement of work
Specifying objectives and audience for evaluations, 72–73
Snowball sampling. *See* Nonprobability sampling
Stakeholders: consultations in evaluation planning, 72–73; different information needs of different stakeholders, 168–169
Stanley, Julian C., 88
Statement of work (SOW), 77–78
Steps in planning evaluations: assessing evaluability, 78–79; formulating evaluation questions, 73–75; selecting evaluation design, 75–77; specifying objectives and audience, 72–73
Stern, Linda, 127
Stratified sampling. *See* Probability sampling
Structured direct observation: example of an observation form for polling station, 150; preparation of observation forms, 149; rapport with concerned staff and officials of program to be observed, 151; steps in planning, determining focus, 148; site selection, 149–150
Surveys. *See* Sample surveys

Sudan: *Let's Talk* civic education program, 93–94

Summative evaluations, 14–17

Supplementing randomized controlled trials data with qualitative research, 107–108, 111–112

Support for data collection for evaluation, 82–83

Sustainability, 12–13

Swedish Agency for International Development Cooperation (SIDA): evaluation of a National Democratic Institute program to strengthen women's political participation, 15–16

Synchronous communication, 189–190

Systematic sampling. *See* Probability sampling

Telephone interviews, 147

Test/pre-test reliability, 37

Terms of reference. *See* Statement of work

Thick description, 128

Triangulation of data and evidence, 128–129

Two-stage/multiple-stage sampling. *See* Probability sampling

Unforeseeable consequences: implications for democracy evaluations, 4–5

United Nations Development Programme: Manual on Monitoring and Evaluation, 57

US Agency for International Development (USAID): elements of a good statement of work, 78; evaluation of democracy and governance program in Albania, 48–54; global evaluation of USAID media assistance program, 23; impact assessment of civil case management in Jordan, 120; impact evaluation of national civic education program in Kenya, 122–123; Office of the Transition Initiative program evaluation in Nepal, 76; program evaluation of electoral assistance to postconflict societies, 9; qualifications for evaluators for a rule-of-law program in Liberia, 81

USAID. *See* US Agency for International Development

Validity, 37

White, Howard, 87, 102, 109

Wilson, James Q., 31

Workshops to discuss evaluation findings and recommendations, 188–189

Wollack, Kenneth D., 1

World Bank: Worldwide Governance Indicators, 40

About the Book

With the international community providing billions of dollars each year to promote democratic institutions/cultures in transitional and developing countries, rigorous evaluations have become essential for determining the effectiveness, as well as the future direction, of democracy assistance programs. Krishna Kumar provides a unique, practical guide to the on-the-ground tasks of evaluating and monitoring these programs—from planning to implementation to preparing and presenting evaluation reports.

Kumar assesses virtually all of the evaluation and monitoring approaches currently in play, pointing out the strengths and weaknesses of each and suggesting alternative approaches where appropriate. Packed with valuable insights, this book will serve as an essential tool for those who are involved in democracy assistance programming and evaluation, those who fund it, and those who simply want to learn more about it.

Krishna Kumar is senior evaluation adviser in the Office of Foreign Assistance Resources, US Department of State. He has been engaged in development and democracy assistance programming for the past three decades and has designed, managed, and conducted evaluations in Africa, Asia, Europe, and Latin America. His recent publications include *Promoting Independent Media: Strategies for Democracy Assistance* and the coedited *Promoting Democracy in Postconflict Societies*.